REFLECTIONS

REFLECTIONS

An Oral History of Twin Peaks

by

BRAD DUKES

short/Tall press
NASHVILLE

 Published in the United States by short/Tall Press, Nashville.

Publisher contact and information:
shorttallpress@gmail.com

Cover, page design, and typeset by Charles Ramsey
charlesville.us

Grateful acknowledgment is made to Howard Miller and John Thorne for permission to reprint excerpts where cited from the following articles originally published in *Wrapped in Plastic* magazine. All rights reserved. Reprinted by permission.

Miller, Craig and Thorne, John.
"1993 Twin Peaks Fan Festival" *Wrapped in Plastic*. October, 1993: 9

Miller, Craig and Thorne, John. "Killer Bob Speaks"
Wrapped in Plastic. December, 1993: 5-6

Complete photo credits and sources at conclusion of text.

LIBRARY OF CONGRESS CATALOGING-IN-PUBLICATION DATA

Dukes, Brad
Reflections : an oral history of twin peaks /

Brad Dukes

ISBN 978-0-615-96883-4 (pbk)
ISBN 978-0-692-28229-8 (kindle)
LCCN: 2014903072

To Jessica

To my mother and father

And to Peyton

AUTHOR'S NOTE

I will always remember a quiet summer night in August of 1990. I was nine years old, playing alone in the upstairs family room with my collection of action figures. I went downstairs for a Coke and noticed my mother was on the edge of her seat, as if she was about to be metaphysically absorbed by the tiny television set on the kitchen counter.

As I inched closer to the screen, I saw a dark figure moving through the woods at night and asked my mom what she was watching. Without taking her eyes off the television, she whispered, "A girl has been killed and they are trying to find the murderer." I didn't dare leave the kitchen until the credits rolled.

In the following weeks, every new episode of *Twin Peaks* enchanted me with conflicted feelings of fear and fascination. I began hiding under the covers as I went to sleep every night, yet at school I covered my journal with drawings of ghostly giants, "Have You Seen This Man?" fliers, and a bespectacled lady cradling a log.

Almost twenty-five years later, *Twin Peaks* continues to fill me with wonder. I am compelled to document and preserve this brief chapter of television history that is unlike any other, before or since. It is my wish that this book brings you a little deeper into the world of *Twin Peaks*, a place that is both wonderful and strange.

CONTENTS

INTRODUCTION

Countless television series have come and gone over the last sixty-five years, but few have managed to lead a profound and perplexing life as *Twin Peaks*. Six months before premiering on the American Broadcasting Company (ABC) in April of 1990, *Twin Peaks* was hyped as "the series that may change it all" on the cover of *Connoisseur Magazine* and a rogue wave of publicity was born.

Defying skeptical ABC executives, thirty-five million viewers tuned in for *Twin Peaks'* broadcast debut. The tale of an enigmatic federal agent investigating the slaying of a small-town homecoming queen bewitched audiences and propelled the catchphrase "Who killed Laura Palmer?" into the national conversation.

A rabid cult of fans was born and a media circus stretched throughout the summer as stars of the show appeared on magazine covers and late-night talk shows with Johnny Carson and David Letterman. The frenzy became intoxicating as *Twin Peaks* received record-breaking Emmy nominations, won three Golden Globes, and spawned a book on the New York Times Best Seller list.

More than a routine crime procedural, *Twin Peaks* was capable of being melodramatic, hilarious, and downright terrifying within the span of minutes. Coffee, doughnuts, and cherry pie were consumed in mass quantities. A middle-aged woman with an eye patch was obsessed with inventing silent drape runners. A ponytailed truck driver attacked his wife with a bar of soap stuffed in a sock. *Twin Peaks* was unclassifiable and undefined, yet still engrossing to both viewers and critics yearning for the next generation of distinguished television.

In its second season, network politics and creative differences induced a string of bizarre episodes and abysmal ratings. Fans were confused, the cast and crew were disillusioned, and the show vanished in a puff of smoke upon its cancellation.

If you speak with the individuals who brought *Twin Peaks* to life, it is evident that something magical happened. Stories of fame, friendship, and inspiration live in their memories along with the show's shortcomings and suspicious demise.

Actors, directors, musicians, crew members, and yes, even network executives transcended the customs of mass media... and the result was *Twin Peaks*.

You might call it a good ol' fashioned murder mystery.

VISITOR'S GUIDE

The world of *Twin Peaks* is full of different people doing different things. Nearly one hundred individual voices are documented in the following text, and it may be challenging to keep it all straight. A brief description of the interviewee's role is included before their first quote, and at the author's discretion. If you require further assistance, please reference the Census of all interview participants at the conclusion of this book.

I.

KAMIKAZE PILOT

Breaking Ground

This oral history begins in a nameless café in Los Angeles, California, where David Lynch and Mark Frost first met. The two cocreators of Twin Peaks *were first paired in the mid-1980s to collaborate on a film adaptation of* Goddess, *a Marilyn Monroe biography by author Anthony Summers. Lynch was a film director regarded for his midnight-cinema mainstay* Eraserhead *(1977) and his feature adaptations of* The Elephant Man *(1980) and* Dune *(1984). Frost was a seasoned screenwriter who had honed his craft working with television trailblazer Steven Bochco on the lauded police drama* Hill Street Blues.

Mark Frost *(series cocreator and executive producer)*: David and I were introduced by one of our mutual agents at CAA [Creative Artists Agency]; I believe it was in 1985. I remember it being at a coffee shop or a restaurant in Westwood, but David remembers it as somewhere else. My first impression of him was that he was a guy I felt completely in tune with. He was remarkably easy to get along with and it turned out we just had very compatible sensibilities.

Ken Scherer *(former chief operating officer, Lynch/Frost Productions)*: Mark is a storyteller and David is an artist, that's really how I saw them perform. Whether it is David's photography, his art, or his films – he's very visual; he's very experiential. He makes you experience things you would not choose necessarily to experience. He sees the world in a very different way than most minds and Mark is a classic storyteller who chose film, TV, and novels to tell his stories. So, the two of them were a perfect combination. David had this vision that Mark could grab a hold of.

Ken Scherer on set with David Lynch, 1991

Jules Haimovitz *(former president and chief operating officer, Spelling Entertainment)*: David and Mark are two of the greatest, most talented guys I've met in this business. Their intelligence level is phenomenal. They were not spoiled Hollywood types in any way, shape, or form. This would be a whole different industry if everyone had their demeanor.

David was just a very creative sort who lets things roll off his back; he wasn't temperamental at all. He lives within his own mind and is just an interesting guy. Mark was more of like a college professor. He was very academic, a strong writer with strong story and character.

Mark Frost: I think the dynamic that David and I established early on is the one we've always had where we learned we could just sit in a room and start talking and things start to bubble up. It's just like making music, a jam session you could say, and it's just a tremendous amount of fun. A lot of hard work and a lot of laughs and it's been the same ever since.

Although Goddess *stalled in development, Lynch and Frost continued their collaboration and co-wrote* "One Saliva Bubble," *an unproduced comedy of identity swaps. As Lynch and Frost's writing partnership progressed, an ambitious Hollywood agent was determined to bring Lynch into the world of television.*

Tony Krantz *(former television agent, Creative Artists Agency)*: I met David because I was an agent at CAA and he was a client of the agency and he was my favorite director. I remember the first meeting I ever had with him was a motion picture meeting, even though I was a television agent. He came into the conference room and met with fifteen agents at CAA and he just talked about things that he loved. He said, "Red lips, rubber, radiators, and leather."

It was like a miracle: my favorite director talking to me about the things he loved the most. His primary agent (Rick Nicita) created an opportunity for me to build a relationship with David and as a television agent I just started talking to him and enticing him into the world of television.

Jules Haimovitz: Tony was one of the most fun agents. He was young, he was very aggressive without being obnoxious, he was cocky without being obnoxious, and he delivered.

Tony Krantz: David and I would go to lunch all the time. There was a restaurant called Nibblers in Beverly Hills and there was Du-Par's – he loved going there. I thought being with David Lynch was like a treat; sitting with him and just being with him was the greatest thing in the world.

Because I was in the television business exclusively as an agent, I loved David's directing so much I wanted to see if we could bring David to television and change the face of TV a little bit. It was an extraordinary and interesting idea: David Lynch, who was such an unusual and genius talent in the world as a film director coming into prime time television.

Lynch struck mainstream feature success in 1986 with Blue Velvet, *an explosive portrait of small-town crime and sexual masochism. In early 1988, Lynch's box office momentum was mired in legalese by the surprising bankruptcy of De Laurentiis Entertainment Group, who owned the rights to a number of gestating Lynch films. Lynch soon acquiesced to Krantz and began to pursue ventures in television with Mark Frost.*

Tony Krantz: We started to explore the possibilities and after a variety of different conversations I took David and Mark in to meet with Brandon Tartikoff, the president of NBC [National Broadcasting Company], on a pitch called "The Lemurians." Lemuria was sort of like an Atlantis – it was considered a continent that vanished from the history of earth.

It was a story about a bunch of FBI [Federal Bureau of Investigation] agents who used Geiger counters and other homemade detection devices to find Lemurians who were intent on rising up and taking over the earth. It was a little bit of a *Ghostbusters* kind of idea and Brandon committed right then and there to a two-hour movie.

David didn't want to do it as a movie and we then went back and started thinking about a different idea. After having seen *Blue Velvet*, I went to Nibblers with David and I told him, "You should do a show about these people, the customers here in Nibblers," and we started talking about an idea for a soap opera.

Mark Frost: The show just came out of us (David and I) sitting in a room until we hit on the idea of the dead girl as a way into the town. That came before we knew who she was or even where the town was, but we thought that would be an interesting way to start to peel back the layers of the onion. That was the entry point.

As the seeds of Twin Peaks *were planted, there was a ripe opportunity at ABC to bring Lynch's quixotic vision coupled with Frost's cerebral storytelling to the network. ABC's audience share had begun to evaporate in the mid-1980s as Brandon Tartikoff led NBC to a ratings monopoly with a prime time lineup led by* The Cosby Show *and* Family Ties. *By the end of the decade, ABC was rebuilding its brand through innovation and more diverse programming.*

Brandon Stoddard (*former president, ABC Entertainment*): We were trying to change - not the image - but the programming of ABC and we were trying to make it a little more adult, a little bit more serious and improve the writing and productions, et cetera, and I think to a degree we did.

Chad Hoffman (*former vice president of drama series development, ABC)*: When Brandon took over the network he brought in a bunch of us, ostensibly to take the network (which at the time was in third place and probably losing money if memory serves me correct) and to really alter the programming style and really give it a sense of purpose and meaning for a viewer, and most important, an identity. The hope was that if we did that, the audience would follow us.

Brandon Stoddard: It's hard to remember exactly what we did and didn't have on the air in the late-eighties. It was *The Wonder Years*, *China Beach,* and *Roseanne*; we put a bunch of stuff on that was different that people hadn't seen before. Some of it worked and some of it didn't.

Chad Hoffman: We really kind of kicked down the doors and let in a lot of fresh air and a lot of interesting people that had never come to the network. We really had to go out and sell ourselves and what we were doing because a lot of people had just stopped coming. They were going to NBC or to other places where they felt there was more of an adventurous spirit.

Our first go-round led (in the dramatic area) to *Thirtysomething* and *China Beach*. Those were the first two big breakthrough shows that I put on the air and then on the comedy side, Stu Bloomberg came up with things like *The Wonder Years* and *Roseanne*. I think if you take those four shows and group them together, that was our first collective batch of series. They were successful commercially and successful in terms of critical acclaim, appealed to a very different demographic, and most importantly said a whole lot about what we were trying to do. No longer was it just us tooting our own horns saying we want to do this.

Brandon Stoddard: Chad was very passionate about his shows. He did *China Beach* as well, which was an excellent show and a number of others. He was a very good developer and worked extremely well with creative people. They liked him, he took risks which they liked, and he had great taste [*laughs*] which they also responded to. He was really a superior development executive.

Gary Levine *(former director and vice president of drama development, ABC)*: Chad absolutely believed in finding the highest quality and the most distinctive programming, and if you build that, the audience will come. "Never pander to the audience and respect the creators who come in." I thought he was terrific.

Chad Hoffman: So by the time *Twin Peaks* surfaces, it's very clear two or two-plus years into our mission (if you will) that people clearly understood in the creative community what we were trying to do. We really were trying to break the fourth wall on television and just do stuff nobody else would be doing.

Hopefully it succeeded, but our feeling was that even if it failed - as so much in television does - the failures would be so interesting and memorable that even those could help serve the company in terms of bringing in more interesting people and ideas and (eventually over time) programming that would be successful.

So that kind of a groundswell on that foundation is what ultimately led Tony [Krantz] to call me up one day to say, "You're the only guy brave and crazy enough in town to do this." He said, "I want you to meet with David Lynch and Mark Frost," both of whom I certainly knew creatively and I said, "Sure, bring 'em in. Why not?" That was kind of my whole attitude always: "Why not? Try things that other people won't try."

The Pitch

The packaged dexterities of David Lynch and Mark Frost were untested in the realm of prime time television, yet tempting to ABC executives eager to continue their programming renaissance. After the resolution of the Writer's Guild of America strike in August of 1988, Lynch and Frost visited the ABC offices in Los Angeles to pitch an embryonic idea of Twin Peaks *to Chad Hoffman and his team.*

Chad Hoffman: Mark's work I had known from *Hill Street Blues* and other things; I knew his reputation quite well. David I certainly knew from the feature business primarily. Interestingly, I had worked at the Nuart Theatre in West LA [Los Angeles] when I first got to California in the mid-seventies and we were running *Eraserhead* there at midnight, so I was already familiar with David from that, and of course from *The Elephant Man* and *Blue Velvet* and really understood that he was a visionary.

He really took a look at the world and saw things a little differently than everybody else, but also in a very artistic and unique style. And the notion of taking Mark (who had really cut his teeth working on *Hill Street Blues*, in that Steven Bochco mold of television programming) with David Lynch, I thought, "Those are two really talented people who just don't look at the world the way other people do." By putting them together, I thought we might be able to come up with something quite cool.

Gary Levine: I remember they came into the pitch meeting and I had seen *Blue Velvet* as David's last movie before the pitch. I was a little afraid [*laughs*] of what David Lynch was going to be about. They came in and I found him to be a very sweet, gentle, soulful person. Mark was a really good partner for him.

Chad Hoffman: I remember it like it was yesterday. They came in and talked generally about the kind of show that they wanted to do. They talked about a real sense of mood of this town in the Northwest where everything was pristine and beautiful, but that behind the curtains was a world with the lives of people that were quite opposite of the environment that they lived in. It was all about secrets and I remember David and Mark talking about what you see in the foreground is not what's going on in the background and what's going on in the background is what's going to capture everybody.

Mark Frost: I remember Chad as really friendly and receptive. He probably had other people there, who I don't recall, taking notes. We didn't have a whole lot to say in that first meeting. Literally that story David has told, "There's this town and this wind..." and he made this gesture with his hands, "and then there's a dead girl and then a whole bunch of stuff happens." It wasn't that simplistic [*laughs*] but it wasn't far from that. Chad was caught like a trout on a hook. He thought it was the coolest thing he'd ever heard and no one was more surprised they wanted it than we were.

Brandon Stoddard: I think if Chad had come in to tell me about a wonderful new drama with wind blowing through the trees I would ask him for a little more detail than that. But, it was really Chad's baby and he did a phenomenal job of developing that show and the pilot. So I wasn't in that pitch meeting when it first got exposed to ABC, but it was David Lynch and it was a bunch of really good guys and we were trying to get really good creators to come to ABC at that point, so under those circumstances - with those good people – we would be willing to take a risk.

Chad Hoffman: We had a great meeting about it and at the end of it I said, "I think you're talking about something that kind of has the feel - for wont of a better TV term - sort of a soap opera, but not in a negative sense. Why don't you go back and take a look at *Peyton Place* (the movie, not the series) and think about that piece with the quaint town and what was going on behind the scenes and just think about how something like that was done; [it] might jive with what you're trying to do and see if there's a connection there. If there is, come back because I'm very interested."

Mark Frost: We hated it [*Peyton Place*], we didn't even finish watching. We watched maybe half an hour. It was just a dead piece of work at that point. It said nothing to us of any relevance whatsoever and we looked at each other and said, "Why are we wasting our time with this?"

Chad Hoffman: So I got a phone call from Tony a few weeks later and he said, "They're ready to talk." We went to breakfast at the old Café Plaza in what was the Westin Century Plaza (it's now the Hyatt). I was with Gary Levine and it was Mark and David and Tony and we had a great breakfast and they talked about the town and where everybody lived and they talked about how all the stories interconnected and it was just captivating. The only word for it: captivating.

Tony Krantz: David drew a charcoal map of the town of Twin Peaks that we unfurled with Chad when we sold the show and gave it to me for my birthday one year. I have it framed in my office. It is television history.

Mark Frost: Tony was a little like Burgess Meredith in *Rocky*. He was the guy who kept slapping us and telling us to get back in the ring: "Come on, you guys can do this!" He put a lot of energy into making the ABC deal happen. I would say from an "agent-ing" side he was clearly the driving force.

Chad Hoffman: At the end of the breakfast I said, "Let's do it." So we hired them to go ahead and write the script and I remember talking with Gary as we were walking back from breakfast to the office. I said, "I don't know if this is going to work or not, but it's not going to be boring. It's going to be really interesting. So we'll take the shot."

Lynch and Frost swiftly delivered a script titled Northwest Passage *to ABC within weeks of the agreement. As promised, the script focused on a small town devastated by the death of the local homecoming queen, Laura Palmer, while the eccentric Special Agent Dale Cooper uncovers all the dirty secrets of the town in pursuit of her killer.*

Mark Frost: We had been writing together for a few years and this thing just flowed like crazy. We didn't work from much of an outline. We had done a lot of work about who was in the town and what the town was like physically, so we just sat in a room and wrote it in about three weeks.

Tony Krantz: It was this perfect synergy of the framing dramatic abilities of television through the *Hill Street Blues* experience that Mark had and the genius of David Lynch in his particular "avant-garde – ness." The two of them came together to create *Twin Peaks*, and the merger of those two things is not to be underestimated.

Mark Frost: We [the Frost family] had (still have) a small vacation home on a lake, thirty minutes east of Albany. Very rustic, a lot of cabins, and a lot of strange characters in the area, some of whom found their way into my thinking about the show. One story in particular that had haunted me was one my grandmother told me about a girl who had been murdered and found on the shore of a nearby lake.

There was supposedly a ghost in the area of this crime that some people said they had occasionally seen. I went down to the city hall and did some digging and found that a murder had taken place there, in either the 1900s or the 1910s. I believe the girl's name was Hazel Grey, but I might be wrong about that. That obviously had a lot to do with how Laura came into our lives.

Ken Scherer: Very few people can work with David; I just feel that way. I could be terribly wrong, but he's such a unique visionary that you have to have a comparable mind to stay up with it and Mark does. Mark was really able to take characters and the general development and turn it into dialogue, turn it into a story.

Mark Frost: Part of that time he [Lynch] was in New York and I was in LA and I remember I had the second or third edition of the Macintosh and we hooked it up on a modem somehow, so I could type and he could see what I was typing on his computer as we talked on the phone.

We had a few writing sessions like that and both thought, "Welcome to the future." After we finished we were planning to let it sit for a couple of days and then read and revisit it. Turned out we both couldn't help but read it that night and we both said, "I think it's working," and we called each other that night and said, "I think this thing is ready to go."

Jules Haimovitz: Tony sent me the script that was done for ABC and it was a great script, one of the best scripts I have ever read. I said immediately that I want to buy the distribution rights to worldwide television, including home video.

Kyle MacLachlan *(Special Agent Dale Cooper)*: I loved the script, first of all. I recognized right away that the character of Cooper was special and that it was something that I really wanted to do. I thought it presented one of the greatest introductions into a film or television project that I had ever had. Just that long, one single take driving up the mountain, talking into the tape recorder pretty much said everything about the character.

Michael Ontkean *(Sheriff Harry S. Truman)*: It must have been 'Be Kind to a Canadian Hockey Player Month,' or something like that. The networks sent me a couple of dozen pilot scripts. *Twin Peaks* (originally called *Northwest Passage*) was far and away the best of the bunch. Light years ahead of the pack. I didn't really want to do any kind of TV series at all. But quickly figured this might be a chance to work with David on a great little movie and not be obligated beyond the initial two hours. There was just no fucking way any broadcast network in those days would ever give this sublime mayhem a slot on their schedule.

Chad Hoffman: The first draft was almost perfect; I read it and closed it. Gary read it and closed it and we kind of all looked at each other and I said, "This is really cool. We have got to do this." Brandon read it very quickly and said, "You're right. It's really cool; it's different. It's a great team but you need to tell me more about the series." I started to and I said, "Wait a little. Let me go talk to the guys. I'll get back to you and give you their vision of it, not just my vision of it."

Brandon Stoddard: I know what I was concerned with about that show from the very, very inception of it. That kind of drama is a "peel-back-the-onion" kind of drama which they're very good at doing. The problem is - it's television - it's not a movie. There's next week and when you're doing that kind of storytelling which is "what's underneath this, and what's underneath that?" you eventually get down to the center.

Chad Hoffman: I talked to them and within a few days they sent me a document that I now have framed called the "Twin Peaks Gazette," and it essentially was the town newspaper laying out the whole arc of the series. It was just funny and dramatic and mysterious and I thought, "Anyone that goes to these lengths to show you what they're doing really deserves a chance." I showed it to Brandon and he had a great laugh and said, "Absolutely, let's make the pilot."

A Whole Damn Town

David Lynch and Mark Frost established complete ownership of the Northwest Passage *property by selling worldwide distribution rights to WorldVision, a subsidiary of Spelling Entertainment. Lynch and Frost then partnered with Propaganda Films to produce the pilot episode for ABC as they began to scout acting talent with casting director Johanna Ray.*

Special Agent Dale Cooper was the first role to be cast, with Lynch's oft leading man Kyle MacLachlan (Dune, Blue Velvet) *appointed as the protagonist. The supporting cast of* Twin Peaks *was populated with a variety of familiar faces from cinema and television of prior decades, including Peggy Lipton* (Mod Squad)*, Piper Laurie* (The Hustler, Carrie)*, and Richard Beymer* (West Side Story).

Kyle MacLachlan: Johanna Ray was the casting director and she put together such a diverse mix of people. Not only just physically, but with their natural rhythms, their speech patterns, even down to their interests – incredibly diverse. At the same time, those initial scripts (particularly the pilot) were so concise and specific that the voices of the characters (meaning what they represented on the page) were so specific that it was very clear to all of the actors what their job was and who they were and what purpose they served in the material.

Piper Laurie *(Catherine Martell)*: A very dear friend of mine had worked with David Lynch on *Dune* and they had become friends. Sometime later she had a dinner party for David and invited me. I'd seen and admired all of his films up to that point and looked forward to meeting him. He was very easy to be with and I just liked him; I liked him a lot.

I ran into him again over the years and my agent told me he and his partner were interested in meeting with me about their television show. I read the pilot script before the meeting. I didn't think there was much in the pilot for me, just a few moments here and there but I thought it would be interesting to work with Lynch. It was not planned to be a TV series at that point, only a TV movie, and our meeting was fast and pleasant.

Richard Beymer *(Benjamin Horne)*: Johanna Ray and I had known each other for some time and she was always waiting for the right time to introduce me to David, but she never had. This came up and she said, "I think you ought to meet David, there are some roles here." I knew of David because I had seen his films, particularly *Eraserhead* which I had thoroughly enjoyed and I knew people working on it back when he was making it while I was working on my own film at the time. They would say they're making this strange baby and all other sorts of things. [*laughs*]

Mark Frost: David and I sat in together on all the various meetings and we didn't have anyone read, we just met with people. Once we met Richard Beymer (who was a friend of Johanna Ray's) we really thought he would be great for Benjamin Horne and then she brought in Russ Tamblyn and we just couldn't resist the notion of reuniting them [from *West Side Story*].

I think Russ may have been wearing his Dr. Jacoby glasses when he came in. There wasn't much to the character as it was written in the pilot, maybe one brief scene, but once we knew we had an actor as great as Russ Tamblyn, our ideas about Dr. Jacoby expanded. That was kind of a favorite moment.

Russ Tamblyn *(Dr. Lawrence Jacoby)*: To tell you the truth, it was just exciting to work. I hadn't done anything in a while and it was great to be back to work. I was able to bring quite a bit of my own creativity to the character; I actually made up the glasses and suggested a lot of the crazy clothes too.

Sherilyn Fenn *(Audrey Horne)*: What was interesting about *Twin Peaks* is that they [ABC] didn't tell David what to do. He did not read a cast. He said, "Here's my cast!" He didn't say, "Here's my first, second, third choice, you all can read them and make them jump through hoops." He thinks an actor having to audition is the most horrible, brutal thing ever.

Ray Wise *(Leland Palmer)*: I had an appointment with David at the Propaganda Films office. We talked for about fifteen or twenty minutes, not about *Twin Peaks* or the script or any of that, but mostly about our first cars that we owned. Mine was a 1960 Alfa Romeo, a convertible. Not a bad first car!

It was a nice interview and then a couple of days later I got a call saying that they think David would be interested in me playing Leland Palmer. I had to stop and think a moment, "Wait a minute? Leland Palmer? I'd originally gone in for the role of Sheriff Truman!" Yeah, isn't that wild? So I had to read *Northwest Passage* again and look at Leland Palmer.

I looked at the first scenes where he discovers on the phone his daughter has been killed and he breaks down and cries. He goes to the morgue to identify his daughter's body and he breaks down and cries... he's up in the bedroom when the sheriff's deputy goes through his daughter's things and he's weepy there too. I thought all this guy does is cry! [*laughs*]

Mark Frost: I just loved Peggy [Lipton]. I mean, she is such a sweet and authentic and warm and wonderful person. She hadn't been working a lot for a while and I had loved her (when I was younger) on *Mod Squad* and it was a dream to cast her. I have nothing but wonderful memories of her and how creative she was. She has a singular warm presence about her that people really gravitate to, and I certainly count myself as one of those people.

Warren Frost *(Mark Frost's father; Dr. Will Hayward)*: I was living in Brooklyn Heights [New York] at the time and I was working on a soap opera. My wife was teaching at a school and we'd only been there for a year and we were going to go down to Florida where we had a house and retire. Mark called one day and said he had this part. I always kidded David and Mark by saying I'm the only straight man in the whole damn thing! [*laughs*] But that's okay.

I met David when I was in New York and he was there for some reason. I went over to a recording studio and that's where we first met. He was supposedly looking at me to find out whether or not to accept me because he didn't know me; I've mainly done stage work for most of my life. One thing led to another and they picked me up in a limo and I went to Washington where we shot the pilot.

Mary Jo Deschanel *(Eileen Hayward)*: I got the part of Eileen Hayward (mother to Donna and wife to Dr. Hayward); she is crippled, in a wheelchair. So I concentrated on working to understand what it would be like not to be able to walk, learning to operate a wheelchair and the relationships and story at hand as written in the script.

One day some people were over at the house seeing someone else and I was in the chair and met them and then a few minutes later I just got up from the wheelchair and started walking around the room and then I saw the strangest looks on their faces! [*laughs*] It took me a minute to realize that they thought I was really crippled and couldn't walk.

Charlotte Stewart *(Betty Briggs)*: I didn't even interview for it. I went in to talk to David and Mark Frost because I had a couple of ideas about Garland and Betty and Bobby which they did incorporate into our characters a little bit. Betty was Catholic, Garland was in the military, and Bobby was screwed! They put a big palm frond cross on our wall in the dining room and things like that.

The Northwest Passage *script offered a delicate balance of characters ranging in age from wise elders to brooding teenagers. To complement an established group of screen veterans, Johanna Ray recruited a promising ensemble of young talent to capture a sense of high school angst met with tragedy.*

Dana Ashbrook *(Bobby Briggs)*: Johanna Ray knew me from this other show she cast called *Amazing Stories*. I auditioned for that show and my picture was in a stack of pictures David was looking at for *Twin Peaks*. I guess he saw a picture of me and wanted to meet me.

Dana Ashbrook and Mädchen Amick

Before I went into the meeting I remember sitting out there with Eric DaRe (Johanna's son) who was running the casting session. He and I had known each other from other auditions. We were laughing about the script with the woman with the patch on her eye and the silent drape runners; we just thought that was so funny. So I took that energy into the room when I met them and it was just amazing.

Mädchen Amick *(Shelly Johnson)*: I had already known David's work from *Dune*. I had gone to see *Dune* with my mom and I thought it was the strangest, weirdest movie I had ever seen so when I knew he was doing this TV show I thought this was either going to be a horrible flop or its going to be brilliant. Once I read the script I thought, "Wow, this is really good," and it reminded me a lot of my home town of Reno, Nevada, in a really dark and twisted way.

I had done a guest part on *Star Trek: The Next Generation* and I had done the pilot for *Baywatch*, neither one had actually aired before I was cast in *Twin Peaks*. Since I had been auditioning for anything and everything I had gotten to know Johanna Ray and had gone in for her a lot. She brought me in basically to meet David and I had gone in to read for Lara Flynn Boyle's part and read with Eric; he was just reading the off-camera lines.

Mark Frost: The other person that impressed us so much that we altered our plans was when Mädchen came in. She was brand new in town and hadn't really done anything at that point, but we were so taken with her that we actually conceived the role for her. The Shelly character was nothing like what it became at that point, but we saw a lot more potential in her.

James Marshall *(James Hurley)*: I had a very youthful look, this boyish look and at the time my photos were terrible, they looked literally like *Teen* magazine. There were a few headshots that looked normal, but he [Lynch] had one of the bad headshots and just refused to see me when he was casting it. So Johanna told me that he broke down and said, "Fine, have the guy in," which made me like, "Oh my God. I'm the only one he's avoiding seeing the whole time." [*laughs*]

I remember David had his hat on and he was just really cool. I don't know what prejudices I had going in, but he was this tall, all-American, kind of cool guy [*laughs*] and he was just so straight.

He was so clear and not what I was expecting. At the end of the meeting he said, "I think we're going to do this and I want you for the part. I wasn't even going to see you and now there's no one I'd rather have. This would be great if you're willing."

Caleb Deschanel *(director, episodes 6, 15, 19)*: They did a great job of finding these really wonderful young actors and I think it went a long way towards making the show that much more interesting. And at the same time, finding these established actors like Kyle and Joan Chen, Richard Beymer. They had a great interest in the history of movies and television in the casting - drawing people from *West Side Story* and other things they remembered as kids. It was kind of fascinating to have the older guard be representative of another time period and then find all these really young actors and match them together in a really interesting way.

Mark Frost: The whole time we had trouble finding a Leo and Eric DaRe had been working with his mom all through the process. I think he was the next to last role we cast. We just looked up one day and said, "What about Eric for this? He's the son of Aldo Ray for Chrissake!" and you know, that turned out pretty well.

Sheriff Truman was the last major character we cast. We looked at a lot of people and I remember one day hearing from ABC that they had a deal with Michael Ontkean and I knew his work primarily from *Slap Shot*. I think David and I met him separately, because one of us had to be up in Washington - which was the only time that happened. But we had exactly the same reaction, that Michael was our guy.

Michael Ontkean: Years earlier I had gone to a screening of *Blue Velvet* with Paul Newman and we were both knocked out by the originality of all the elements. For unknown reasons David had not done another feature since then. It was winter when we first met. I had on a coat that Mitsuhiro Matsuda made for me to resemble and replace the worn-out biker jacket I'd been wearing since 1961 as a teenage member of The Black Diamond Riders motorcycle gang in Canada. David's birthday is only two days before mine so there was some sort of immediate affinity, but he offered me the part of Sheriff Harry S. Truman just to be able to see more of that motorcycle jacket.

Welcome to Snoqualmie

With the majority of casting completed in Los Angeles, David Lynch and Mark Frost traveled to Seattle, Washington, to scout locations for filming. Communities in all directions from the downtown area were scrutinized to fit the specific needs of the Northwest Passage *script, resulting in a majestic exterior backdrop for the production.*

Mark Frost: I remember David and I just having a ton of fun on that trip, excited that we were actually going to go make this thing. Washington seemed like the right place; David had grown up in that part of the world and it felt right to him. This local scout drove us all over and we didn't see anything for the first two or three days. We had one day left, and he finally said he's going to show us this area around Issaquah and Snoqualmie, and the minute we got there everything we'd written showed up in front of our eyes.

There was a sawmill, the diner by the railroad tracks, a hotel by a waterfall, the gas station. It was all there like we'd been looking through some kind of magic crystal and seeing this place from a distance, then we get there and find it's exactly as we'd written it. So it was a great last day and we came back on the wings of that scout knowing we'd found the place where we could bring it all to life. Everything was already written in stone at that point. We just knew we had found everything we needed and we didn't need to alter anything.

The Seattle area also offered a handful of local actors to fill in seemingly small but distinctive roles, including Wendy Robie as Nadine Hurley and a young stage actress, Sheryl Lee, as the dead homecoming queen, Laura Palmer.

Sheryl Lee *(Laura Palmer)*: I was very young and had no experience in TV or film and at that point wasn't even thinking about pursuing television or film; I was just interested in doing theater. I went in and met David and he was wonderful and kind and welcoming and funny. I was so nervous; I sat on my hands the whole time [*laughs*] because I was shaking so badly. He was just so joyful and put me at ease. He didn't tell me a lot about the project, except that it was a pilot and that I would be playing a dead girl and I would have to be wrapped in plastic and probably put in freezing cold water. He asked if I could handle that and he said there would be a few flashback scenes.

At the end he said something along the lines of "okay, let's do this." I didn't know what that meant and the casting director walked me out and just said very quietly, "I think you just got this, but don't say anything," and I said I wouldn't. I had walked down to the audition and it was blocks and blocks and blocks. I remember that walk home like it was yesterday because I was so excited! The excitement wasn't so much, "Oh, I'm going to be on the TV show," it was because he was so nice and so creative and that's what was so exciting and interesting to me.

As filming began under the direction of Lynch in February, 1989, the landscape and ambience of the Snoqualmie Valley established an ethereal setting for Northwest Passage. *Thirty miles east of Seattle, the area provided memorable filming locations including Mt. Si, Snoqualmie Falls, and a vast Weyerhaeuser lumber mill. The towering Douglas fir trees and grey skies of the Pacific Northwest played a central part of the production as the cast and crew settled into their surroundings.*

Warren Frost: I did a lot of television with Andy Griffith and a lot of *Seinfelds*, but pilot-to-pilot (in terms of unusual) it was wonderful and it was all on location. I think the main thing is that it came out of Mark and David's sick minds! [*laughs*]

Piper Laurie: I remember that the location in Washington was lush and beautiful and we stayed in cheap motel rooms with views of the gas station! [*laughs*] I was probably nervous because I always am when I begin anything. If David was nervous I didn't know him well enough to know. He seemed very much in control and we got through it.

Joan Chen *(Jocelyn "Josie" Packard)*: I had very little to do when I was there; I just remember coming back telling people that I had so many dreams. Like every night, there were interesting and weird dreams because that was Indian sacred land or something. I remember it to be very watery and very green; it had some kind of mythical feeling to that place. I just remembered having all sorts of very strange dreams as if you're on something - that was my memory.

Kyle MacLachlan: I was born and raised in Yakima, Washington, which is a couple of hours east of Seattle, in what is Eastern Washington. Snoqualmie and the areas that we filmed - that's all on the western side of the state, on the other side of the Cascade Mountains. So I knew the area pretty well. I was much more familiar with Seattle, having gone to school there for five years at the University of Washington.

On a number of occasions I had driven between Yakima and Seattle and at the time you had to pass right through North Bend, which was the site of the diner. I didn't give it much thought in those days; it was just a point on the map. I never really stopped in. It was all changed of course when the setting for *Twin Peaks* was based right there; I was surprised.

It was a lot of fun to return to Seattle to work in a city that I knew so well in a previous life (as a student) where you struggle to make ends meet, and it was a real treat to be back in Seattle and be able to really enjoy the city and go to some restaurants and do some nice things.

Sheryl Lee: I absolutely love shooting on location, especially when the location is able to be where it is (meaning you're shooting in Washington and it's supposed to be Washington). Sometimes you're in Vancouver and it's supposed to be Chicago. But when you're able to shoot on location in the location it is supposed to be and it is allowed to breathe as its own character – creatively - it's an absolute thrill. I love it because you can be so present with everything you're seeing and smelling and tasting in the air. The energy of the land and the trees and the stories that they tell - it just had so many layers of such richness.

Michael Horse *(Deputy Tommy "Hawk" Hill)*: Sometimes the atmosphere is as important as the characters in the show. It's like Monument Valley in Westerns, people are excited because there's nowhere else that looks like it and *Twin Peaks* had that. I have a lot of friends up in Washington and there's stuff out there in those forests. There's spirits that live up there. We all knew we were doing something special. There were no egos at all, and we all knew that we were a part of David's and Mark's artistic balance.

Mädchen Amick: Just the visual part of *Twin Peaks* is so unique. The way we filmed it, we were all put up in a little motel outside of Seattle. It was about an hour and a half from Snoqualmie, so that in itself was fun because it was kind of like camp with all the actors in the hallway and raiding the kitchen. I wish we could have filmed more up in the Northwest, just having the waterfall be a character in itself with the trees and the forest.

David and Mark had a dinner for the cast and they were so relaxed and encouraging. We were able to hang out and get to know each other and that sticks out the most - the bonding. And the appreciation too, after being in the business for twenty-five years [of] how unique that was and how they set up the show and how we were able to work with each other. It was very special.

Mark Frost: I went out of my way to create a really positive work environment for people. I've been in plenty of situations where the studio was being oppressive, using Stalinist tactics, pinching every penny and treating people kind of badly. Since this was our show and our company we were determined to do it differently. We wanted a place where people wanted to come to work and I was always really happy to hear that that's how most people felt about it; they believed in what we were doing.

David J. Latt *(producer, pilot episode)*: We weren't being told by a studio how to do it or where to do it, so it was just the inventiveness of the producers and director. Ultimately we came in under budget and ahead of schedule, even though we had gotten freakish weather like hailstones the size of softballs, snow, and then there was a blizzard that shut down the whole Seattle area.

We were stranded in the Snoqualmie Valley, sleeping on the floor of some of the locations. Really the only problem we had was the blizzard which prevented flights coming in for two or three days. Even that didn't prevent us from doing things we need to do. Not even a word changed on the script, perhaps a few Standards and Practices things were changed, but that was it.

Russ Tamblyn: I was looking forward to going up to Seattle to film the pilot; I took some hiking boots with me and was ready to go into the woods and see some beautiful scenery. The plane landed in Seattle, a car drove me to a hotel along the freeway, and that's where I stayed the whole time. I just did one scene in an old, abandoned hospital, then they drove me back and I flew home. I never saw a tree!

Sherilyn Fenn: I was ecstatic; I had the best time of my life. It snowed; I grew up in Michigan so I was running down the hall waking people up: "It's snowing!" [*laughs*] I took a car once and almost drove all the way to Canada. I was listening to music [and] I had this great job and a great part written for me and all of a sudden a sign said you need to have chains on your wheels and I had to turn around. It was great; it was beautiful. Everyone was dressed up and cozy and David was yelling at them because they couldn't find saddle shoes [for Audrey to wear] and he was so insistent. They found an Oxford and had to paint them. [*laughs*]

Gary Hershberger *(Mike Nelson)*: It was a lot of fun and it created an environment for everyone to really get in to their characters and get into the mood of this place. We showed up in Washington and everyone was getting to know each other and it was just a moody place. Kyle MacLachlan's character was constantly talking to Diane; he was talking about the trees, the waterfall, the people, and the birds - that's how it was. It was a little bit spooky up there. [*laughs*] These trees were dark and tall and it was kind of like we were at camp, trying to explore what David's vision was for *Twin Peaks*.

James Marshall: Without a doubt, real magic was in the air. Everybody was sort of swept away, even David. Everybody was so connected, even if someone had a little attitude it would float away and it wouldn't matter. When we read the lines it was like we were zapped into a dream and just speaking what we were feeling.

A Beautiful Thing

The six-week production of Northwest Passage *was steeped with David Lynch's raw instinct and affinity for 'happy accidents,' amassing many spontaneous inspirations that live on in* Twin Peaks *lore. The cast and crew recall an intimate and prolific experience with their trusted director.*

Sheryl Lee: A lot of it starts at the top and dominoes down, and David is kind. He respects what each department brings to the work. He listens to his actors and all of his departments and is open to hearing suggestions and ideas and he really makes it feel like a collaboration, like each person and their contribution is just as valuable as the next.

Ray Wise: David just had an uncanny way of beginning the day and I just love it when he says, "...and it's going to be a beautiful thing," no matter what he was talking about. Whatever was going on in the scene – as long as he ended it with that little phrase – I was happy and comforted by that. He had the uncanny ability to be able to say just the right thing before you had to do a scene, and it sort of triggered everything that followed.

Gary Hershberger: David was great; the entire time we were up there I felt spoiled rotten by his direction. He would explore scenes with you and it felt like you were finding your way with him instead of getting to where he wanted you to go. There was so much care; it was like shooting a feature. I remember when we were filming the scene in the bar, there was the theme song called "Falling" being sung and David was showing me the lyrics for it. I think he even wrote them. He was involved with every little detail.

Sherilyn Fenn: David is not weird in the way everyone wants to say he is. He's eccentric, kind, and he never yells on a set. It's always relaxed and it's very, very abstract. He's not there to tell everyone what to do. He describes it like there's a soundboard in front of him and he turns up the volume, turns something else down, and then adds a little more bass. He hires the people he knows are essentially right for the role and makes little adjustments.

Leslie Morales *(set decorator, pilot episode)*: David is not difficult to work with, but he absolutely has to have what he wants. He's not a rude person or a screamer at all. He's very much a gentleman, but he has to have what he wants. The only times I could see him act completely differently was when he was speaking with studio executives about more money or an extra day – he was very different than the David you worked with as a director.

Mary Jo Deschanel: I remember one time that someone told David we were over budget or over schedule and he just ripped pages out of the script without looking to see what they were. I was right there when it happened and it was a great moment. Now it's possible that was just a gesture, but it felt very close to how David really worked. And it was a great laugh at the time.

Richard Beymer: I didn't have much to do in the pilot; I was originally cast to play Dr. Jacoby – that's who David thought I was going to play. Then he called and said I would be Ben Horne, this business guy. I was a bit disappointed. I wanted to be the crazy doctor, but I'm sure glad it turned out like it did.

We were up at the hotel and David had us sitting on this couch in front of the fireplace and it felt rather strange, just sitting there. I asked David if I could just get up and lean on the mantle. He said, "Yeah, that'd be really neat, but when you get there you should hock a big 'loogie' right into the fire." I said, "Okay..." [*laughs*] and I gave the subtle version and went on talking. If I could go back I would have gone further with the [*very loud gargling and spitting sound*].

Ron Garcia *(director of photography, pilot episode)*: We were at this old hospital when Kyle was digging under Laura Palmer's nail and found the letter *r*, I believe. We had a problem with the balance in the light and they started flickering. I said, "Ah! I've got to get rid of this flicker!" David walked in and it was like *Frankenstein*! I said, "David I'm really sorry, but we're working on this problem." He said, "I like that Ron! Can you do that all the time?" I had this conception you had to be proactive and David taught me to be reactive. It was an amazing awakening for me.

David J. Latt: David wasn't afraid of letting people get emotional and he was just willing to let things go. So the actors certainly liked the latitude he gave them. He certainly had a clear vision of how he wanted it to all be. There was that wryness and David's willingness to hold on the awkwardness of the moment.

Grace Zabriskie *(Sarah Palmer)*: Certainly I had not been able to intuit from the text of that scene [when Sarah learns of Laura's death] how extreme David would demand my performance to be. I was pretty sure he was wrong, leading me in an over-the-top direction, but I went with him, and learned I had been right to trust him so completely. (Which is a horribly egotistical way of saying that I learned that he had been right.)

It was my introduction to David and the world of *Twin Peaks* as it was to be performed, as opposed to whatever it seemed to be on the page. Later, you can see that everything was implicit on the page, but not in the beginning, when the director is deciding what of that which seemed implicit will be used, and what will not. Looking back, it seems to me that each of the actors was used by David in a slightly or very different way. He saw in me the ability to be so earnest that my performance could be pushed into a really dark kind of humor. And he has found other ways to do that with me since.

Wendy Robie *(Nadine Hurley)*: I was just going to be a day player and we shot this scene where I'm inside the house and I'm flipping the drapes. They were shooting from across the street in the little flag store that was converted to look like Big Ed's Gas Farm.

I was working these drapes and I could hear the walkie-talkie headset that the PA [production assistant] had, who was crouched down in the corner. I could hear David laughing as he was shooting and I thought that has got to be good if you are making the director laugh! I was being very much an automaton so I just kept doing it for all I was worth. It was very painful with these skinny little ropes I was pulling up and down, up and down and I just kept doing it because he kept laughing and kept shooting. My hands were actually bleeding; it was so painful but I wouldn't stop. After that I was convinced Nadine would be interesting in the series.

Dana Ashbrook: I just did what they told me about the character and what was written. Of course a little piece of you comes through in a character in TV because you're doing it so much and you want to stay true to what they want. I remember in that first meeting with David and Mark it was pretty affable and David goes, "You know, Bobby doesn't smile that much," so I said, "Okay, I'm not going to smile!"

James Marshall: Everybody's parts were a little somehow of them. The only preparation I had to do was just be available for it and admit to my own self that there are certain parts of me that are like that character and to live in that during that time period.

It was a very Hemingway kind of vibe. The Bookhouse was actually called Hemingway's before they changed its name. I already knew how to ride dirt bikes, but I'd never ridden a Harley [Davidson] before, so I learned how to ride that up there which also helped. It was about being available and knowing he [Lynch] already saw in you what you didn't know was there.

David J. Latt: There was a scene at night with Lara Flynn Boyle out in the woods and she gets very upset. It was a very late night, very cold, and we were out in the middle of (what looked like) a wooded area. At the time I think Lara was eighteen or nineteen and I just remember how David kept working with her until she got to the right emotional pitch. He got her to a place emotionally where the intention of the scene totally came through her. She was so vulnerable and involved and I thought the audience empathized with her. It was really wonderful to watch him do that. It really showed what a deft hand he had and why actors really love working with him. That really sticks in my mind.

Mary Jo Deschanel: Lara was perfect for the part of a young woman being quite wonderful but wanting something more, something else, something exciting, but then finding out that the 'other,' the something maybe more thrilling is also dangerous and perhaps even evil and destructive. It's the growing up experience that she played so well in this show.

James Marshall: Believe it or not, my favorite part of the whole thing was James and Donna's scene in the woods from the pilot. David was so into it; we did it literally hundreds of times. The whole mystery between them and the intimacy we had – it was something that most teenagers can relate to. That time in one's life where you feel really alone, yet you get with somebody and that person doesn't turn out to be the right person and all of a sudden you end up with someone else, where you've both been watching each other from afar. It's so explosive. When that got played out, I thought it was really cool.

Leslie Morales: The other thing I haven't encountered with other directors was that David rehearsed in private. He'd always have people leave completely when he was speaking to an actor and that was a very private time for him and the actors. I think that might have spoken to some of the ability of getting sides out of the actors that you never saw again on-screen from some of those actors. That was just sacrosanct and you didn't know. Nobody ever sat around and said, "Do you know what he said?" [*laughs*]

Ron Garcia: David was very parsimonious [*laughs*] with his comments one way or another. With his actors, with me, with everybody creative – he just cut right to the chase with simple descriptive words that seemed to hit our psyche and we understood right away.

Joan Chen and David Lynch

Joan Chen: I remember that David was very spontaneous and he wanted to see what could happen; he was curious what would come out of you. I remember once he asked Richard Beymer to whisper something in my ear. Richard whispered, "You're a cunt." I wasn't expecting that and my English wasn't good enough; I didn't understand what "cunt" was. I thought, "Did I not know the script?" I did not know what that meant! [*laughs*] So David didn't get what he wanted because I didn't understand!

I walked by thinking, "What was that supposed to be?" and sat down and finished the scene. Richard came rushing to me and said, "I'm really sorry Joan, but David wanted me to do this!" I said, "What did you say? What did that mean?" I didn't understand! [*laughs*] I wish we had to make a project where I had two and a half months with him, a feature film or something. David is an extremely interesting man, but our time together was very limited.

Dana Ashbrook: He [Lynch] basically is the kind of guy that you just trust so much that you will walk through fire. If he tells you to do anything, you do it. You'll go through anything with him because you trust him and you believe in him. As a kid, being around someone like that, it was great. It was like having the best sort of father figure and person to look up to as an artist, to just watch and see the way they work with people. He was loved by everyone on that set, down to the last guy. He was such an amazing force to work with. I still love him.

Unsolved Homicide

In the opening moments of the Twin Peaks *pilot, the earnest fisherman Pete Martell (played by Jack Nance) discovers the body of Laura Palmer, famously drawling, "She's dead, wrapped in plastic." Until Nance's mysterious death in 1996, he was a staple of nearly every David Lynch film beginning with his starring role as Henry Spencer in* Eraserhead.

Many key themes from Eraserhead *percolated into* Twin Peaks, *including lonely figures singing cryptic songs, zigzag floors, and tumultuous domestic issues. The filming of* Eraserhead *persisted for five years at the American Film Institute in Beverly Hills and initiated other future* Twin Peaks *alumni into the Lynch fold, including Nance's wife (at the time) Catherine E. Coulson and Charlotte Stewart.*

Catherine E. Coulson *(Margaret Lanterman a.k.a. the Log Lady)*: I got teased about the fact that Jack's wife in *Twin Peaks* was named Catherine Martell. I think David did that as kind of a 'poke a little joke' in the way Jack used to say, [in Nance's voice] "Caaatheriiine" to me and he still said it in *Twin Peaks*. By the time we did the series, Jack and I were back to being good friends. We stayed friends after we weren't married. We got married way too young but stayed friends doing the series, which was fun.

Duwayne Dunham *(editor, pilot episode)*: Jack was a beautiful human being; I worked with him on *Blue Velvet* as well. There are some crazy stories about that guy, but he was a wonderful soul. I understand why he and David were so close. David is a wonderful, kind soul. Jack Nance, a kind soul. He played it quirky, he played it honest, and I chuckle every time I see him in the beginning of that pilot episode.

David J. Latt: Finding Laura Palmer's body was pretty depressing to film, I must say. It looked on the screen the way it did in life: cold, desolate, foggy and creepy. And poor Sheryl Lee - it was just creepy! [*laughs*] Everything you saw, we were feeling.

Sheryl Lee: I was just like a sponge; I had studied a bit of meditation prior to that and I used any tools that I could to just really, really slow down and go into a quiet, still place. I had never been on a television or film set, so I was really soaking up what was going on around me: listening and feeling and learning. Playing a dead person is a fantastic education on set because you get to listen and hear everything and everyone kind of forgets that you're there, so you learn a lot.

Duwayne Dunham: I thought finding the body on the beach (the way David shot it) was pretty powerful. Jack walks out there in this funny way to go fishing and it makes me chuckle every time I see it. Isn't it peculiar that he is the character that finds the body? In my opinion, he's the one that lets the audience know how you are supposed to react to this. That is not easy acting.

Gary Hershberger: The words "wrapped in plastic" continue to echo through me. [*laughs*] A line like that is supposed to be brutally sad or foreboding and every time I hear it (the way he says it) strikes my funny bone. David would always do things like that. He combines two opposites together in the same scene and you just never knew what to expect.

Catherine E. Coulson: Jack was very taciturn; he was not a big talker. When Jack got hired for *Eraserhead* I remember we went over to

David's house and Jack didn't talk much. It wasn't until we were doing some kind of timing of the scene or something that Jack made his mark. I don't know if David was absolutely positive that he wanted Jack to play Henry.

Jack Nance as Pete Martell

I remember Jack seeing the rack that David and his brother had built on David's Volkswagen Bug. It was a really good rack and Jack and I had a Volkswagen; he was so taken with the rack and he was saying, "Man, this is a great rack!" And that made David really like Jack. That was really the deciding moment, I think. He always kind of goes for his gut feeling about a person (David does) and I think if a person can act he can zero in on whether they're right for the part just by talking to them.

Charlotte Stewart: Jack was funny. He was kind of cranky and he and David always had secrets of some kind, you know, giggling and stuff because they spent so much time together. Jack was a character. He loved to watch those quiz shows (*Wheel of Fortune* and stuff) and he would laugh hysterically when people answered wrong and lost their money. He loved it. He was an old codger before it was time for him to be an old codger.

Catherine E. Coulson: I think David just knew Jack would be right; his kind of quiet power is what made him so good as Henry. I don't think there was any question he would be Pete Martell. Jack was in everything David did. He was in *Dune*, *Blue Velvet*, but he wasn't in *The Elephant Man* since they were all English except for Anne Bancroft.

I think he and David just had a quiet understanding and David would say very few words to Jack in terms of direction and Jack would pick up on it right away and go with it. Jack was a deeply thoughtful, soulful guy. A man of few words, unlike me! [*laughs*]

Duwayne Dunham: I was introduced to David's work - specifically *Eraserhead* - when I was working as an assistant editor with George Lucas at Elstree Studios in London on *The Empire Strikes Back*. Stanley Kubrick was on the lot doing postproduction on *The Shining* and invited us to a screening at the theatre there on Friday night of *Eraserhead*.

Neither George nor I had heard about it but were anxious to see it, so we did. We went in the theatre and Stanley Kubrick, George Lucas, Gary Kurtz, and myself watched that movie and it was quite a screening. Kubrick said it was one of his favorite films and that he'd seen it thirty or forty times. [*laughs*] Hard to imagine!

Tony Krantz: I would take girls that I was dating to see *Eraserhead* and depending on how they reacted, I would know if I wanted to date them again. That was literally my litmus test.

Piper Laurie: Jack was a very peculiar guy; I admired his presence on the screen in David's movie *Eraserhead*, which in my mind gave him some sort of authority. In reality he was very soft and silly... soft and puzzled. He seemed unsure of everything in front of him. [*laughs*]

Joan Chen: Jack was very open, easy to talk to. Because I was so shy and I don't talk to people, I did remember talking to him. Then in between there was this deep melancholy that sometimes took over. He seemed so everyman, but actually a very deep and complex person - that's how I felt about him.

Michael Horse: Jack Nance was also a friend of mine. My first agent handled me and Jack Nance and Viva, one of Warhol's actresses. I miss Jack because Jack explained everything. It all made sense through Jack's eyes. I would say, "Jack, I'm a pretty far out guy, but I just don't get this," and Jack would say, "Well, see, this is how it all works..." I just miss looking at everything through Jack's eyes.

Catherine E. Coulson: Jack worked all the time and he could have worked a whole lot more. It's unfortunate that he died so young. It's still an unsolved mystery. He was a great guy. Jack was kind of oddly religious, he knew his Bible stories from growing up, and he grew up in Texas for heaven's sake, so he knew his stuff. He just made Pete Martell an extension of himself and pushed the envelope with his laconic delivery, his very unembellished directness, and his kind of slow-talking ways. I think he did a great job.

Excalibur

Angelo Badalamenti *(conductor and orchestrations)*: I had a little office across the street from Carnegie Hall and that's where David Lynch and I would work. I had a Fender Rhodes piano there in this little room and David would come in and sit next to me, on the right. He said, "Angelo, I'm going to do this show. It's called *Northwest Passage*." I said, "*Northwest Passage*? David, that's something I read when I was in grammar school. You can't use that title!" Before you knew it, it was changed to *Twin Peaks*. [*laughs*] That must have hit home.

Angelo Badalamenti was a critical figure in the artistic development of Twin Peaks, *conducting and composing the rich and arresting music that underscores the series. Badalamenti's soundtrack experiments with jazz, blues, and classical styles to create an essential element of the dreamy and menacing aesthetic of* Twin Peaks.

Mark Frost: If the show was a boat moving along, Angelo's music was the river that carried it. It helped create and support the mood of the show. It gave you a very specific sense of time and place that felt outside of real time and real place. It helped elevate the show into a mythological realm that really separated it from the usual TV view of what the world is.

I can't imagine the show without the music. Angelo is such a fun guy and so great to work with, he's just as important in the *Twin Peaks* tapestry as anybody else's contribution and you know, that turned out pretty well.

David J. Latt: Every layer and level adds more to the impact of the material and to the effectiveness of the material. The most exciting to me is when the music comes on. David's visuals are very haunting without sound, but then you lay in the sound effect mix together with Angelo's score and you reach an almost operatic level. If you had the ability to hear only Angelo's tracks, it would be pretty amazing on its own. So in terms of postproduction, the final layering of that music was really something.

The music of Twin Peaks *came to life on the East Coast with Badalamenti leading a small circle of session musicians in New York City. Badalamenti and Lynch's musical partnership commenced with* Blue Velvet, *leading to the 1989 album* Floating Into the Night *with vocalist Julee Cruise and the Brooklyn Academy of Music stage production* Industrial Symphony #1. *These collaborations produced multiple tracks that later served as the bedrock of the* Twin Peaks *soundtrack.*

Angelo Badalamenti: I did all the music in New York - a little studio called Excalibur with Artie Polhemus, a brilliant engineer who could do magic. At the time it was not a world of out-and-out digital stuff; he would record everything on tape and do these incredible edits. Both me and David were in awe of what Artie would do for us.

Art Polhemus *(engineer)*: I built my second studio [Excalibur] in '85. It was in a six-story building that was very dilapidated; it's gone now. It was a very odd, old building that was very spooky and the lobby looked very foreboding. I had it very dark inside, which I always prefer. David liked the atmosphere for it. It was right off Times Square – back when it was completely different, when it wasn't Disney World. There were all the porno shops and those old theaters from the previous era when the great plays were done. Everybody settled in and got accustomed to it and everything ironed itself out.

Al Regni *(tenor saxophone)*: Excalibur was one of the funkiest studios in New York located in an equally funky building on a funkier corner of Eighth Avenue and Forty-Sixth Street. It was really a great place to be creative for many of those same funky reasons, and it was also a great place to record because of the recording engineer, Art Polhemus. In that era - and to the present - he remains one of the top guys I have worked with. I swear he could hear paint drying!

Kinny Landrum *(synthesizer)*: The funny thing is that with the *Twin Peaks* pilot, the music was done before we ever saw a lick of film. We never scored the picture; that was all laid in after the fact. I don't think I'd even seen the name. Working with Angelo, one of the things I like is that he knows what he wants but he's open to input from his musicians.

Julee Cruise *(vocalist)*: [I met Angelo] from an HBO series that came out. I was a resident actress at the theater and HBO came out and filmed it. It didn't translate well. But, I was a rather larger than life actress and the director said he wanted me to meet his friend Andy, "Andy Badale," who was a tunesmith in Nashville. He thought Steely Dan was a guy and Pink Floyd was a guy and he got successful really late in life. He's 100 percent Sicilian and family means everything to him.

I didn't know David and I didn't like *Eraserhead* either, I didn't care – but I did like Andy and all of a sudden everyone is calling him Angelo. I just fell in love with him and thought he was fantastic. He always has a smile on his face. Then a year later I met David. It was in *Blue Velvet*. They were sitting beside me [at a screening] and every time Frank Booth would squeeze Isabella's [Rossellini] boob or something, David would turn and look at me and I knew this guy had a really childish and funny sense of humor, you know? [*laughs*]

Angelo Badalamenti: Julee is a remarkable, multi-gifted talent. After David and I wrote "Mysteries of Love" for *Blue Velvet*, I asked Julee if she knew a female singer that could sing delicately in an upper register, to do the vocal on the song. Julee sent over to me some singers, but they weren't quite what David and I were hoping for. She then said, "I think I could do it the way you want."

You see, I only knew her as a singer in the show, which necessitates a big, loud, show-chest voice which she projected. I then said to her, "Alright, practice it, and come back in a couple of days, and we'll give it a listen." Needless to say, she came back, sang the song for me, and she knocked me out. David and I had now found our angel voice. It was love at first sound.

Angelo Badalamenti's Fender Rhodes piano

Julee Cruise: He [Lynch] came into the booth and would direct me, in an acting way. Some days he'd have to get me on track. Angelo would say, "You're flat! You're sharp!" and I would say, "How? I have perfect pitch!" We would argue, but it was a good argument! It was the best. It was when everything converged at the right time and we had a master with a plan and we followed it blindly. If only everyone could set their ego aside and do that, they might come up with something that's timeless. Angelo deserves the Mancini award and all those things.

Art Polhemus: Whatever you wanted, Angelo had a good knowledge of it and could go in any kind of direction. It was easy for him because he's accomplished in every different kind of music. Just playing a little bit of whatever mood you want and he can take it from there.

Angelo Badalamenti: David always believes things are more beautiful when they're played slower. There's a lot of great music out there that he feels is not as great as it could be because it's played too fast: "Just slow things down and it becomes more beautiful."

When we wrote "Laura Palmer's Theme," David sat next to me as I played and said, "Imagine you're alone in the dark woods and you hear the soft cry of an animal or an owl in the background. There's sycamore trees blowing softly in the wind and the moon is out. A girl appears from behind the tree and pauses for a moment. She's walking towards you and looks into your eyes..." And as he's talking, he told me to visualize it and I did. I started improvising and playing with the opening of those dark, C minor, legato chords [*hums tone*]. He said, "Angelo, that's beautiful, can you play it slower?" It's like how slow can you play? [*laughs*]

I slowed down and kept playing for a minute and a half and he said, "Let it build, let it build, she's walking toward you and she's very sad," and I segued into the main theme and kept going up the scale, a very kind of strange scale in a way. He said, "Now get it to reach each a climax." I did and he said, "It's beautiful! It's beautiful, Angelo! Now come down again! Slow it down and then go back into the dark wood where you were." I did that and I don't know how long I played it. We recorded it; David has this cassette in a vault. He needs to make me a copy. [*laughs*]

We did one take. I said I'll go home and work on it. He said, "Angelo, don't change a single note." You could see the hairs on his arm were standing up and his eyes became just a bit salty, if you know what I mean. He said, "Angelo, this is *Twin Peaks*. I can see it." And that was it; it became "Laura Palmer's Theme."

Kinny Landrum: "Laura Palmer's Theme" is quite an interesting piece of music. If you know about theory, it goes through that whole climbing sequence - three different tonic relationships (or keys if you will) only to arrive at the major version of the minor key which it starts in, which is called parallel major as opposed to relative major. [*laughs*] At some point it reminded me of the main theme of *Last Tango in Paris*, that's a tune by [Gato] Barbieri, a great saxophone player. When it reaches the climax and goes into the high part...that's so Italian. It's a surprising piece of music.

Angelo Badalamenti: Just by talking and whispering in my right ear as I'm at a keyboard, David describes a mood and I'm able to take his words and translate that into music. It has its own identity. It's been kind of incredible to work so closely together, and the fact we're on the same musical wavelength, it's very special if and when that happens.

It's also great for David - because he's told me this a bunch of times - even in *Twin Peaks* before he would film or shoot a scene he would have some demos of the themes I've written and he would play it for the actors on the set and it would put them in some kind of a mood, even as they speak their words. The style, the mood, and the pace - it helps the director with the actors. The music becomes an integral part of the story.

Green Light

By the fall of 1989, Brandon Stoddard and Chad Hoffman had departed their respective positions at ABC. The fate of Twin Peaks *was now in the hands of the freshly minted President of ABC Entertainment, Robert "Bob" Iger. As ABC delayed its decision to order a series, Lynch and Frost enacted a public relations campaign to boost exposure of the pilot as it debuted at select screenings.*

Chad Hoffman: There was a screening at the Museum of Television Arts and Sciences prior to its airing. I was invited to go sit on a panel with Mark and David and the cast and we showed it to maybe (I think) a thousand people and they just couldn't get over it. They were applauding and [there were] standing ovations at the end and then we sat up there and talked about it and answered a lot of questions. I remember backstage we were just kind of pinching ourselves and we were saying, "What is going on here?"

Mark Frost: After we finished the pilot we'd only seen it with a few small groups of people, and we did a big screening at the DGA [Directors Guild of America] long before the show ever aired and the reaction was extraordinary; people just went nuts for it. So that's the moment when we looked at each other and said, "Holy cow, we might have something here."

It just rang people's bells in ways they hadn't been rung before and it was so cool to see that happen. In addition to writing fiction I'd worked in the theater for a long time, so I was used to live audiences but you don't get that very often in television, so to see the show received exactly the way we hoped it would be – for the first time – was an amazing experience.

Harley Peyton *(series screenwriter and season two producer)*: One day Mark called me up and said, "Look, I did this pilot with David Lynch and we're going to screen it at the Directors Guild," and I knew nothing about it. It was such a great way to see it. I was obviously a big David Lynch fan and thought, "Wow, how awesome David Lynch would even do television," particularly back then when there was a huge wall between the feature world and the television world. So I go to the screening and sit down, and like everyone else in that room I spent ninety minutes going, "Oh my God, this is the best movie I've seen all year - forget that it's good television."

Angelo Badalamenti: I saw the pilot and it was simply outrageous. It was like nothing I or (I believe) anyone else had ever seen. I was fascinated with the mysterious, off-center, off-the-wall characters which were perfectly cast and most of all, with the hypnotic, haunting quality of the piece. It really got to me.

Kyle MacLachlan: It's the kind of horrifying vision or surprising moment that is very hard to create on television where the hair on the back of your neck stands up when that glove reaches in at the end to pick up that necklace combined with the musical cues. It just makes you sit bolt upright and say, "Oh my gosh! What did I just see?" That's hard to do on television and they had a number of moments like that on the pilot.

Chad Hoffman: There's two favorite moments that come to mind, one is where they see the Log Lady and I think Kyle says, "Who's that lady carrying the log?" The sheriff answers, "They call her the Log Lady." I remember laughing out loud the first time I saw that. And then the scene where Russ Tamblyn comes out of the elevator and he's got wine corks in his ears - I thought was just brilliant - just little pieces of business in the midst of all that's going on that just made me giggle. Those two in particular just jumped out at me and I said, "Where else are you going to see this?!"

Tony Krantz: It was difficult to get anybody to agree to any sort of series commitment for anything, but the pilot was so absolutely undeniable; it was so new. The famous quote that Brandon Tartikoff gave about the show was that when he saw *Twin Peaks*, he knew that "tried and true was dead and buried."

Gary Levine: I thought the pilot was terrific and odd, but ultimately very compelling. It's interesting when you're a network executive - you're the buyer when the creative community comes to you, but you slowly turn into a seller of the show to the corporate brass. So that's where our energy turned. We thought the pilot was really as good as it could be.

Chad Hoffman: I had a discussion with Bob [Iger] before I left ABC and he asked me about a few things and I raved about it and said, "You have to put this on the air and see what happens. The show and these guys are too important. It's your decision; you have to decide what you think is best," and that is sort of it.

Michael Saltzman *(former publicist, Lynch/Frost Productions)*: From the very beginning we didn't have an airdate, but we kept sending the tapes of the pilot out to as many places as we could think of: airline magazines to travel magazines to entertainment magazines. Whenever we had a tape returned to us I said, "Let's find another place we can send it to." We really saturated the market and there wasn't a lot we had to tell them other than "watch the show." That was kind of fortuitous that we were that aggressive about a program.

Each and every time Lynch and Frost backed our publicity efforts to the hilt. They backed us up and there are not a lot of people in my twenty-five years to have the backbone to say "let's do this." If anything, I would say (without patting myself on the back) that publicity forced the hand of ABC to program and schedule the airdate of the show because I'm not sure when they were going to air it.

Piper Laurie: I was asked to sign a contract in which there was a clause about a series, which of course every show wants but never gets in a million years... so I signed without much concern about being tied up. But lo and behold we were suddenly a series. [*laughs*]

Tony Krantz: I remember it vividly. I was in New York at the Regency Hotel in the CAA war room (if you will) where we had all our pilots that we had brought to New York. Ted Harbert (the president of ABC) came over to meet with me and maybe one or two of the other agents and told me that *Twin Peaks* was going to be picked up as a series, but not until midseason for seven episodes in addition to the two-hour pilot. I actually thought that was a good thing because it wouldn't require everybody to dive in and make so many episodes so quickly. It would give everyone a chance to do it in a more relaxed atmosphere.

Philip Segal *(former programming director, ABC)*: They ordered the show and the delay was the fact that when they saw it, no one had ever seen satire like that before. You have to remember in those days we were at the tail end of a tired formula for television series other than what [Steven] Bochco was doing. There was not a lot on ABC that was out of the box. It was all very safe.

David J. Latt: There really wasn't a place for that material on network television. To the credit of the ABC guys (whether or not they thought it would be a success) they felt positive enough that they wanted to give it a shot.

Brandon Stoddard: I have a memory that it didn't test well. There was a pretty big battle because I think some of the research department wasn't exactly behind it and a few other people like the owner of the network, Tom Murphy. It was a battle and the programming department won and it went on the air.

Alan Wurtzel *(former vice president of research, ABC)*: I just remember we were on a management retreat (every year in Phoenix) and we were going to get a rough cut of this show. So the rough cut comes in and a small group of us (sort of senior management and program guys) sat and were watching this show, and we actually couldn't follow it. Not everybody, but a number of people thought we were seeing reel three in place of reel two. We were trying to follow a linear story and it was anything but that.

Chad Hoffman: I don't think there was ever a thought not to schedule it, as far as I can remember. I know there were some disagreements with the research people with what they thought the initial audience would be. I think the feelings on the creative side of the network were that it's something special and it needs to find a place, and where can you put it on where it's not lost in the clutter of all the new shows in the fall.

David J. Latt: The cost of the pilot wasn't that exorbitant. There were no big stars, it was all affordable, and they figured, "Eh, there's a lot of movies of the week. It's no big deal." So the financial downside wasn't too difficult. Then they sat in the screening room and thought, "Oh my God, this is haunting and evocative. We ought to take a shot at this." It was one of those instances where they had enough reasons to take a chance on something that wasn't normal and they could pat themselves on the back if it paid off.

Harley Peyton: I can't confirm this, but I did hear that when they screened it for the network brass (in New York, I guess) an old pro, one of the top corporate guys said, "This is not going to ever appear on ABC. This is garbage. This is horrible. This will never happen."

Brandon Stoddard: Fortunately, the deciding factor in most of those battles is the quality of the show and it was really, really wonderfully done! It was a hell of a pilot. It was really good, it was fresh, and it was different. You hadn't seen anything like it before. It had wonderful casting and it was fun to see some of those old TV people back, and it just had a totally different feel to it. It was really well done and beautifully written. It grabbed you. At the end of that thing you wanted to see more, and I think that was the reason it got on the air.

James Marshall: I was so ecstatic. If the pilot hadn't even aired I was still thrilled and satisfied, so when it got picked up it was like, "Are you ready?" We really weren't sure if it was going to continue, so it was very exciting. We were aware of how special it was while we were doing it.

Gary Levine: When I flew home from New York to LA after we had made the scheduling decisions and ordered *Twin Peaks* from a pilot into a series, I came back to LAX [Los Angeles International Airport] and had a car waiting to drive me back home. As happens at airports, the drivers of the cars wait with a little sign with your name on it by the baggage claim. When I arrived at the airport having just ordered the series, the guy holding the card with my name on it, the driver was the actor [Harry Goaz] who played Deputy Andy in *Twin Peaks*! [*laughs*] I was able to tell him he now has a paying gig as an actor on the series. I even offered to drive him at that point.

2.

WELCOME TO VAN NUYS

Warehouse

ABC's order of an abbreviated season prompted excitement and action as David Lynch and Mark Frost completed scripts for the following two episodes. Over the summer of 1989, Lynch began work on his next feature film Wild at Heart, *while Frost steered the day-to-day direction of the newborn series.*

Mark Frost: We knew it was a short order, seven additional episodes to make an impression. We just decided we were going to keep doing what we'd been doing: "We're filming a novel here, so let's just go write the first two chapters." I tended to think of the episodes as chapters, not episodes.

The model (particularly then) for network television was you cranked out episodes like sausages and the closer they were to being identical to each other without being identifiable as such, the better it was for the company you were making it for. But we weren't making this for a studio, we were making it for ourselves and we wanted to break that mold and said, "Let's make a nine-hour movie." And that's how we proceeded all the way through that first season.

Frost assembled an infrastructure to facilitate production and hired two of his friends to script select remaining episodes. Although both Harley Peyton and Robert "Bob" Engels had no prior television writing credits, they offered stunning contributions to the first season of Twin Peaks *and beyond.*

Mark Frost: I had known Bob for a long time; he had been a student of my dad's at the University of Minnesota, so I'd known him for nearly twenty years. I had known Harley for six or seven years at that point, and I just felt each of them would give us something interesting. I had never worked with them before, they were just friends.

Harley Peyton: I was working and doing primarily movies in development. I had adapted *Less Than Zero*, so that was my first screen credit and I knew Mark Frost through a fantasy baseball league and he and Bob Engels were a team. I can't remember the name, but something from Minnesota since they're both from there. They were like great friends and I knew Mark sort of socially through that and that was pretty much it.

Robert Engels *(series screenwriter and season two co-producer)*: Well, I was friends with Mark (still friends with him) and he said, "I'm doing this series with Lynch and I think you'd be perfect to write one of the episodes." I hadn't seen the pilot, but I was on board to do the first six or seven episodes. I had just met David briefly.

Mark Frost: I didn't give them a lot of freedom, in that David and I had broken the main story, and then I did all the final passes on the episodes, but they definitely made some great contributions. But David and I had set the template, and he and I still talked a lot about the stories and everyone had to adhere to that through line.

Robert Engels: I had never written a television show, so I got sort of a crash course from Frost on how to do that. He's the master, the best. A very lucky break, where most guys would start writing *Saved by the Bell*... actually I like *Saved by the Bell*! That's a bad one to pick. [*laughs*]

Mark Frost: Harley has a wonderful and wicked, caustic, cynical-slash-romantic view of the world and Bob had this Midwestern... what's the right word? Not simplicity, but a practicality that fit the profile of our town.

Harley Peyton: When you were writing an episode it was very detailed. You would sit down with Mark - act by act, scene by scene - and your job was to fill in the blanks. If you had ideas he was open to them, but one thing Mark was really great at was identifying when your work worked and when it didn't. He didn't rewrite everything because he felt like he had to. I wrote the episode and I remember my phone rang at midnight. I thought, "Who the hell is calling me at midnight?!" and it was Mark who had just finished the script and he was thrilled and asked me to write a second one on the spot.

Washington State offered abundant filming locations and landscapes full of character, but the series production of Twin Peaks *was transplanted over one thousand miles away to sunbathed Southern California for budgetary reasons. With filming scheduled to recommence in October of 1989, Mark Frost tapped another friend to literally rebuild the town of* Twin Peaks *from the ground up.*

Richard Hoover *(series production designer)*: I knew Mark Frost when he was a kid in Minnesota; I worked with his dad who was at that point an actor, but also teaching at the University of Minnesota. I had just gone to the Telluride Film Festival and saw this pilot (*Twin Peaks*) which had Mark's name on it and I was amazed. When I got back into town I called him up and I said, "Hi, how are you?" He said, "What are you doing?" I said, "I'm looking for work." And he said, "No, what are you doing now? Come on over. Let's talk."

Mark Frost: We shot in so many practical locations in Washington when we shot the pilot, Richard's primary job was first and foremost to translate all those original places we'd found into sets in LA and he did a brilliant job. I had known Richard for almost twenty years at that point and knew how capable he was, and what a great and tireless worker he was. As we went along and there were more things he had to create from scratch, I had complete faith in his art and craft.

Richard Hoover: I had two construction coordinators on two different stages at a warehouse by the Van Nuys airport. Working in warehouses is sometimes common here because of the expense of real stages. It was about six weeks until we had sets standing and we were ready to shoot; it was pretty quick. I had never done anything like that before, but it was a great way to learn something.

Harley Peyton: We had this world Hoover had created. One of my favorite things was leaving the office and walking down into those empty sets and kind of exploring, soaking up those feelings you would later put into the script. What he did was perfectly in sync with Lynch and Frost, in that he took the existing world and turned it about 30 percent into another direction. Anything he did - even something simple like Donna's house - he got a great sense of that entire world.

Richard Hoover: All the sets are Americana in their own Northwest idiom and the colors were buttery and warm. I think the color in the piece is interesting because it's not necessarily film noir. It's warm and fuzzy in a way, yet at the same time there is something dark lurking in there and that was kind of on purpose. Each one of the sets had its own visual comfort and color and life... and a lot of other mysteries you never know about.

The sheriff's department they found on the pilot was a lumber company head office and it was near a lumber mill. It had a lot of design aspects of wood and entryway, and it was very fifties and comfortable and brightly lit. The wood was there and we ended up replicating a lot of that with the sense that down the hall somewhere was where the jail cells were and there might have been a basement. It was very country, not urban. It wasn't like a cement world, it was more like a dentist's office [*laughs*] in essence.

The hotel became elaborated from what it was in the pilot. It needed a dining room and we added a check-in counter. We ended up finding a lumber company that would rip three-quarter material in half so we could get a lot out of the material on the walls and it wasn't as heavy. A lot of the beams you see were real, and some of the big supports were pieces of trees we got from a lumber guy up in the [Angeles]

National Forest who would take trees that had already fallen and help clear the forest.

We wanted the Big Pine Lodge [Pete and Catherine's home] to be a big, open, roaming space as much as we could with reflecting cabin instruction. The thought was that it was a strange, rangy, big room with a river rocks fireplace. It was exploring that world of the log cabin with a lot of reverence to people who live up in the woods and have money and build these big things. They weren't broke, so all the objects reflected that aggressive earthiness and the people in it sometimes didn't quite fit that. It was counterpointing what's going on in the piece.

The Palmer and Hayward homes were adapted from the actual living rooms from the pilot. They were very normal and "stucco-y." The doctor's house was more of a craftsman style with painted woodwork (American style) with a living room and dining room connected. It was all about family. The Palmer's house was sort of cheesier, but a real study in that normalcy. David has liked to artistically explore that world in his past. He comes from the Midwest and lived in it and found a way to express stories in it, so that's why they were that way.

Aside from the construction of new sets, Twin Peaks *required further adaptation through cinematography, costume design, and exterior photography to sustain the visual aspects of the pilot episode.*

Frank Byers *(series director of photography)*: When I first started the show and I saw the pilot, my take on the whole photographic direction was the Orson Welles picture *Touch of Evil.* It is black and white and it was shot with wider lenses and longer takes and that type of contrasting photography. I said, "This is it, this is what I need to translate." *Touch of Evil* was the blueprint for me.

They liked what I was doing right off the bat, so they just let me go. I very rarely heard from David, but on his episodes he would be specific about certain things. The other thing about *Twin Peaks* which is totally different from now is we shot [with] one camera, so that means you're not compromising anything to get your second camera in. Maybe once in a while we had a second camera. The first season I operated the camera and I was really happy to do that. The minimum day was sixteen hours. By the time those seven episodes were done, my health was going. It was really, really hard.

Mädchen Amick and Chris Mulkey on the set of the Double R Diner

Sara Markowitz *(series costume designer)*: My thoughts going forward after the pilot were of a small town in the Pacific Northwest where the people would hold on to their clothing for years and years. They were practical, hard-working folks whose money was not spent on expensive clothing. I felt they shopped at local Goodwill stores or at most, Horne's Department Store. Perhaps they even made their clothing. There were a few characters like Catherine and Josie who were much closer to modern-day fashion. I always dreamed of Nadine Hurley's character having a variegated yarn sweater that perhaps she made.

Costume design is not what is in *Vogue* magazine. It is about the psychology of the character, not unlike someone's home or office environment which is a reflection of who they are and I believe clothing is no different. Patty [Patricia Norris, production designer and costume designer, pilot episode] had done a beautiful job of starting to lay the foundation of who the characters were, which was a great jumping-off point for me.

Frank Byers: We shot exteriors mainly in Malibu Canyon and it was a pretty good place to shoot. The harshness of the sun I had a problem with - sometimes I'd win and sometimes I'd lose - but we shot a lot at night so that was better. We actually shot more on location than you'd tend to think. We would go to the Bookhouse and the hospitals; we were out a few times an episode. It wasn't all stage. They were great locations.

Jonathan P. Shaw *(series editor)*: They shot out at Malibou Lake for Leo's house and stuff and it's very Southern Californian, so you really had to take a certain amount of care to cut around and make it look like the Northwest. It also helped having those tools and sound design elements and great stock footage of establishing shots like the falls. There was very little to compare it to, this creepy vibe that was always there.

A Wide Road

Twin Peaks *ushered in a savvy roster of directors known for their work in feature films, including Tim Hunter* (Rivers' Edge), *Tina Rathborne* (Zelly and Me), *and respective Oscar nominees Caleb Deschanel* (Being There, The Natural) *and Lesli Linka Glatter* (Tales of Meeting and Parting).

With an unusual amount of creative freedom in network television, these directors were licensed to distill the world of Twin Peaks *with their own individual style. In his professional directorial debut, Duwayne Dunham was entrusted to direct the first episode filmed in Southern California.*

Duwayne Dunham *(director, episodes 1, 18, 25)*: That first episode was really about getting everyone together and reacquainted with who they are in the story. What made it so interesting is David left and he was not that involved very much in the very beginning - maybe from a distance - but I know he was busy prepping *Wild at Heart*.

I'm pretty sure my script for the first episode was about seventy-five pages long, and after two or three episodes we found that for *Twin Peaks*, thirty pages was the ideal length for the story. So we shot a lot of stuff that wasn't in the first couple of episodes because of that. Mark greased the rails and kept everybody comfortable. Everybody gave it 100 percent and it was really great to see.

Tina Rathborne *(director, episodes 3, 17)*: There we were in the valley in this warehouse with very little money as far as I could see. There was a big space where the sets were built and then there was this hall of small rooms with no privacy. Everybody became very familiar with everybody quite quickly. That was another reason the first season was so much fun: we were all piled up on one another and all working together. Everybody was really great; there weren't cliques or people throwing tantrums.

Tim Hunter *(director, episodes 4, 16, 28)*: It was very exciting material. It skewed Americana in that special David Lynch way, but with a really good central mystery that even in its off-kilter context kept the suspense up and the audience going. They really seemed to have a handle on how to keep it going in that first season. The material was really exciting and everybody knew it was.

Lesli Linka Glatter *(director, episodes 5, 10, 13, 23)*: David and Mark were very involved; they were the best possible collaborators. It was a constant open door, running into their offices to say, "Hey I have this idea or what do you think about this?" It was an idyllic kind of situation in terms of many creative artists of all disciplines working together. But when you were directing, no one was staring over your shoulder in any way but they were always available as great springboards.

Caleb Deschanel *(director, episodes 6, 15, 19)*: Most shows tend to be pretty hard-nosed about the way the script is done - it's locked in stone and that's what you do. The impression I got from David is that they were very much director-centric in that sense. There were scripts, but they were welcome to input from the directors so it made the environment that much more creative and more fun. I think that really made a big difference in the director's experience.

Mark Frost: What I would tell directors coming in was to study the pilot, look at the storytelling style we've evolved here, and figure out what you can bring to it. We were hiring really talented and interesting people and I didn't want them to just come in and feel like they're stamping out engine parts at a Chrysler plant. I think everyone understood that was the assignment: work with the house style and the mood that David had so brilliantly created and then bring whatever you can of yourself to add to that. And I would say nine times out of ten that worked out really well.

Philip Carr Neel *(series associate and co-producer)*: We would play a lot of scenes (editorially speaking) in one wide master. Whenever you shoot a scene, you shoot a master and then you do closer and tighter shots (or over the shoulder shots) and then you have all this material to edit together in a pattern to tell the story. A lot of television shows today will cut five times within a line of dialogue to bring up the pace and make it more visually stimulating, but *Twin Peaks* followed a very deliberate pace with less cuts which David established. That created a real mood and tension and made it a little more theatrical.

Jonathan P. Shaw: Each and every episode felt like a minimovie and they were treated that way from the way they wrote the script and the time directors spent on shooting and postproduction. The consciousness of the show was really well taken care of.

As editors we were able to just play. I don't recall anyone telling us, "Don't try this or that." It was a constant collaboration to steer the ship. How long you held on a shot was equally as powerful. You sit there and say, "I'd never hold a shot this long," but with Angelo's music underneath it and the sound design... that's just powerful stuff.

Paul Trejo *(series editor)*: David described it as, [*in David Lynch's voice*] "You've gotta give my directors a chance to make a one-hour movie. They're going to drive down a wide road." And that's what they did. It was really unique for television because most directors just come in and leave. Typically, preproduction and shooting was barely three weeks, but with David and Mark, it was their plan to allow the directors to see the postproduction all the way through and come to the sound mix, which was kind of unheard of at the time.

Lesli Linka Glatter: It was very much like doing a film. Once you turned in your director's cut, they didn't change very much. There was a very tight shot I did in Jacques Renault's cabin of a needle going into the groove of a record and I remember David saying to me, "Les, that is a great shot. Can't we hold on that much longer?" The shot was on the screen for an inordinate amount of time which would just never happen now. That was a very *Twin Peaks* kind of image - the details of life.

Tim Hunter: It was very good for directors to work on because David and Mark set the tone, certainly David through the way he shot the pilot. The tone was very clear and within that they were very encouraging to directors to come up with good ideas, make it visually interesting and a little bit stylized and I think the directors on the show took advantage of that.

Caleb Deschanel: It was a slow show, but you never felt it dragged. You always sensed there was something going on under the surface that you had to find. The leisurely pace of it felt like there was a time bomb in a bag in the side of the room. It had this sense that at any moment something terrible could happen, or something exciting or wonderful could happen. It just created this wonderful reality.

Tim Hunter: The llama in my episode was the kind of thing they just encouraged directors to do. We were scouting locations and we got to the vet's office and I don't know if I'd seen a llama farm that day - I just thought it would be a good gag. I asked them if I could have a llama for the waiting room and miraculously they said yes. So that's how the llama got in. There's one beat where Kyle and the llama clearly make eye contact which was my favorite part of it.

Mark Frost: I also wanted to include what became known as 'Easter eggs' in the video game industry a few years later, where people would be rewarded for heightened scrutiny of what they were seeing. You would see that in character's names or in relationships or pieces of casting. Honestly, I didn't know if anyone would ever notice, but it was certainly fun for us to do.

Waldo [the myna bird] was a reference to Waldo Lydecker who was one of the principle characters in [the Otto Preminger film] *Laura*, as is Laura for that matter. (I think Waldo's actually the one who murders Laura.) I thought it was fun to have a bird as an eye witness [*laughs*], we just hadn't seen that before.

Caleb Deschanel: The myna bird was a really great idea and I think that the one idea I came up with when he got shot was there was an obsession of doughnuts in the sheriff's office, so I thought, "How is there a way to include all the elements in the office?" I thought, "What if the bird's cage was swinging over the table and what if the blood was dripping on to the doughnuts?" You're just trying to find every sort of "Hitchcock-ian," oblique way of demonstrating the death of this bird. It was such a fascinating idea to think that the bird was a potential witness or element in this story.

Duwayne Dunham: In episode 1, there was a fish in the percolator and that came from a story where my wife and I had taken a trip with our young kids. She poured some tea for me. In the middle of the night we were driving down the desert highway and I went to have some tea and it tasted funny. I couldn't figure it out, but I knew something was wrong. Maybe we had changed brands. Then I sort of poured some more into the cup and this one-inch piece of bloated hot dog poured out! [*laughs*]

One of my kids must have been sitting on the counter while the tea was seeping. I guess they dropped a hot dog in there and it cooked itself. Sometime during the editing of *Twin Peaks*, I told David this story and sometime later that scene showed up and Pete had gotten the fish in the coffee.

Lesli Linka Glatter: Actually I was in *Twin Peaks*. I don't know whose episode it was. It was a joke. I was a servant in One Eyed Jack's helping Audrey get ready for work and I had a humpback and a huge mole on my face with hair sticking out of it. [*laughs*] Red lipstick everywhere but on my lips and no one recognized me at all. Finally I was like, "Guys! It's me!" That was pretty funny and then everyone had their picture taken with me!

Richard Beymer with Lesli Linka Glatter as the One Eyed Jack's servant

Tina Rathborne: The minute I started working on the episode I called everyone in the cast and asked if they would rehearse and many did. Michael Ontkean sort of said, "Who are you?" and there was no rehearsing done. [*laughs*] I think it was the last day of shooting - we had three sets going and I simply walked between them all, spending the majority of my time working with Leland. I realized there was someone standing behind my shoulder and it felt like they had been there for a little while. I turned around and it was Michael. He said, "Tina, I don't want to do my close-up without you." There was some pleasure in getting people's confidence. It was very rewarding to me.

Duwayne Dunham: The whole experience of *Twin Peaks*, especially the first season was extraordinary and probably the most fun I've had in my entire career. It was made that way because of David and Mark. The way everybody approached those first seven episodes, I believe still any of us could call one another and it would be like family. Very close bonds were formed for whatever reason and we didn't know we were making something special. We knew it was unusual, but it was the camaraderie of everyone that David and Mark were able to put together. It was an extraordinary bunch.

Elementary

As a Washington State native and established leading man in David Lynch's Dune *and* Blue Velvet, *Kyle MacLachlan was the quintessential choice to portray Special Agent Dale Cooper when he was cast in the role just months shy of his thirtieth birthday. In a series full of young stars and proven screen veterans, MacLachlan was the undisputed leader of the versatile cast.*

MacLachlan's Golden Globe-winning performance of Agent Cooper brims with keen intuition and impeccable humor, laced with an undercurrent of mysticism and resolve. Rarely judgmental or coarse, Cooper is the moral compass of the series and the ideal outsider to engage with the dark secrets of Twin Peaks.

Kyle MacLachlan: I was pretty fresh out of acting training school and David thought that I would be the right guy to play Paul [Atreides] in *Dune*, and that experience led directly to *Blue Velvet*. He actually presented me the script while we were filming *Dune* and I read it and I thought it was very disturbing.

At this time I had probably read three scripts in my life, so I didn't know what to make of it. I knew that it was incredibly powerful and dangerous and sort of frightening... and thrilling at the same time. And those are the kind of responses you look for when you read material. It often doesn't happen, but in this particular case it did.

When we finally finished *Dune*, we were supposed to start right away on *Blue Velvet,* but it got postponed and we finally came back and did it, started in the summer of '85. But those two working relationships with David led directly to *Twin Peaks*. David could easily have turned his back on me after the response to *Dune*, but he didn't and he stayed with me which is really a testament to his loyalty.

Tim Hunter: Kyle was just the sweetest guy in the world. He was such a good actor and such a good collaborator. I think the directors actually liked Kyle so much that we really had some loyalty to him in terms of being the anchor of the show and how good he was. The character of Cooper still ranks as one of the great TV cops, as off-kilter as he is. It's also kind of a unique "Lynch-ian" character with his formalities and all his quirks.

Billy Zane *(John Justice Wheeler)*: I loved working with Kyle; he was such a lovely fellow. I spent some time with him in Manhattan and LA after the fact. I've been a fan of his ever since I saw him in *Dune* and he was great to work with; we had that scene sharing a drink. I thought Cooper was a weekly example of great nobility and a tender masculinity with purpose; there was righteousness without self-righteousness.

Wendy Robie: People were quirky in different ways and Agent Cooper respected them and found value in them and you know, the Log Lady was Margaret and she had things to tell him. He treated Lucy as a real professional and her problems were serious.

Lesli Linka Glatter: Look at Dale Cooper as a character. This guy was so unique! He's this guy who travels with special ear plugs and knows all about the trees. He is a man of detail and observation. Kyle was brilliant, created a very indelible character, and it was all about keeping it real and grounded.

Kyle MacLachlan as Agent Dale Cooper

Duwayne Dunham: Dale Cooper is a quirky character, but in all the work David has done, I believe the sensibility and the tone of *Blue Velvet* is very similar to *Twin Peaks*. Jeffrey in *Blue Velvet* finds an ear and takes it to the detective and he says, "Yeah, that's an ear alright." He plays it straight, but that line gets a laugh from the audience. You have a similar theme in *Twin Peaks* where Kyle MacLachlan plays it by the book. Yes, he's solving crimes, but in a very fresh way. There were interesting detectives before like Columbo, but this one was very peculiar in his speech and mannerisms.

Agent Cooper provides a personal narrative of the series through many Dictaphone monologues to Diane, Cooper's unseen assistant. These recordings document Cooper's philosophical views of life and his indulgences of nature, coffee, pie, and doughnuts – all while constructing a dossier of the town's suspects.

Kyle MacLachlan: So much of Cooper was already on the page in his unique observations of his surroundings and his relishing of the sights and the sounds and the smells of the Northwest. Cooper really took time to engage in all his senses and I always felt that was a nod to David, who really does enjoy the world around him.

Caleb Deschanel: Kyle is great; he's obviously sort of a muse for David because he's been part of his movies over the years, so I think there was probably a lot of David in him, in a "Golly gee willikers" kind of way. With Kyle, the character was very much like a young kid who was making discoveries: "Oh, wow! The pie, the coffee..." There was always a childlike response to it. All the images of him sort of meditating over things - it was very much David where he's drawing out these crazy ideas with the sheriff and everybody going along with it. It was definitely part of that. It was really kind of interesting.

Richard Beymer: Kyle always knew his lines. [*laughs*] He could scan three or four pages in about a minute and a half and just know it. We didn't have many scenes together as I recall, but he was always open and friendly and what he did in this piece (I think) was just perfect; that character was David.

Kimmy Robertson *(Lucy Moran)*: I think Kyle knew David better than anyone else and knew what David would want when he wasn't there. He even looked like a young David [*laughs*] and was just a perfect fit.

Kyle MacLachlan: David Lynch is a painter, a filmmaker, an artist, a writer. I mean, he's a true Renaissance man and he really does take everything in as an artist would. Cooper's sort of acute and focused attention on detail is also something that I think David has in terms of his qualities. There were some mannerisms I adapted from David as well, like the hands clasping together and some speech patterns.

Mark Frost: We've always thought Cooper was a weird amalgam of David, Kyle and myself and that's how I remember the process. I wrote a lot of the Cooper monologues after the ones David and I had done together. Of any character I'd worked on to that point, I was writing Cooper in something close to my own voice. Probably [with] his curiosity, his analytical nature and the underlying interest in mythology and spirituality which comes out of him more and more as the series go by.

Kyle MacLachlan: I think Mark Frost has a very dry sense of humor and kind of a wonderful way with words, which I'm sure found its way into Cooper on the page, and that was part of him as well. I couldn't really tell you where David started and Mark picked up in the character - he was really an amalgam of both. Knowing David as well as I did, I think I was more prone to shade my characterization more towards David's physicality and way of speaking over Mark's.

As Sheriff Harry S. Truman, Michael Ontkean portrays the conventional foil to all of Dale Cooper's idiosyncrasies. Truman's steadfast and secular approach to the law contrasts with Cooper's instinctive techniques, but a genuine friendship forms between them in the pursuit of Laura Palmer's killer.

Mark Frost: We obviously knew that Kyle was going to be our guy pretty early on and we knew that character in and out. Sheriff Truman was more of an unknown; we had written him a little more loosely because he was so laconic he didn't have as many words. Then the moment we saw the two of them together, we knew the chemistry was fantastic because you had these two great archetypes: a fast-talking urban Sherlock and this slower small-town guy whose fundamental decency made up for whatever he lacked in mental acuity. They were a classic duo and they really enjoyed each other's company which helped a lot.

Michael Horse, Michael Ontkean and Kyle MacLachlan

Kyle MacLachlan: Those two characters were pretty much established from the get-go. I met Michael and he's a very sort of gentle and soft-spoken guy who moves at his own pace and his own rhythm. I think we both (being good actors) intuitively knew who these people were and what that relationship should be.

Michael Ontkean: As we all know, David is adept at the ancient art of alchemy. The first day of rehearsals for the pilot take place east of Seattle at the Red Lion Inn. Just the three of us in a room, David-Kyle-Michael. The Lynch sorcery is subtle, easy, refined, and full of fun. David and Kyle have done two movies together and are already half way home. I mention the sheriff's cadences (as written by Mark and David) remind me of this friend of mine from Missouri who's a fisherman and a lumberjack.

I ask Kyle the name of his favorite band. Instantly he says Led Zeppelin. David says this is the happiest day of Agent Cooper's life. David doesn't direct. He plays drums and bass guitar and a dozen keyboards. We're immediately launched into a kind of magic mushroom melodic lark that feels like a Thelonious Monk jazz riff. This culminates in David bringing us to his rental car and playing that forever haunting *Peaks* theme written by Angelo Badalamenti. Pure pleasure. This cements for Kyle and Michael, in a completely visceral way, the essence of David's vision for the movie. A home-made circus in an offbeat church.

Kyle MacLachlan: I think there was kind of (on Michael's side) an appreciation for Cooper's eccentricities. He had tremendous patience with Cooper, because sometimes Cooper's ideas were moving pretty quick and were certainly unusual compared to what he was used to. I think Cooper also appreciated Sheriff Truman's sort of dry manner and matter-of-fact approach to the world and for some reason the dynamic seemed to work really well and that was pretty much what we established right on day one.

Kimmy Robertson: Michael was so handsome and so independent of anything and anyone. I liked how he wasn't needy and he had no ego. He acted like the sheriff the entire time, even when he wasn't on camera. He listened and he was kind. He was not judgmental in any way and I thought that was so unusual, but David and Mark picked unusual people to be in that show.

Joan Chen: I like Michael Ontkean a great deal; he's so different. He's such a dreamy guy. He's soft and soft-spoken and he didn't have any aggression it seemed in him. Just a really nice, gentle, decent guy. He's a poet and I remember him reading me his poems and he was a really sweet man. He was different from showbiz, very laid-back and sweet and into his poems and songs.

Michael Horse: Kyle and Michael were very, very nice to me and they were so funny. They understood and played off my character. Hawk was kind of the soul of the whole place. A lot of people didn't know what was going on, but Hawk did. It was such a heavy piece, but there was a lot of humor going on there.

Miguel Ferrer *(FBI Agent Albert Rosenfield)*: I was really friendly with Michael, but I became good friends with Kyle. We all got along beautifully. We just got along very well, never a rough moment, never a bad mood, nothing. I think all of us were really happy to be there. All of us had a sense we were doing something special. No one was making any money. Kyle and Michael might have been, but if they were, they were the only ones. [*laughs*] You know, we were all quite honored to be asked to be a part of that thing.

Jimmy Stewart on Acid

Kyle MacLachlan: The most fun was when David came to visit because things would be changed around and his eye would see things no one else would be able to deliver because David was the creator. He could do whatever he wanted. I think he felt the freedom of that and we all really enjoyed it.

David Lynch returned from the set of Wild at Heart *to direct episode 2, a pivotal development in the search for Laura Palmer's killer that blasts open the mystical sphere of* Twin Peaks *and turns the tables on conventional network television storytelling.*

Randy Barbee *(series assistant director)*: I read somewhere where David Lynch was described as Jimmy Stewart on acid, and he really was. He came off as being so straitlaced. He would come in wearing these pressed khaki pants, this white, pristine, long-sleeved shirt buttoned at the collar and this long, duck-billed hat, also khaki colored. He would say, "How ya doin' mister?" or "Golly gee," and he talked really like Jimmy Stewart, but he came up with these concepts where you would go, "Where is he going with this?"

Richard Beymer: A lot of times David would go to his trailer to meditate, and when he would come back he would have an idea and he wasn't about to explain why. [*laughs*] He'd just come back and say, "I have an idea, let's do this."

Gregg Fienberg *(series producer)*: David just has this really crazy take on the world, but it's grounded in a strange reality. A lot of people think he's this strange guy, but he's the most brilliant person I've ever been on a set with, to this day. I've never seen anyone command a set and have people eating out of his hand because he's such a gentleman and so entertaining and fun. It was unbelievable, the experience on the set with that man.

Wendy Robie: It was lovely working with David. He would go to each actor in a scene and he would have a word for you, a private magical word, and it was yours to use. It was kind of like a secret and it would be completely unexpected and often I would read a scene on the page and think this is hilarious and he would see it completely differently. He would see the horror and the pain and the sorrow and grief in something and take you to that place and yet, you would still see the humor.

Philip Segal: Lynch was just a fascinating person. He didn't like to prep the episodes, so he just walked in and shot them. One particular day he was an hour and a half late because he was pulling into the studio and had seen a license plate that started with 666, so he drove around until he saw another one that would cancel out the bad mojo from the first one.

Robert Bauer *(Johnny Horne)*: David wanted the actors to inhabit the skin of the characters and have a sense of themselves within the characters. There was no playing a scene wrong, because if you were in the skin of the character, whatever came out of you is what came out of you.

I remember he asked me if I should play with my food. So during the scene I just started fucking around with my food, which led to me tossing mashed potatoes around the table. The other actors had no idea this was coming, so their reaction to it was real and very much this wonderful sort of feeling of being in the moment, but at the same time you're fulfilling the needs of the ensemble of the scene.

Chris Mulkey *(Hank Jennings)*: My first scene is the phone call from prison and Lynch said, "Hey Chris, take this domino, here... just Hank has a domino." So I said, "Okay, sure." I was waiting around to shoot, so I stuck it in my mouth. He goes, "Yeah, that's it! Roll!" I can't tell you about the domino though, there are two or three things I'm not supposed to talk about and the double four is one of them. It adds up to eight, which has something to do with balance in the universe. You'll figure it out. I did eat a lot of doughnuts on the show.

Richard Beymer: So when it came to this baguette scene, as I recall, that was in the first season and I was still getting used to different directors, particularly David. So my brother brings me this baguette back from France and he's saying how great it was and he gives it to me and I have certain dialogue while I'm eating.

David said, "Really take a big bite out of that baguette when you're talking." He did another take and said, "No, no, really fill your mouth up with that baguette." And I'm thinking I'm a rich and sophisticated guy and I've got this certain character going and all of a sudden I'm eating this thing and I just couldn't get it. I didn't understand how this connected with this character, but he wasn't going there with me.

He kept cutting and saying, "No, I want *more*. I don't care if I even hear the words." So I finally did it more, but ultimately as I got to know David I realized he probably wanted a *lot* more. I could have stuffed that in my mouth and [*loud nonsense*] and he would have been really happy. But, I didn't go that far, I kept pulling back because I didn't know how far I was supposed to go. I think he got about 65 percent of what he was looking for.

Sherilyn Fenn: The day where Audrey dances in the diner I came to the set and David said, "We're going to get some cappuccinos and rewrite this scene and at the end you're just gonna stand up and start to groove to this really cool, sexy, jazzy thing that Angelo and I just wrote! It's Audrey's theme, you're just gonna get lost in that music!"

I said, "What do you mean? I just worked this scene out with my teacher!" I was so nervous, [*laughs*] but I love him and trust him and said okay. I didn't know sometimes what I was doing, to be honest. He knows the world and if you trust him and go into it, you'll fly if you don't think about it too much.

Mädchen Amick: There was an episode where I'm on the phone and Eric has just called me to threaten me and it was scary and I didn't know he was able to get a hold of me. So at the end of the phone call, David just kept directing me saying, "Okay Madge-kin, keep staring off into the distance, keep staring off... okay Madge-kin, just slowly, slowly start to look up at the ceiling..." [*laughs*]

So I'm slowly looking up, right? And he just had me hold there staring at the ceiling until he finally said "cut". So I went over and was like, "What am I doing? What was the point?" David said, "Oh it just looks good, Madge-kin!" I was overthinking it and he thought it was just a really cool shot, and that's David. Sometimes it's really simple and yet, brilliant.

Ray Wise: I remember David was always so thrilled when a glorious accident would happen and it added to everything that was going on. I remember a scene where I'm listening to my phonograph and I pick up my daughter's picture off the table and start dancing around with it in the room and crying. Then Grace Zabriskie comes in and tries to stop me from dancing and we sort of wrestle around with the picture and smash it on the coffee table accidently.

I remember I cut my hand on some of the glass in that picture and the blood dripped onto the picture itself and I remember smearing the blood with my fingertips, like I was finger painting. It was my *Apocalypse Now* moment, like when Martin Sheen has that scene in his hotel room where he gets wasted and drunk and starts smashing the hotel room around and actually cut his hand on the mirror when he broke it.

Kimmy Robertson: David Lynch's set is different than anyone else. He creates a little world, or a 'bubble.' He gathered us all together and said we are going to do a scene that has to do with Tibet. He explained a little bit and I didn't understand, even though I had been reading a Joseph Campbell book. He was talking about something more advanced than my evolution, but it created an atmosphere of palpable magic. If you had the right eyes, you could see the sparkling energy within the bubble.

Mark Frost: David and I shared an interest in Tibet and mysticism so we made that an interest of Cooper's and thought it would be interesting to fold into the traditional, Western-logical detective process we've seen in many characters over the years. Cooper has a layer of intuition that relies on alternate ways of knowing beyond simply being the smart guy and figuring stuff out. That [the "Tibetan Rock Throw"] was the first scene where we had some fun with that, but also introduced it as a central character trait.

Jonathan P. Shaw *(editor, episode 2)*: There was a lot of great coverage for it, but there was this metaphor for baseball, such as how we pace off ninety feet and you're actually seeing this twisted logic play out. That struck me. Again, this is episode 2 so you're sitting there and you have Cooper throwing rocks and Truman is at the chalkboard calling off names. It really set another tone for the show, and it was of course funny.

Kyle MacLachlan: When that script came through and I have a whole long speech about Tibet and this whole thing, I knew we were really going into uncharted territory in terms of television. Sure, the pilot set the tone, but in terms of just pure, eccentric, and unusual scenes, that's got to be one of the top ones, and it is one of my favorites. I remember we all laughed and took a chance throwing rocks. Someone was really good, I don't know if it was Kimmy or one of the other girls, but she hit the bottle first.

Michael Horse: My favorite scene is when I went to pick up the big iron pot with the rocks we're gonna throw. I put on these oven mitts and said, "What does this mean?" Lynch said, "Nothing, we just thought it'd be funny to see you in oven mitts." [*laughs*] I was picking up the pot and said, "Remember when he picks up the big hot pot and brands himself in *Kung Fu*?" and everyone laughed. There were a lot of funny things and it was very organic. You throw people into this magical world of David's and things happen you don't think would happen.

Kyle MacLachlan: I remember we shot a lot of film, trying to get the rock to hit the bottle because we wanted to do it in a wide [shot], just so you could see that the bottle actually broke. I came close a number of times, but I think I finally hit it but it took a long time. Then, they set up a shot closer to the bottle to see it hit, which is what they probably should have done in the very beginning. [*laughs*]

Kimmy Robertson: I remember David said to Harry [Goaz], "He's going to throw one at you and almost hit you. Do whatever you want Andy!" (He called us by our character's names.) So he threw one and Harry had picked up a rock unbeknownst to anybody. He reached up when Kyle threw the rock and the rock flew out of his hand so it looked like it hit off his forehead. I almost peed my pants; I almost died laughing because I wasn't on camera! I literally went down on one knee. Harry's so brilliant.

Michael Horse: Being on that set was like watching it on television; sometimes you're working on something and then when you're not, you're watching others do dialogue and all that stuff. When you were watching the filming on *Twin Peaks* you were in the consciousness of *Twin Peaks*. It was hard to just break that and go sit down. When we were in there filming we felt it just like you saw it on TV and I think that's why it worked. There was an honesty there. We weren't trying to do something odd or weird like I've seen some people try and do. We were just thrown into this artistic environment and that was the magic of it.

New Blood

The rich palette of characters in Twin Peaks *broadened in the first season as intriguing personalities continued to join the cast. After David Lynch worked with film and stage troubadour David Patrick Kelly on the set of* Wild at Heart, *Kelly was cast as Jerry Horne, the wild and worldly brother of Ben Horne.*

David Patrick Kelly *(Jerry Horne)*: Mark and David gave me such creative freedom. They let me design Jerry's haircut and we talked a little bit about the Kennedy brothers back in the day. The Horne brothers always represented to me every bad thing you may have read about the Kennedy brothers. When I say that, I have to tell you that I'm a Kennedy Democrat. I love the Kennedy brothers, but if you read the *National Enquirer* and you believed all the bad things that were said about them, I sort of wanted to be the evil doppelgängers of the Kennedy brothers.

Harley Peyton: For those two guys [the Horne brothers] it was like watching an absurdist tennis match, they were so great going back and forth, so you would try to find that humor. It came so natural to the two of them, and because they played it so well you also got to do comedy in ways you did in other parts of the show.

David Patrick Kelly: I based Jerry's affinity for food on a restaurateur here in New York – I would always go to this store that was attached to the restaurant. This guy would be walking through the restaurant tasting different foods. So I based some of Jerry Horne on that. There's a scene where Ben and I are walking through and I say, "I didn't know what it was, but I ate it anyway." [*laughs*] I heard this restaurateur say it once so I added those things in. It was just a great aspect of the character; people claimed influence too in that kind of a character - sex and food – that's what Jerry was about.

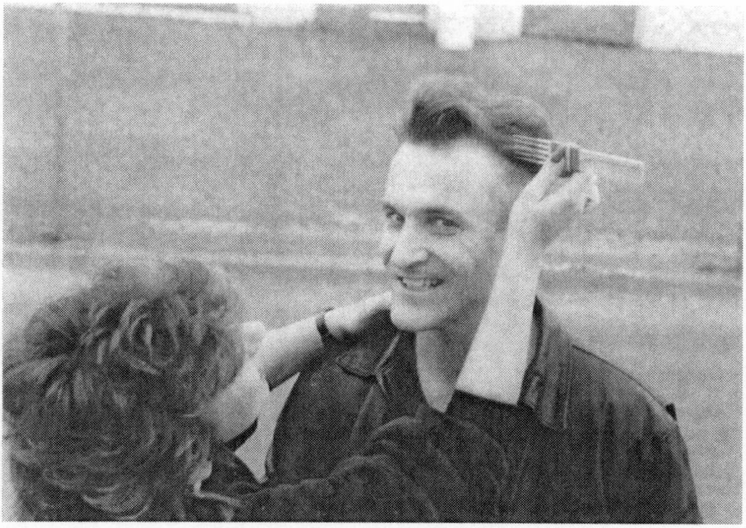

Annette Fabrizi-Coccarelli and David Patrick Kelly

Mark Frost: Writing the Horne brothers was a lot of fun, as Richard and David had great chemistry which we discovered from the first day they worked together. It was almost like writing for a comedy team because their timing was so great and they played off each other so flawlessly. Those were some of my favorite scenes to write. They had a rhythm and pattern to them that was almost musical. You gave them something and they knew exactly what to do with it and it was really fun, those were always some of my favorite dailies to see.

David Patrick Kelly: Working with Richard Beymer was one of the great highlights of my career. He was so generous and inventive. He and Russ Tamblyn being *West Side Story* alumni was a thrill for me. Russ was in the original movie of *Peyton Place* and Richard was in [*The Diary of*] *Anne Frank*... I mean, just the actors in *Twin Peaks* were very inspiring to me.

Miguel Ferrer made his Twin Peaks *debut in episode 2 as FBI Agent Albert Rosenfield, a callous but brilliant forensics expert. Rosenfield's arsenal of insults and barbs earn the ire of Sheriff Truman and also measure the depths of Agent Cooper's tolerance.*

Miguel Ferrer: Mark Frost gave me a VHS copy [of the pilot] and said, "Go home and look at this and call me and we'll talk." So I went home in the afternoon and put it in the tape player and watched the whole thing. I then called up everyone I knew and said, "You have to come to my house *right now*," and I showed this to about five or six friends. I'd never seen anything like it, obviously nor had anyone else, certainly not on TV.

There's a guy I grew up with who has since become sort of the main guy in the world of personal protection. If you are Lady Gaga and have a stalker, you call this guy's company. This guy reminded me of what I thought Agent Rosenfield should be like, so I thought of my friend who is this super personal protection person. His name is Gavin de Becker and that is the person upon whom I based Albert Rosenfield.

Gavin de Becker: I spent my teens as a 'brother' of Miguel... and I still am. I was taken in by his mother and family after the death of my mother. Of course I saw the show. I didn't know until later that Miguel was doing a sort of impression of me. I was blind to it, beyond a strong feeling of loving the character.

Kyle MacLachlan: Miguel is one of my favorites. I think the dynamic, the energy, the rhythms – the character of Albert was so opposite of Cooper and it gave Cooper a chance to reveal his patience and his understanding of human nature. Albert is obviously not easy to be around, but Cooper appreciated and enjoyed him for who he was and his abilities and wasn't really bothered by Albert's abrasiveness and straightforwardness. He actually embraced it and sort of enjoyed it.

That relationship was a great way to indirectly reveal more about Cooper, I felt. I just enjoyed working with Miguel so much, he's so smart and he's fearless. I love his choices and his intensity and everything about him. He's just one of my favorites and that dynamic was great. Harry didn't really understand what was going on, but Cooper made it all okay.

Harley Peyton: Ferrer was so good and that character was introduced in an episode I wrote. The insult comedy was something I loved. Mark and I wrote most of the scripts to a certain extent, so some of those lines are his but it was really fun to write that guy and write with that attitude. It was not one that I was unfamiliar with since I was from the Northwest and I came from a small town there and had a good approach to how that character would react. I remember later my wife had found a website dedicated to his insults.

Miguel Ferrer: I remember getting the scripts and about every second or third episode it would fall to me to explain everything that had come before, so that if you just came in from Mars and had never seen an episode of *Twin Peaks*, I'll explain the whole thing for you. And that happened, I don't know, about half a dozen times where I would sit there and have columns of exposition just explaining what had gone before with names and dates, people and places, things and events and stuff.

The most awful words in the English language that a director can say in a moment like that were "let's get it in one." I would see that coming and [sigh] it was just so torturous! Sometimes it would be me by myself, sometimes it would be me and Kyle just exchanging these massive, massive chunks of exposition and those were just so hard. So I remember those and being so happy when they were successfully completed.

Robert Engels: I remember Miguel saying something about the music business and I said, "How do you know anything about the music business?" He said, "Oh, I've got a member of the family in it." [*laughs*] A perfect Rosenfield line, and I thought, "A member of the family? Oh yeah, Rosemary fucking Clooney!" I was completely unaware that she was his mother, but Miguel would never say that, he would just mess with you.

Tina Rathborne: I loved all the scenes, but there was one that was so much fun. It was the one in the hospital with Agent Rosenfield with Laura's corpse on the gurney. Working with Miguel, we were always laughing when we made that scene. It had something to do with the drill. I think it was the kind of drill you would use to put screws into the wall and when you press the trigger it would go [high-pitched drill sound] and we would all crack up. It was hardly surgeon's equipment! [*laughs*] I was looking at the scene and realized there was an undercurrent of silliness, especially with the drill. Everybody was laughing out loud as we did that. That was the most "fun."

Miguel Ferrer: I remember I had the drill and I kind of revved it up close to Sheryl Lee's face. [*laughs*] I remember saying "Listen, I'm really being safe with this. I'm being careful. So please don't worry, you're not going to get hurt. I'm really going to be responsible!" She just smiled at me and said, "Do whatever you want. I'm not worried."

Then I remember we got to the point where Truman slugs me and I wind up lying on top of her. I landed on her pretty hard and I was really concerned. I said, "Is that okay with you? I'm trying to be careful!" She looked at me again and gave me a big smile and said, "Do whatever you want." And that's my clearest memory of that day. She was so trusting and lovely, and such a sweet person and that was fun.

Sheryl Lee returned to Twin Peaks *in episode 3 as Laura Palmer's cousin, Madeline "Maddy" Ferguson, to attend Laura's funeral. Visiting from Missoula, Montana, Maddy opts to stay in Twin Peaks and joins James and Donna's quest to unmask Laura's killer.*

Sheryl Lee *(Madeline Ferguson)*: I had been hired for the pilot for a week in Seattle and I stayed because that was the end of my job on *Twin Peaks*. Months and months later David called me and said, "How would you feel about moving to LA?" I had been in LA when I was eighteen and I was not going to come back without a job. I said, "I'm dead." And he said, "Don't worry, I'll figure something out." I came down and I was a little bit like a deer in the headlights.

I was not in my element at all. I was very shy and intimidated, trying to navigate myself through this whole new world and this whole new city that felt very overwhelming to a kid from Colorado. When you start weaving all of that together, I look back now and think, "Oh my God, I don't know how I did it!" [*laughs*]

Chris Mulkey: One day I was in craft services and Sheryl Lee (who is just a knockout) walked up to me and she looked at me very seductively and said, "Chris, do you believe that there's a devil?" I looked her in the eye and said, "Sheryl Lee, I absolutely do and I think I'm talking to the devil *right now*!" [*laughs*]

Sheryl Lee: Maddy was a collaboration. We wanted her to be very different, so physically we started there. For me it was about figuring out what Maddy felt like energetically compared to Laura. There was definitely a difference for me in how they felt when I was portraying them. Laura, I had to find from deep within myself, but Maddy I found more from the outside going in.

James Marshall: The character of Maddy was a trip; I liked it in a way because it was such a classic sort of twist. That kind of thing has been done throughout the ages and it gave me something to work with as an actor. At the time I was looking at it going, "Is anyone going to believe she's identical to Laura?" It was always like that on *Twin Peaks*: "Are they going to buy this?" [*laughs*]

Ray Wise: Sheryl and I became very close and she's just a wonderful actress. Working with her on camera was really so easy and such a joy. She's just such a generous and giving actress, completely open. I like to operate that way myself. During the making of that pilot she gave me a picture of her (from when I believe she was in the fourth or fifth grade) and I kept it in my wallet the entire time I was playing Leland Palmer. We were and still are very close and enjoy each other's company when we get the opportunity to be together.

Sheryl Lee: I was constantly in awe of Ray and Grace. Ray's versatility is absolutely phenomenal. He is a brilliant actor! Grace is the same way. I couldn't have had better parents on that show than those two. [*laughs*] I was lucky to have such good actors and actresses to work with, and most importantly, kind people - really, really kind. I keep using that word, but it's an important word for me. We felt safe with each other and felt comfortable with each other and thank God, because a lot of what we had to do and where we had to go – it was a gift and a blessing to have that kind of safety with each other. It really was a wonderful way to work.

Amen

After directing David Lynch in his first credited acting role in the 1988 film Zelly and Me, *Tina Rathborne was invited to direct episode 3. With* Zelly and Me *charged by domestic turmoil, Rathborne was a sterling candidate to tackle the spectacle of Laura Palmer's funeral. Notable as the only scene to feature the entire regular cast of the series, the friends and family of Laura gather to bid a final and unhinged farewell.*

Warren Frost: When we were back in LA there was a funeral scene at a cemetery and they had to get a whole bunch of pine trees because the cemetery was full of palm trees, so they had to get them in boxes or big pots so you couldn't see the palm trees! It was kind of a bizarre day, but they were very inventive, everyone was.

Tina Rathborne: I went to the location a couple of times. I saw the palm trees and just thought, "Oh, my God! This is Seattle? I've got palm trees in the background!" I was told by Gregg [Fienberg] I had to do the whole scene in a day and I just sort of said, "Okay, if that's what you need!"

There's not one shot of the entire cast in the whole scene, so that was definitely the most challenging scene to cut. Toni Morgan was the editor assigned to me and we were given an editing machine -

it was kind of like the Alien [Ridley Scott] - it looked prehistoric to me! I had never even seen such a machine. It was nowhere even near the Steenbeck flat-top film editing machines.

I did do some long tracking shots of the cast walking towards Laura's casket. I didn't use any of them as you can see. If I remember correctly, it really was Toni's idea to do the beginning of the scene with nothing but close-ups. Once I saw that, it made sense to me and I took it.

Ray Wise, Grace Zabriskie and Richard Beymer

Grace Zabriskie: I remember walking between Leland and Ben Horne, being led to my daughter's gravesite. A bit wobbly, clearly, from sedation. I got excited by an idea that Sarah should also be trying to smoke, as was her wont, further complicating an already precarious walk, as both my arms were being held onto to keep me from stumbling. I suggested this idea, and was told, "Oh, that might be a bit too much." (After all these years I still don't think it would have been too much.) But, I was excited by the chance to work a scene with so many of my fellow actors, and remember the day very fondly.

Tina Rathborne: After we finished and it was logged, Toni told me, "Tina, I didn't want to tell you this but I've never edited anything in my life!" She was a writer and a journalist and just an extraordinary person. We loved working together. We finally condensed it as you saw (to the expressions of the mourners) and that was not at all what I had originally in mind.

Michael Horse, Kyle MacLachlan, Wendy Robie and Everett McGill

Wendy Robie: We just spent the whole day in the great outdoors being these people, hanging out [*laughs*] and I remember wandering around. We shot in the cemetery and they had added gravestones and they must have paid a lot to do that. There were some rather humorous ones like "I told you I was sick!" I wish I could remember some of them [*laughs*] but I was vastly entertained that day. I remember I hung out with Sheryl Lee; it was a fun day.

Robert Bauer: We were all there and it was chaotic; it was a funeral scene and there was a lot of moving pieces. A few days before the shoot, I went to a bookstore and bought a used, first edition of *Peter Pan*. That was my bible; the thing that Johnny held on to as sort of an anchor to his topsy-turvy world.

The cast and crew on the funeral set. Sierra Madre, California

Charlotte Stewart: There was no script to the funeral. We were just all gathered out there in a circle. So I thought, "What would Betty, the eternal optimist do?" So I wore a "happy face" button on my suit. Nobody noticed it except for the fans watching it later.

Mädchen Amick: I was so excited because the whole cast was together filming something because all of our story lines were so separate from each other. Sometimes you wouldn't see cast members for a long period of time unless we got together for some promotional event. It was exciting and kind of like a class reunion in a way.

Tina Rathborne: I really enjoyed working with the characters who had a greater range of emotion in the scene than other scenes where they didn't have to give a strong emotion. I have to say I really enjoyed everyone I had to get down in the foxhole with. [*laughs*] I really did put everything I had into it. It was a pleasure.

Robert Bauer: It was a really cool day and Dana Ashbrook just exploded on to the scene, coming off of Johnny's line "Amen." He was young and raw and fucking fantastic. We met that day and became best friends to this day.

It was another one of those instances of it not being rehearsed to a tee, so all those actors responding in a very visceral real way was in reaction to things that happened in the moment. No one necessarily knew the highs and lows of what it was going to be. Everyone's at a really weird, fucked-up funeral where it's supposed to be somber yet all hell breaks loose.

Dana Ashbrook: I really just did what was written. It said Bobby screams at the funeral, so that's what I did. As far as that day it was the first time the whole cast had been together since coming back from the pilot. It was a big mess of a day, so many people to shoot so many things.

Tina Rathborne: Dana was wonderful to work with and was really into the part. Dana's amazing part where he breaks out of the pious mourners and assumes the town's responsibility for Laura's death is really one of the brilliances of the series to me - which is that it's infinitely layered. There's nothing pat about the dynamic in the town.

Dana Ashbrook: I remember being extremely nervous having to do that scene in front of everyone. These are all the people I love and respect and I wanted to do good and all that; just super nervous having to be the focal point in front of everyone else. But it was a fucking fun scene. Who gets to yell and scream in the middle of a funeral and fight? You don't get to do it every day.

Tina Rathborne: I remember when we were editing that [the funeral fight], the scene didn't move me enough. Then I saw the scene in slow-motion and it suddenly came together for me. It ramped the emotion of the media up to a human level in the scene. I was shooting so fast I only had one or two takes of Dana and James [*laughs*] and I probably used the slow-motion when I realized that those two shots just weren't going to cut it.

Sheryl Lee: I just remember the weirdness of that day and how surreal that was because I was at my own funeral. [*laughs*] I remember thinking this is probably the only time I'll do this in my whole life.

Tina Rathborne: It was definitely Leland's idea to throw himself on the casket; I remember saying, "Great!" Putting the casket on the scissor lift and having it go up and down was what made Leland throwing himself on the casket into its own moment. It really went to the center of the scene. I thought looking up at Grace and having her say, "You're not going to ruin this too!" added another level to the scene. The way Ray has his hands and his head on the coffin – it was irreplaceable. That angle to me totally fits with that extreme.

Ray Wise: I thought it was a marvelous idea. I remember as a young child going to several family funerals and funerals of friends of my parents (that sort of thing) and I saw some interesting reactions of family members when they were viewing their deceased loved one in the casket. Sometimes there were some emotional outbursts. I remember a man who was looking at his dead brother and was overcome and overwhelmed with grief and picked his brother up in his arms and just kept hugging him. He picked him up right out of the casket! So Leland throwing himself on the casket seemed perfectly logical to me [*laughs*] and it didn't require any selling myself on being able to do that. It came pretty naturally.

Twin Cities

The roots of many cast and crew members can be respectively traced to the University of Minnesota and the Guthrie Theater in Minneapolis, Minnesota. In the late-sixties and seventies, Mark Frost and his family bonded with many trusted collaborators in the community who later brought their collective talents to Twin Peaks.

Warren Frost: I had a few good years out west, but found out that Hollywood wasn't interested in me becoming the new Clark Gable. So we moved on back to Minnesota. The Guthrie was an interesting place. We did some great stuff and it wasn't all classical. Wonderful actors would come and go. Minneapolis was an interesting place; Mark grew up there.

Mark Frost: I was working at the Guthrie from the age of fifteen all through high school as an intern; it was fundamental education. An immersive experience in theatrical storytelling, staging, writing, acting, directing, as a way of life. I just took to it like a duck to water, the start of my apprenticeship in the business of telling stories. I don't know if there's a direct correlation to what I brought into *Twin Peaks*, but that's where I started to form a sense of what it is to have an artistic point of view and an artistic sensibility and how to implement both when you're trying to creatively tell a story.

Lance Davis *(Martin Padley as Chet Weems)*: I won a McKnight Fellowship to the University of Minnesota where one of my professors was Warren Frost. Warren was from the business and not academia so he had a wonderful practical knowledge of what worked. Mark was the kid playing with trains on the floor. We had no idea he was going to be the wunderkind.

Richard Hoover: I remember Warren taught a class on television directing. I think I was his worst student. It's a mental process I don't have. I remember I did a [Bertolt] Brecht play and he used that video as the teaching tool of what not to do.

Warren Frost as Dr. Will Hayward

Peter Michael Goetz *(Jared Lancaster as Evan St. Vincent)*: Warren and I worked together at the University; he directed me in some plays and we acted together at the Guthrie, and since have been very close friends. I met Mark when he was (I believe) four years old and he spilled spaghetti in my lap the first time I met him.

Chris Mulkey: I was a wrestler at the University of Minnesota my freshman year and my friend said an athlete should take an arts class, like an acting class. It's easy and it's an elective. I did and I fell in love with acting immediately, it was crazy. I met Warren Frost who was a wonderful actor. He taught directing and acting at the University of Minnesota and before I knew it, I was doing plays there and at the Minneapolis Arts Institute.

Warren Frost: It was an interesting place for the theater and the arts, amazingly so - considering it was in the boondocks in some people's minds. I enjoyed teaching but I did not enjoy academic life, so that was a dichotomy that wasn't terribly good. I remember Lance Davis and Bob Engels very well, we became very good friends and they've done quite well.

Robert Engels: I look back on that stuff and there certainly was a Minnesota contingent to that. I'm not sure who decided it, but it's always nice in any show when you can use a friend who's really good! It's like a double whammy. It wasn't a situation where you had to lobby. On the other hand, you're like, "Wow, what if they fuck up?" [*laughs*]

Mark Frost tapped a couple of Minnesota associates along with his brother-in-law, Rick Giolito, for the production of "Invitation to Love," an inane soap opera watched by certain characters on Twin Peaks. *The 'show within the show' playfully mirrors and foretells different events of the first season.*

Mark Frost: We had one day to shoot all the segments. We booked the Ennis-Brown House, the famous Frank Lloyd Wright house in Los Angeles to shoot in. We had twenty or twenty-five scenes sketched out and some others we just improvised, with actors that I knew and had a lot of faith in, so we just winged it. I don't think we did more than one or two takes of any scene because we had so much ground to cover. I remember it as a really fun and productive day.

Rick Giolito *(Jason Dimbo as Montana)*: Mark asked me if I'd be interested in doing a small part in a 'show within the show' called "*Invitation to Love*," a soap opera. He wanted me to play the archetypical cad character. I was an actor in LA, fresh off of two years on *As the World Turns* as a psychotic rookie serial killing police officer... so I jumped at it. Happily, I found out that he had also cast several of our mutual family friends who were some of the most incredibly funny people I've ever met: Lance Davis and Peter Michael Goetz.

Peter Michael Goetz: I think that when Mark was doing *Twin Peaks* he created a character named Peter and he mentioned to me that he hoped I could play Peter when they were in the early stages of developing the pilot. I had a series going and couldn't do it. I read a few excerpts Mark was working on and of course I remember it jumping out at me with its quirkiness.

I was only available for the soap opera section inside of the show. In a sense, the soap opera was a counter to the real scene which was sometimes played in a soap opera in a comedic way – and we were the real ones in the background. A total opposite of what you would expect. You had to be very careful about not hurting anything in the house.

Lance Davis: My favorite moment was shooting the gun. We didn't rehearse. We were racing to get everything in. So we set up the shot. Got ready for my moment. Now I'd never shot this gun before, nor had Chet, and I was in no way prepared for the gun to be that loud in a living room. I'd obviously not realized that the crew were all holding their ears. So Chet shoots and instead of feeling any compassion or fear he reaches for his ear: "Ow..." I think in retrospect it was perfect for Chet.

Rick Giolito: It was the most hilarious day I've ever spent on a set. Peter and Lance took turns making Mark lose it as he 'attempted' to direct the scenes. All I can say is that it was an incredibly memorable day and the performances turned in by Peter and Lance were off the charts funny. I played the heavy and had a blast doing it.

Since it was a spoof on traditional soap operas, everyone had license to take it to the limit and we did. I think Erika [Anderson] was a little shocked by the whole thing. The poor girl. I say that because Mark, Lance, Peter and I spent the entire day cracking each other up. She had no idea we were all close friends just having a good time, but she caught on pretty fast to the inside joke.

Lance Davis: Given that we shot it in a day I thought it had possibilities. I loved the idea that the soap would mirror events that were going on in the town. But I heard that David didn't like video and that the cast had grown to such a size that they couldn't afford to have a whole separate plot line going on for the soap. I was disappointed when it went away, but I certainly understood. I thought they did a great job with a lot of it.

Rick Giolito: People did not really know the breadth of Mark's capabilities at that time, but he had tried some strange stuff in the past. David was known for this kind of work, Mark however was not. You might ask him about the musical comedy he wrote and staged in his formative years in Minneapolis based on Ugandan Dictator Idi Amin's life. I think he called it *Make Room for DaDa*. Now you know the type of mind necessary to come up with a show as fantastically twisted and original as *Twin Peaks*: "From the minds that brought you *Eraserhead* and *Make Room for DaDa - Twin Peaks*!"

Shenanigans

With filming ensconced in a San Fernando Valley warehouse, the cast and crew worked at a grueling pace to produce the first season of Twin Peaks *over the course of two months. During the intense weekly filming schedule, friendships and laughter were by-products of dedication and artistry.*

Mary Jo Deschanel: I might overuse the word "fun" to describe *Twin Peaks*, but it really was. There was a lot of respect for everyone, for the creative process, and for the story. There wasn't a star per se; it was a communal experience. Mark and David were responsible for that. The attitude on a project comes from the top.

Mädchen Amick: *Twin Peaks* always had its little worlds and we would get to know the people in them. I have the greatest collection of Polaroids from filming; one day I'll have to make a coffee table book out of them or something.

Dana Ashbrook: Mädchen was just this cool girl and we happened to really hit it off - it was just luck. She had a boyfriend at the time that she is now married to, to this very day. We always had good chemistry on-screen and that was it. We are great friends offscreen. I remember we would have these kissing scenes and if David was directing we would always ask him, "So... on a scale of one to ten, ten being the hottest, where should we put this kiss?" and he would say "eleven!" He made it so comfortable and fun, not weird.

James Marshall: Lara [Flynn Boyle] and I were like buds; we genuinely loved each other as friends because we did hang out and stuff. We were like brother and sister for the years we were shooting. Offscreen too, we hung out and would go to movies and shop for shirts. [*laughs*] So that was very alive.

Chris Mulkey: Kyle MacLachlan and Lara Flynn Boyle were living together and they lived seven houses down the block from me in Venice. We were all neighbors. Kyle was great; he and I had already done *The Hidden* together which was a wild show. It was great to be part of that incredible ensemble of actors. There was so much energy involved.

Working with Peggy Lipton, it was really like being married. We spent a lot of time together, but it was always as those two characters. It was Norma and Hank. It was so bizarre because we were so those characters. She was cold and distrustful, but would melt when I'd do certain things and vice versa. It was really like being those people.

Mädchen Amick: Peggy Lipton was so great; really our relationship that you see on-screen is similar to the way we were together. I really looked up to her and thought she was so beautiful and smart and talented. I was just in awe of her, like Shelly was in awe of Norma. I would hang out with Peggy and her daughters, Rashida and Kidada. Peggy was like a mentor to me and would give me advice as an upcoming starlet to keep my head screwed on straight. [*laughs*]

A favorite scene of mine is when Shelly and Norma go to the beauty parlor to get all made up. We get our hair and our nails and makeup done, feeling really spiffy and fancy and we have these horrible bouffant hairdos and terrible turquoise eye makeup. It was really fun to play these silly girls that thought they were so hot! [*laughs*]

Gary Hershberger: You know who I loved working with? Warren Frost. Loved Warren! We hit it off great. I didn't have too many scenes with him, but he was just great on set. He was just warm and he was one of the older guys on the cast so he was like a father figure. He'd been around awhile and had a good sense about him. I think his work is really understated. With so many showy characters he's like the only normal guy in town who has a shred of common sense. Everyone else was into something weird, but Warren stands out to me.

Joan Chen: Looking back, all these people - I wish I had just talked to them. I would hide in my trailer and I didn't get to know anyone. I was free, living my life, and because I only worked a couple of days a week at most, I was enjoying Los Angeles. Other times I would be unemployed in Los Angeles and employed out of the country. I never really got to enjoy it, and that was the only time I really did.

Wendy Robie: Everett [McGill] was really my teacher in all of this. I always teased him and told him that I was the star student of the 'Everett McGill School of Television Acting.' I had never been on television and other than a very bizarre commercial for JC Penney pantyhose I had never been in front of a camera.

Everett just gently guided me through all those mechanics where I had no idea. Just stuff you wouldn't think of, like if you look at someone up close in the way you would normally, on camera it can look like you're cross-eyed. I would memorize all the text so I always knew everything I said and everything he said, so when we would shoot he would quiz me and say, "What do I say here, honey?" and I would give him all the lines. He always thought that was funny I memorized these pages of dialogue word for word.

Richard Beymer: Working with Piper [Laurie]... was like working with a diva. [*laughs*] In the script it said we're having an affair and that I am supposed to just maul her - we're rolling in the bed, covers are flying and we're going crazy, you know. We're getting ready to do the scene and she says, "Oh no, you can't do that, my lipstick will smear and we'll have to put my makeup on again." So I looked at the director and said, "What am I supposed to do?"

She didn't want to do the romp in the bed and she was making all sorts of reasons why that couldn't happen. I couldn't do this, I couldn't do that. Finally I got to the end of the bed and I said, "Piper, can I at least kiss your toes?" [*pause*] She said that would be alright. So that's why I kissed her toes. That's not how it was written. We were supposed to really just be devouring each other. [*laughs*]

Piper Laurie: It was very pleasant working with Richard, but in some ways he was puzzling too. I don't know if he was putting us on or if he was just truly naïve about some of the lines that were supposed to be very suggestive in the motel scenes. The front office wanted us to make changes.

There was a line where Richard, barely dressed, gets up from the bed where we have clearly just had sex and moves toward the bathroom saying he's going to wash "Little Elvis." The comment was just too much for the front office. The remedy that David and Mark came up with was for the prop department to make a little Elvis doll about eight inches long [*fifteen seconds of laughter*] and they gave it to Richard to hold up as he says the line!

So Richard said the line beautifully and walked to the bathroom with his doll. When the scene was over he said to all of us, "I don't get it, why am I carrying this doll?" I don't know if he was putting us on or what. It appeared he didn't get the joke but he went ahead and did it anyway! [*laughs*] He's a very mysterious and nice man. I read his book [*Impostor*]. It was beyond me.

Robert Engels: I think "Little Elvis" was Mark's idea. I'm not sure who came up with the line, but the censors as I recall said, "You can't do that; that's not going to fly." Now, who would give a shit? [*laughs*] I think it was Mark that came up with the idea of getting literally a little Elvis doll. It would make less sense, but it no longer referred to "penis." So the little statue was pretty funny. Then I think we got a call from the Elvis estate saying "you can't use that image." I can't remember how that got resolved, maybe Mark would know. I don't think we paid them anything.

Michael Horse: The writing was wonderful. Hawk was a Native character that nobody had ever seen. He was funny, he was insightful, and held a mirror up to some stereotypes and did away with others. Being a Native actor, there's hasn't been a character like that that's came around. All Native characters are pretty much the same person. They let me do stuff and they didn't question it. The censors would ask if they had run this by the Native community and the writers said, "Yeah, we've got Michael!" [*laughs*]

Robert Engels: People have told me they've used Hawk's speech to his girlfriend [episode 4] at their weddings and I just think, "Oh, Christ. You're kidding!" [*laughs*]

Lesli Linka Glatter: We were trekking through the woods, shooting a scene in which the police team was searching for Jacques Renault's cabin. I remember Michael Horse, who was the Indian tracker, all of a sudden bent down and looked at a piece of grass as if he was picking up some kind of a sign from the universe and then pointed straight ahead as if he now knew the right direction to travel. We all held it together till I said "cut" and then everyone burst out laughing! It was so spontaneous, brilliant, and appropriate for the character and so very funny.

Michael Horse: Michael [Ontkean] was a vegetarian and he had some gas, and he wouldn't even acknowledge it. We're about ready for the first time to go into Jacques Renault's cabin. The camera is on the inside and we're going to go in and see evil, with Michael going in first, Kyle, and then me. All of a sudden Kyle looks at me with the strangest look and all of a sudden I get wind of what Mr. Ontkean has done. I just went "oh!!" and my eyes started watering. [*laughs*] They said "action!" and we went through the door. So that look you see on Kyle and mine's face... that's pretty much the surprising look we had. [*laughs*]

Tim Hunter: The cast in *Twin Peaks*, they were really cast for their characters so there were quirks in all of them. The actors tended to be in real life like nice actor versions of the characters and so it was fun to just see them spin it out on the set. It always had that nice edge of humor to it. It was a dream to work with that cast; everybody in it was so vivid and so great looking. They were all really great and eager to collaborate.

Chris Mulkey: The bridge between reality and the fantasy that was the show was so complete that when you got there to the set, everybody was so much their character. Even at parties, I would really relate to people in respect to my character. We all just had this relationship. It was bizarre.

Sheryl Lee: I just feel so fortunate that I (at such a young age) got to work with such an incredibly talented cast of actors. Everyone was so unique and creative and had such depth. It was a group of actors that could do the most intense drama and at the same time be wickedly funny. You can't put any of them in a box.

Kyle MacLachlan: In those initial few scripts (perhaps even the first seven) the characters were very clear and they cast beautifully. Each one of them from Michael Horse, Harry [Goaz], and Kimmy [Robertson] - they were all very, very unusual and yet, you really believed they were a team. There was a real feeling of camaraderie and of everyone getting along and a real pleasure and enjoyment out of the creative process that existed not only among the actors, but also with the creators too, in the beginning.

Flying Blind

As 1989 drew to a close, so did the concentrated production of the first season. Written and directed by Mark Frost, the season finale brings every story line to a boiling point and leaves most characters in mortal peril, including a shot and wounded Agent Cooper as the episode fades to black.

Paul Trejo *(editor, episode 7)*: I remember working on the first season finale; it was Christmas week in '89, but I distinctly remember being the only one at work that day. I remember watching a cut with David and Mark, and David's only comment was, "*Twin Peaks* was awfully busy that night, wasn't it?" There was so much going on with the fire and the mill, people getting shot.

Mark Frost: I remember all of us having so much fun. We were working really hard and it was at the end of the shoot and everyone was really gassed but we found a finishing kick where you can sort of "smell the barn" and everyone rallied and gave us the best energy for that final push. It was really great. I knew that I was going to do it [direct] because it was really the only one I had time to do, it was such hard work prepping the rest of the episodes that I couldn't afford to take time away from that process. So we jam-packed it with all the cliffhangers, and it was just a riot to shoot.

Piper Laurie: I loved working with Mark. He could tell me to do things that I wouldn't allow other directors to do, vulgar specific things like rolling my eyes – in my old Universal days when I was eighteen it would drive me crazy when directors asked to do fake or superficial things. But I was confident enough and trusted him. He would give me these tiny little tidbits to fill the moments in scenes to make them funnier. I was timid about doing it, but he encouraged me. I really enjoyed working with him, and of course in his movie [*Storyville*].

The Packard Saw Mill

Ray Wise: That first season finale was another great moment for me. We shot it at a hospital in Burbank where Leland kills Jacques Renault [Walter Olkewicz]; he smothers him with that pillow. That was a very striking moment for me, killing Jacques [Renault], and then I do the silent scream which was my idea. And that was before Al Pacino does it in *The Godfather: Part III*, so I think I may have done the first silent scream. [*laughs*] Anyway, I enjoyed doing it and thought it was pretty effective. Walter Olkewicz is another old buddy of mine, a fine actor, and we had a good time that day.

Wendy Robie: I didn't realize it, but in the scene that Mark directed [when Nadine tries to commit suicide] I was mouthing a word. I was saying "goodbye" and Mark wanted to hear it.

He asked me before we shot that scene, "What music always makes you cry?" and I said Patsy Cline singing "Crazy." [*laughs*] So I remember they used that on the playback while we did this scene and he had to make this camera go around my head and he wanted me to cry so that as the camera came around to the left side, the tear was coming down from under my eye patch. It was really tricky! [*laughs*] So that's what we did.

Mark Frost, Kyle MacLachlan, Carla Fabrizi

I was in my own little world saying, "Goodbye! Goodbye!" So I had to go to this recording studio with my little cassette of Patsy Cline. So this technician who has no idea – he has to play this over and over while I'm in the booth listening to Patsy Cline singing "Crazy" over and over in different ways saying "Goodbye!" and crying so Mark could put it in later.

I was saying goodbye because I remember watching this *National Geographic* story on TV with my daughter in my lap about the polar bears and it was called "Say Goodbye." This was ages ago, and this hunter had shot this polar bear and the little cubs were on the mother's body. As the camera pulls away you see these little cubs trying to wake up their mother and my daughter Samantha was in my lap crying and saying "Goodbye!" So that's a shameless use of sense memory to save that scene.

Chris Mulkey: I turned Leo into a vegetable! I shot him through the window and put him on a respirator in that episode. Hank Jennings was such a dick, but he was so fun to play! I could go on and on, but there was one hilarious scene (maybe Mark Frost was directing) and I was cutting Josie's hand and becoming blood brothers and we're drinking each other's blood. When I start talking my head is perfectly aligned with this deer's head so the beginning of the shot appears as if I actually have antlers coming out of my head! [*laughs*] We did subtle visual stuff like that.

Richard Beymer: Mark Frost is really the one who put everything in gear for me. I was at One Eyed Jack's and we were celebrating something with Blackie [Victoria Catlin] and we were pouring some wine and having some cigars. When Mark gave me the cigar, that prop absolutely let me know where to go with Ben. Ben Horne just entered. Before, I was floundering. I was spitting in fireplaces and I thought I was some straight kind of business guy. Holding it, working with it, just what it brought out in me when I would arrogantly puff on it – the cigar really loosened me up.

James Marshall: It was easier to work with Mark than a lot of the other directors because he was the creator of the show with David. You were working with one of the 'parents.' Mark is different from David, obviously, but he was an incredible person to work with because he let you do your own thing. There was no stroking of the ego, but everything was always positive.

Paul Trejo: I loved working on Mark's episode because I was juggling a lot of different balls in the air at the same time to make that final episode. That moment where Cooper answers the door and looks down was a jarring moment and I remember playing it a lot of different ways and coming up with the way we did it. It was another peak for me in terms of the whole run. It was a huge moment obviously, a real cliffhanger.

Setting up as many cliffhangers as possible and offering no resolution to most story lines (including "Who killed Laura Palmer?") placed pressure on ABC to continue Twin Peaks *beyond its first season. In a bold maneuver, producers submitted a false script to the network to mask the true intentions of the season finale.*

Gregg Fienberg: There were certain things we did along the way that were really bad, like sending them [ABC] scripts that were completely fake. I think it may have been the end of the first season. We didn't want them to know what we were really going to do, so we wrote a fake script and sent it to them saying this is what we'll shoot. Eventually I had to tell Phil [Segal] that was not what we shot. When Phil found out, I had put him in a really bad position, so he's like, "Well now what the fuck do I do? How do I tell my guys you sent me a fake script? They're never going to trust you again." So we had to find a way to get around it.

Philip Segal *(former director of programming, ABC)*: It took me awhile to figure out what was going on. It started where whole scenes were being hidden from us, so the scripts that were coming over were these dull, kind of bizarre scripts that weren't being shot. By the time it was in the can, it was too late.

Frank Byers: Gregg really held it together under very difficult circumstances. I can't even imagine his conversations with ABC. I just can't imagine them, the poor guy. [*laughs*]

Gregg Fienberg: I don't remember the details, but we smoothed it out. Rather than him [Segal] going nuts, he knew how to orchestrate it and he wanted to support the filmmakers and also take care of his guys at ABC. Ultimately, I think he did a really good job. He was aware the network didn't know how to handle the show because it was just a unique project for a network and that the nature of the show just wasn't what the network was used to handling, or the people - in Lynch's case.

Philip Segal: It became very difficult to get any kind of degree of management out of it and it was a very bizarre experience for me anyway because there were all sorts of walls in place to keep us away from the content. There were all kinds of muddiness surrounding that and it was all designed to confuse. It was a group of people who you have to understand had never made a television show and they didn't care. They did what they wanted to. It wasn't coming from a group of people whose intent it was to keep a show on the air for five years. It was an experiment.

With its peculiar disposition and intricate episodic approach, the cast and crew had few expectations of what the eventual audience reaction to Twin Peaks *would be, or if the series would even continue past its initial nine hours upon airing in the spring.*

Wendy Robie: I was so excited to see America get to share what we were enjoying. I can remember shooting that first season [and] I would get a script for the next episode and I wouldn't just go to my scene to see what I had to do, I would read it to find out what was going to happen. I loved it.

Lesli Linka Glatter: I was so thrilled to be working on the show but it felt like we were involved with this wonderful indie project that may or may not ever see the light of day. Was ABC really going to put this on network TV next to *Baywatch* or *Saved by the Bell*?

Frank Byers: I had no idea how it would be received, none. The crew, everybody on it was enthralled: "Where is this going?" We wouldn't see the script until almost the day we would shoot, and sometimes we wouldn't see them at all because they weren't ready. We were amazed every day. We would rehearse the scenes and our mouths would be open. The story was so compelling. We were hooked, we were all hooked.

Ken Scherer *(former chief operating officer, Lynch/Frost Productions)*: Because of being at AFI [The American Film Institute], I had seen David's work and his early projects and knew where he was in the spectrum of mainstream filmmaking and storytelling. I just knew it was different, everyone knew it was different. It was eerie and it had great music, it was shot in a different way. You don't ever know [how it will be received] and the truth is [*pause*] I don't think any of us understood it.

Kyle MacLachlan: Well, it was fun to do the stunt with Cooper getting shot, but you just don't know because it's all well and fun to shoot something, but unless you're a director or you're the editor, it's difficult to imagine what the finished product is going to be. So we just sort of had fun with these characters not knowing how the audience was going to respond or react to what we were doing or which characters might become audience favorites or not. It was pretty much like flying blind. I wasn't sure if they knew where they were going with it, but it was a great way to end the short season.

Lori Eschler Frystak *(series music editor)*: I remember finishing the final episode of the first season. Nothing had aired on TV yet. Not even the pilot. Everyone worked their asses off that first season. We were on the dub stage with David and Mark and some of the producers and most of the postproduction crew. After watching final playback, we all just looked around at each other. We all knew it was so different and weird and very special and everyone was really proud. David said something like "Well, I hope they like it."

3.

THE HAPPY GENERATIONS

Phenomenon

Michael Saltzman *(former publicist, Lynch/Frost Productions)* I don't think that the network believed in it from day one, but all of the publicity forced their hand to do something. ABC called me (an executive who will remain nameless, because I frankly don't remember) on Thursday or Friday morning before the pilot aired and basically said, "You've done the greatest magic trick ever in the history of television. We're going to watch the first half hour on Sunday night with people tuning in and they're going to say to themselves, 'What the fuck is this thing about?' and slowly, by the end of the show no one's going to be watching, but I just want to congratulate you for all of your great work."

On April 8, 1990, Twin Peaks *made its American television premiere on ABC to 34.6 million viewers, equating to a third of the national viewing audience. After six steady months of positive buzz and a strategic media blitz, curious viewers took a chance en masse. This historic debut ignited a wildfire of popularity that spread internationally throughout the spring and summer of 1990.*

Tony Krantz: When *Twin Peaks* debuted, it got a thirty-three share in the last half hour. That's in a pre-cable universe, but it was still unbelievable. It was as if the earth shifted in the television business for a minute and the notion of doing something quirky and different and odd and weird became something that could be possible in TV.

"Quirky" never was something that existed in TV before that and that's what David and Mark did with *Twin Peaks* and it just was a... shocker.

Chad Hoffman: I remember that the research that had been done indicated that by the end of the first hour of the two-hour pilot that half the audience would drop away and it was the opposite - I think the audience built and it was the highest rated two-hour movie or pilot of the year.

It felt great and it was a vindication for everything we had fought for and strived to do. The ratings for the first six [episodes] - given it was at Thursday night at nine o'clock - did comparatively well given that it was against *Cheers* and that mammoth NBC lineup.

Billy Zane: I remember the pilot episode and how it struck me as the most sublime and beautiful thing on television with the color timing, the saturation, and the warm tones – it was like nothing I had seen on the box. The underscoring - that fabulous jazz beat as the camera panned up from Audrey's pumps in school – it had me from that moment! The fifties eye makeup and hairdos, it was all very sexy.

James Marshall: It was that feeling inside of when we were shooting the pilot - I thought nobody's going to see it or it's going to drop jaws. We didn't expect it, but we had this consciousness that it could happen. Then it turned into the whole water cooler thing where everybody talks about it at work and it just grew and grew.

Piper Laurie: It was fun; it was unexpected. I didn't quite understand it. When you're close to something you don't really get it. My relatives and my nephew were so proud and would huddle around the water cooler with everyone else and have parties to watch the show. I thought that was delightful; I enjoyed it so much.

Joan Chen: I thought it was very different; it was very beautiful. I didn't know it would take off like that. Even when I was in it, I didn't know it was that big of a deal. I didn't understand these things. I was simply naïve and I was a very shy person. I basically don't reach out to people. If they didn't talk to me I didn't talk to them. I didn't realize the impact it had until it was done, basically.

Caleb Deschanel: I thought it was a little off-center for the public, but often times you get surprised by the success of certain things that you think are either too subtle or sophisticated for a mass audience. It was actually quite encouraging to see its success because it was a good show. It was something that required your attention, to watch it in sequence and see it evolve. I suppose you could have jumped in on the fifth episode, but I think it was much better if you saw it from the beginning.

Gary Hershberger: The detail, the substance, the character, and the mood - it was a great combination of all those elements to make for a fun night in front of the TV with coffee and cherry pie. It created a whole culture of making television fun and serious... and an event.

Todd Holland *(director, episodes 11, 20)*: David did a brilliant job with that pilot and it was so accessible. I do credit Mark Frost for keeping David's genius accessible in that pilot and bringing him to earth a bit. I think that's a dance they did so brilliantly: their collaboration of grounding and extraordinary inspired weirdness. It was grounded and heartbreaking and I remember crying during that pilot when I watched it on network TV the first time. The sense of loss in this small town – it was so vivid and human.

Miguel Ferrer: I thought people would either like it or hate it because it was so extreme and took such a radical point of view. I thought people would either really, really appreciate it or just say "I don't get this" and it would bomb. I had no idea, but when there were pie and coffee parties at colleges and it became this thing. It was just great; I loved it.

Lesli Linka Glatter: Once it started airing there were *Twin Peaks* parties; everyone would get together to watch it. It was an event, and then you discussed it the next day. Water cooler TV. I never expected it to have a cultural impact like it did. I thought it would be this obscure little indie project we had all worked on in Van Nuys in this weird area where you only go to have your car seat covers repaired! [*laughs*] Who knew it was going to go out into the world in a big way?

Scott Frost *(Mark Frost's brother; screenwriter, episodes 15, 21)*: I think I remember talking to Mark once and originally he and David thought it would only be a seven-episode series about a murder that happened in a little town. I don't think there was a big expectation it would continue beyond that half season and suddenly it's the talk of the nation, and I think that caught everybody by complete surprise.

Kimmy Robertson: During the first season we would get together at Dana Ashbrook's house. It was packed! People were everywhere: on the couch, on the floor, hanging off the balconies and another one was where Sheryl Lee was living in this huge, old, old house in Beachwood Canyon and God - it was so cool because it was a very *Twin Peaks* kind of place. There were always so many interesting people because everyone brought their best friend. Except for me, everyone's best friend was really cool.

Richard Beymer: I was always surprised [as a viewer] because half the time I didn't read the script. I just read my part. I didn't want to know anything because as a guy in this town, I wouldn't know what's happening somewhere else in Twin Peaks. I only knew my world, so it was always fun to watch and to see the other performances and what the other actors were doing.

Miguel Ferrer: It was one of those things that was so much fun when you're part of something successful like that. It's happened a couple of times to me and it's just great fun and the times that that's happened I've just really enjoyed it and taken it for what it is - not taken it too seriously - but really, really enjoyed it and realized this moment wasn't going to last forever.

Michael Saltzman: I'm an early riser and I got into work Monday morning [after the pilot aired] at seven thirty or a quarter to eight. We had twenty-five employees and probably a dozen phone lines. Throughout the day and the entire week our phones rang morning, noon, and night. Everything from fans to writers who wanted interviews with David and Mark, "What's going to happen next?" "Who is Laura Palmer?" With the exception of Kyle MacLachlan and a few others, there were a lot of brand new familiar faces and most of the actors and actresses didn't have a publicist. We were inundated with calls for everyone from Catherine Coulson to Peggy Lipton.

Harley Peyton: It's hard today to understand what it was like to be in the midst of that hurricane. Sherilyn, Mädchen, Lara Flynn Boyle - they were all wonderful and they were in a crazy situation. Surviving that and to be as young as the girls were - everyone handled it really well. There was no one on that set who was difficult in the way you thought they might have been.

James Marshall: It's hard to explain or tell you how that feels because the only thing I could say is that it changes your life and it alters things. Suddenly you're able to get your calls taken by people and suddenly they're able to move a little easier. I didn't feel like I was all of a sudden made this star; it had the feeling of being a part of something that was bigger than me. That was huge and it enabled me to get into auditions easier and have other situations pop up. And that was fun.

Mädchen Amick: To be honest, it was scary because on one hand it was everything that I dreamed about, wanting to go to LA and become a famous actress. All of a sudden I was there and it was so intense. You don't ever think about that as a starstruck young person in a small town; you don't think of all the negatives that come with that: the really strange stalkers and death threats, the mania of places we would go and all the paparazzi. It made me quickly realize that the fame part of the business was what I didn't want and what I really wanted was to just be a successful working actress that could hopefully not be in the public eye too much.

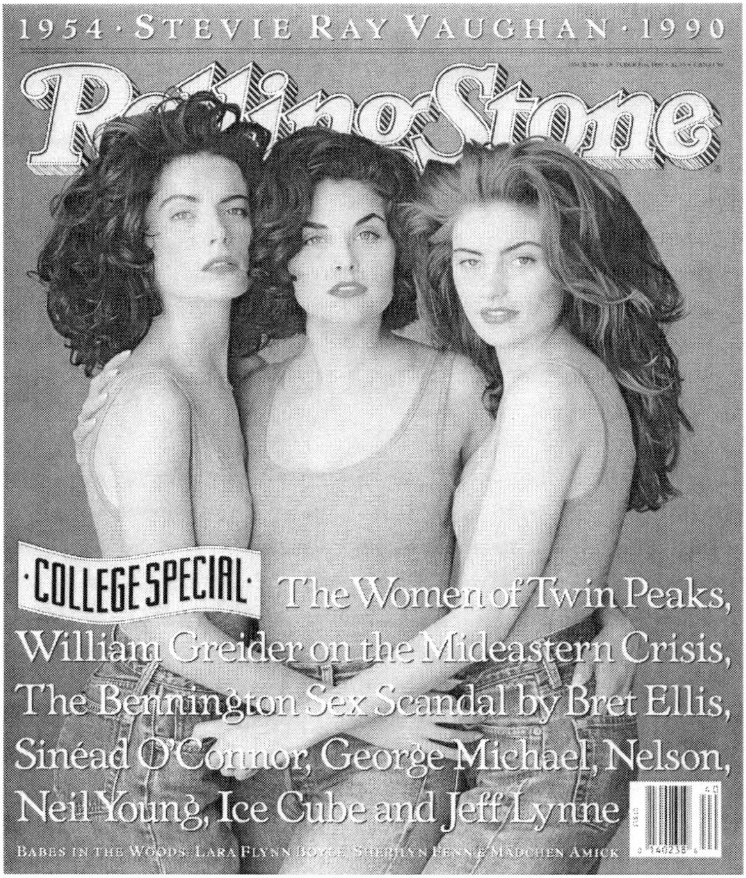

"The Cover of Rolling Stone"

Sheryl Lee: I was really young and I had no experience, so I was very shy and I'm an introvert by nature so I was intimidated. It all happened so fast and I didn't have the experience that a lot of the other actors had. There's no handbook that comes with how to all of a sudden be on a hit TV show. It was all very new to me and when I go back and try to remember it, it's almost like a blur. It just went so fast. I wish I could have slowed it down and been able to experience the moments more, [*laughs*] but it was a whirlwind.

Robert Bauer: Dana [Ashbrook] was - at the time – one of the most famous guys around. He was in every fucking teen magazine out there. He was great looking, young and rich. He'd stay at the Plaza [Hotel] in New York City and girls would chase him down the street. He was like a fucking Beatle. He was a heartthrob; he had that moment where he was definitely 'it.' He took it all in stride and didn't puff himself up too much. He's one of the most grounded, soulful people I have ever known.

Harley Peyton: There were a lot of great actors on that show and each served a different purpose - like Michael Ontkean was the professional that you so need on a set. There were all these young kids and actors who were getting all this sudden attention and fame. It's easy to go off the rails; it's very emotional and Ontkean was just awesome because he had been through all of that. He was Truman and he was so good and so solid. Ray Wise was a little bit like that too.

Michael Horse: I was a musician before and I was used to it. I like being recognized and as an artist and as a sculptor I'm used to people coming up and saying "I really like your work." It wasn't like, "Oh you are on television!" It was, "We like what you are doing." It was nice. I wasn't famous, I was respected.

Angelo Badalamenti: I received a call from Paul McCartney's office when *Twin Peaks* was riding high in England. It was maybe even bigger there than America. They said, "Paul would love for you to come and work with him at Abbey Road Studios where you can add some of your *Twin Peaks* sound on something that he's doing. He loves it so much and would love your direct input."

So I'm rehearsing this piece I had rescored with the orchestra at Abbey Road and Paul comes over to me and said, "Angelo, it sounds great. Let me tell you this story. I was invited by the Queen's [Elizabeth II] office to perform forty minutes of my music to celebrate her birthday at Buckingham Palace. I'm about to go on and she comes by and says, 'Oh, Mr. McCartney, it's so lovely to see you, but I can't stay!'" Paul said, "What do you mean? We're celebrating your birthday!" The Queen said, "You see, it's five minutes of eight; I must go upstairs and watch *Twin Peaks*." Paul turned around and punched me on the left arm right on the conductor stand and had a few choice words. [*laughs*] I thought that was incredible! David Lynch and I both like the Queen a lot as a result of this.

Golden Goose

Alan Wurtzel *(former senior vice president of research, ABC)* I think that if you're a broad, mainstream audience, you're interested in the narrative and you're interested in the "whodunit?" and that was the kind of thing you'd expect. After all, what was TV in those days but "there's a murder and at the end of the hour, somebody solves it." This was so far beyond that. If anything, that story was what Alfred Hitchcock used to call a MacGuffin. It was just an excuse to get you into this world."

The mystery of "Who killed Laura Palmer?" was instrumental in capturing an audience and briefly launching Twin Peaks *to the forefront of pop culture. With production shrouded in secrecy, inquisitive viewers from all walks of life were becoming anxious to know the true identity of the killer.*

Randy Barbee *(series assistant director)*: We had *National Enquirer* reporters going through our dumpsters trying to find old script pages. They were putting out numbered scripts with your particular number and if a photocopy showed up with your number somewhere, you were basically out of a job. We obviously had to sign non-disclosure agreements and all that stuff.

Jonathan P. Shaw: I'm from Buffalo, New York, and I had people calling me from the newspaper there. The entertainment editor knew me through a connection and called me saying, "You've got to tell me who killed her," and I said, "I wouldn't tell you if I knew!" [*laughs*]

Harley Peyton: When did I know [who the killer was]? Oh boy. I really didn't bother asking that much, I mean, we're getting into the sands of time here! Maybe Mark and David knew who it was in the first season. If a gun was put to my head, I don't think they did.

Gary Hershberger: With David and Mark, you never knew who the guilty one was. For all I knew, it could have been me. They never really told you who was doing what, which kind of helped because you could say, "Well, I'm playing this like I'm the murderer or I'm playing it like I'm not." They never really let you know what was going on. You just had to trust what you had in front of you and do the best you can.

Lesli Linka Glatter: None of us knew who the killer was; there were multiple scripts and we didn't know for a very long time. Suspects were everywhere. The town was so full of secrets and nobody was who they appeared to be. It could have been anyone.

Russ Tamblyn: I wasn't sure in the beginning if my character had killed Laura Palmer because David Lynch told me from the beginning that Dr. Jacoby was like a sex addict who was having affairs with his clients - and with Laura Palmer. When we got around to doing all the scenes with Agent Cooper I think I said that I was not having an affair with her and I remember I wasn't sure if I was lying or telling the truth! [*laughs*] I never did really know. Later it was explained that I was a red herring. I felt that it was kind of a mistake that they didn't reveal the killer at the end of that first season.

Kimmy Robertson: The mystery of Laura Palmer was the whole show. People would always ask me, "Who killed Laura Palmer? When are they ever going to reveal it?" and I've come to realize that people don't like things resolved. They like things to hang from a nail from a second-story in a television show *and* in life.

Piper Laurie: I think it was amazing because no one knew what was going to happen. I think David and Mark were just going by the seat of their pants, improvising and making up new stories. Maybe they just didn't want it to end. That's my personal opinion.

Mädchen Amick: We all talked about it, like, "Who do you think it is?" We would all get different pages of the script and they didn't want us to know what scenes would make the final cut for the show, so we were all tricked the whole series! [*laughs*] For a little while I thought it was Leo, but then it goes to the ridiculous theories, like, "Did the teapot do it? That teapot is looking pretty good right now!" [*laughs*]

Caleb Deschanel: Everything revolved around this one murder and yet somehow within that town there was an absolute underlying malaise about all the things that went on in the town that ended up commenting on the realities of what this murder was and how it came about. There were just so many people you could suspect.

Wendy Robie: I remember being in the grocery store and someone would come up during the show and say, "Okay, I really didn't understand when such and such happened," and I would always try to give them a thoughtful answer.

Jonathan P. Shaw: There was a lot of secrecy. After we transferred the footage from film to the tapes, a gentleman showed up in a truck. He pulled up in front of the editing room and stood outside and no one could go in the truck. He had this mobile editing rig in there and we would load it up there and even he couldn't watch!

David Patrick Kelly: At the time I was working on the first season, I was going for a very high belt in my karate skill. I'd be on the floor doing knuckle pushups and my teacher would come over and say, "If you don't tell me who killed Laura Palmer, I'm going to make you do fifty more pushups." [*laughs*] So, the mania was pervasive all over the place. It was really fun; it was like being in the Beatles for a short time. It was really something, quite a phenomenon.

Dana Ashbrook: People came up to me and were like, "Who did it? Who did it?!" and it took me by surprise that people wanted to know who did it because it just didn't matter to me. As I read the pilot and acted in it I cared about the characters and it did not matter one fucking bit to me. Then it put that in a different light when the marketing people got a hold of it and they did this amazing job with it.

Gregg Fienberg: You just got so sucked into the world and I (like everybody else) and the fans were like, "I've got to know what happens. I can't wait to see the next episode." It was really fun to be a part of it and watch the world get caught up in it.

Jules Haimovitz: *Twin Peaks* aired in Russia and Mikael Gorbachev [President of the Soviet Union] was a big fan of the show. [*laughs*] We had sold half of our company [Aaron Spelling Productions] to Carl Lindner (the financier) when we bought WorldVision. So Carl owned a half of Spelling and had been a big supporter and fan of George H.W. Bush, they were friendly. One day, Aaron gets a call from Carl Lindner who wants to know who killed Laura Palmer. Aaron was not that involved with the show on a day-to-day basis, so he calls me up and he said, "Who killed Laura Palmer?" I said, "No clue." He said, "It's really important."

I called David and he says, "I can't tell you." I don't want to press David, so I call Aaron back to say, "David won't tell me, who wants to know?" and he says "President Bush." What happened was Gorbachev called Bush, who called Karl, who called Aaron, who called me. So I called David back and I said, "This isn't going to go anywhere, it'll be a secret. You have to tell me who Laura's killer is." That's when I realized David had no idea who killed Laura Palmer. [*laughs*]

Sweet Dreams

John Wentworth *(postproduction coordinator and associate producer)*: The episode where Mike [Anderson] was introduced and people started talking backwards and all that stuff: "That gum you like is coming back in style." It was just monstrously great and beautiful. My proudest moment on that show was taking the master videotapes with those episodes over to ABC, delivering them to the network, and handing them off to these seasoned ABC professionals and saying, "Why don't you take a look at this?"

One of the marquee moments of Twin Peaks *takes place at the conclusion of episode 2, as Agent Cooper dreams of Killer Bob (Frank Silva), the One Armed Man (Al Strobel), and a room surrounded in red curtains, floored with chevron. Looking aged and wrinkled, Cooper sits with the Man from Another Place (Michael J. Anderson) and his cousin, a beautiful woman (Sheryl Lee) who looks just like Laura Palmer. The man speaks to Cooper in a warped tone, offering hints to Laura's killer and waltzing to Angelo Badalamenti's "The Dance of The Dream Man."*

Mark Frost: You see a glimpse of the red room in the closed ending of the pilot, and that's where it came into being. Since we were contractually obligated to round off the pilot if the series didn't go forward, it initially functioned as a deus ex machina, a way to lift the story out of its normal trajectory and impose an ending. So we came up with the idea of this other-dimensional place and these out-of-time characters as a way to facilitate that.

Kyle MacLachlan: That is the moment I think when most people sort of felt the electric bolt through their bodies when they were watching the show. It was suddenly flipped into this other dimension and I think people were like, "What in the world did we just see?" I think that exploded the show, that you could have another dimension happening at the same time."

Angelo Badalamenti: With "Dance of the Dream Man," I just fell naturally into a slow, jazzy, quirky, bluesy kind of music that has a bit of that film noir feel. With the added alternate beat finger snaps, our 'dream man' (we'll call him Little Mike) just danced his way into another surreal world. It was the perfect piece of material for him. The way he danced, the way he moved his body – the tempo of it was just so perfect for him. It took us all to another place. A place you may not want to visit.

Al Regni *(tenor saxophone)*: I remember that "Dance of the Dream Man" was recorded on a Wednesday afternoon between Broadway matinee and evening shows. I arrived at the studio a half-hour early and when I got there they were mixing a Ron Carter bass line. I was in the studio by myself and just playing over that minor "blues-ish" line to warm up for the session. After playing through the chorus nearly twenty times, David Lynch rushed into the studio very excited.

He was so thrilled and said he would use the recording he had just made, unbeknown to me. I didn't think it was any good at the time and was really just warming up in the style that I thought would be needed for the date. I really didn't think it was very good and asked David if I could record my part again. He said, "No, no, I'm going to use that." It was just one of those things that you could never plan for and it is also an excellent example of how alert David is for capturing creative thoughts and transferring them to his imagination for visual effects.

Mark Frost: David realized it so brilliantly on film, and given that the series was not exactly planted with both feet in kitchen sink realism, this opened a door to an alternate, mythological way of steering the story and changed our idea of what the narrative could be. It was pivotal in a lot of ways and led us to more otherworldly experiences that really informed the series.

Kyle MacLachlan: I don't know to this day who thought up the red room - I'm going to imagine it was David - but it was truly brilliant. I think in some ways it was predicated on the fact that that second episode also contained material that was initially supposed to be the end of the pilot. We filmed the pilot as a two-hour movie so it had an ending, but when ABC bought it they said, "We don't need to end it, we want to turn this into a series," so that piece was then moved to the second episode and they were able to mess around a little bit with how that integrated into the show.

Duwayne Dunham: There's so many things that David does where my first reaction is, "Oh my goodness, what is he thinking, he's out of his mind!" And time and again I've been proven so wrong in my limited view on that because I don't share David's overall vision and not many people do. David is brilliant in that way.

Ron Garcia *(director of photography, episode 2 dream sequence)*: David wanted those curtains to glow and they were heavy red curtains. I said, "Wow. That's gonna have to be a lot of light!" So I'm lighting these backlit curtains and we're getting it down in rehearsals and I filmed it. David looked at it and (we had video playback at the time) he said, "Ron, I need a spotlight going across these curtains. Can you do that?" I said, "Well, I've got a lot of light hitting these curtains. I'm going to need an even brighter light to make this circle," like a spotlight from outside the set.

So I had to rent a Super Trouper which they used for lighting stadiums and big venues. They brought it in and David looked at it and said, "Ron, can you put a shadow of a bird on that circle as it goes through the curtain?" [*laughs*] At that time I was pulling my hair out: "You've gotta be kidding me!" The prop department figured it out. It was a group effort.

Al Strobel (*Philip Michael Gerard/the One Armed Man*): Well, I asked if there was a script. David seemed a bit taken aback, but quickly recovered and asked an assistant to fetch his notebook with... you know... 'the poem.' Fifteen minutes later a fully typed-out side with my complete scene arrived. Ten minutes later David came back and asked if I was ready as the crew was all set. I begged for a little more time, panic setting in. He gave me ten more minutes.

When he came back I had the lines memorized but still had no idea who this character was. There was this crazy monologue that clearly established that I was not portraying an ordinary person. Mark Frost said the hair stood up on the back of his neck when he saw the rushes. That was not only the key to my character, but as it turned out, a major clue to understanding the whole project.

Jonathan P. Shaw *(editor, episode 2)*: I had seen some of the dream sequence because it was in the [international] pilot. They shot that and it wasn't used, so I was aware of it and Duwayne was telling me about it before I saw it: "You won't believe what David's up to now!" So I took it and made it fit a little more into our story. I thought it was very clever and it obviously got a huge amount of press and acclaim. It was another thing in that world we all inhabited.

Duwayne Dunham: With the red room, it was Little Mike and the whole idea of him walking backwards and talking all of his lines backwards, then to reverse print it so he's moving forward almost normally, but in a very strange way with a hitch in his step. The dialogue was so weird, but that fit with how strange and unworldly that red room was. With Angelo's music, I think it became hypnotic and it definitely worked.

Sheryl Lee: We actually had to learn the phonetics backwards: "cat" wasn't just "tac." It wasn't easy and it wasn't comfortable, but it really stretched me creatively and it put my brain in this very different place.

It turns things kind of upside down and I love to be challenged like that. I love to find different ways of thinking or communicating or expressing myself and that was certainly one of those places: the red room suspended in this place of non-reality. We never knew what was going to happen, [*laughs*] but it was always really fun.

Ron Garcia: There were no effects for sound or visual. I didn't even know if a Panavision camera had the ability to actually record backwards, to reverse the film through the gate. I actually had to call them. Getting technical, there was the ability to take the eyepiece of the camera (they call it a pellicle) that you could flip, so it was just a mirror so you could look into the film plane and I had that upside down. So I was operating the camera right side up with the camera upside down and then shooting what they rehearsed with everybody talking backwards.

On top of that, the pellicle lens broke, which allowed me to operate the camera right side up. It was late at night and all the equipment houses were closed. I figured out how to set the eyepiece, but I had to be *literally upside down* so I could operate it and see the image. I'm upside down, everybody's talking backwards, and I'm thinking I'm in the strangest spot I've ever been in my life! It was the most interesting, exciting time ever spent and hasn't been surpassed in my forty-seven years of cinematography. [*laughs*]

Jonathan P. Shaw: I was so engrossed; I thought it was so trippy. It didn't completely catch me off guard because I was always getting caught off guard by unique stuff! [*laughs*]

Dana Ashbrook: When the show was on I watched it every week, there was stuff I didn't know about because a lot of stuff with Cooper and the dreams was shot late at night. I remember watching the first dream sequence and being totally blown away, thinking this is the best thing I've ever seen on television. It was so creepy and so freaky and so amazing. I had nothing to do with it, but it was great to be a part of something so amazing.

Mark Frost: The second week the show aired I was down in New Orleans, prepping *Storyville* (the movie I directed). I was playing golf at the New Orleans Country Club which is kind of a deep south/old guard place down there. I was playing with a friend of mine, the head of the film commission and a CEO of some big local company (I can't remember which one) and at some point the subject came up that I was with the show. This guy must have been in his early sixties, kind of a square, buttoned-up businessman dude, and he started doing Little Mike's dance on the edge of the third green. [*laughs*] I realized that maybe we had made a little more impact than we knew.

Firewood

The success of Twin Peaks *spread beyond Nielsen ratings and critical acclaim as audience demand spurred the release of Angelo Badalamenti's soundtrack in the summer of 1990. An instrumental version of Julee Cruise's "Falling" accompanied the opening credits of the show and became an unlikely radio hit, winning Badalamenti a Grammy for Best Pop Instrumental Performance in 1990.*

Angelo Badalamenti: David had written the lyric (for "Falling") and I wrote the music to it and then we also put Julee's vocals on top of it. We did the instrumental first and it was marvelous, creating that original hook. If someone was at home doing the dishes and they heard those three notes, they knew it was *Twin Peaks*; it had an incredible, instant identity.

Kyle MacLachlan: With Angelo, the music was a huge part of the success of *Twin Peaks* right from the get-go with that haunting theme, which really sets the tone and the mood. It lets you know you're in a different place and time. It was haunting and mesmerizing and truly, truly brought people into the world of *Twin Peaks*. He was integral to *Twin Peaks*.

Angelo Badalamenti: Much to my surprise, David said, "Angelo, I'm going to use this instrumental for the main title theme. I love it." He was thrilled to death with it. I think he always had that in mind from the very beginning. By the way, the song "Falling," with Julee's ethereal vocal, became a number one pop record in a number of countries around the world.

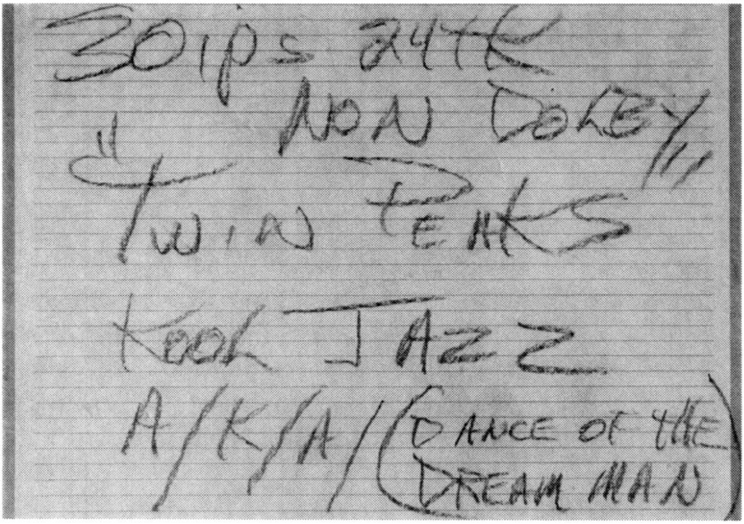

Assorted master tapes of the Twin Peaks soundtrack

Kinny Landrum *(synthesizer)*: After we had finished recording "Falling," David turns to me and says, "I need something that sounds fifties." There were low notes but no independent bass part per se, so I said, "David, I've got this twangy sort of Duane Eddy sound. What if I pitch it down and play it in the bass register?" David said, "Let me hear it." I think I played it once and that was it.

The key of this whole story is that I played only three notes on an Emulator II and David said, "That's it, put it down." He didn't hesitate. Most other producers would make you jump through a lot of hoops and he did not. That's an example of how it was.

Angelo Badalamenti: Kinny was fantastic, a great musician and he was wonderful with sound. Kinny found that incredible bass guitar sample which we all loved. Also, his keyboard performances were always stellar. With his synth we used a string-piano combo sound, but I did one thing different. I figured out a way to darken that sound with the equalization and I took the edge off; I took the top off of it and David just flipped and he loved it. It became the seamless, legato sound of *Twin Peaks*.

Duwayne Dunham: I believe the title sequence itself is completely hypnotic; it casts a spell. You may as well be looking into those rotating circular umbrellas: you're getting dizzy, you're getting sleepy, it's hypnotic and beautiful. With Angelo's music, every time I see it I refer to it as "liquid gold." It just flows and it's beautiful. David shot that stuff and I edited it, and it was David's idea with those saws. We didn't know what it was going to be.

Paul Trejo: The actors are all listed alphabetically and there are the waterfalls and the lumber mill [in the title sequence]. It's so David because he loves woodworking and spent part of his time in Missoula, Montana. I like the slowness of it a whole lot. I think we actually even slowed down the waterfalls in that shot. It's just evocative. And with Angelo's music, what can you say? It's classic.

Lori Eschler Frystak *(series music editor)*: My favorite track is still the theme used for the main title and the song "Falling." It has such a bittersweet longing and sadness and hope at the same time. Watching that shot of the waterfall with that music still makes me cry over twenty years later. It's just perfect.

The Twin Peaks *soundtrack was assembled from a vast archive of themes and variations from Badalamenti and his collaborators. Badalamenti composed a minimal amount of scene-specific orchestrations, but his approach to recording provided endless musical possibilities for each episode.*

Angelo Badalamenti: Once the pilot was picked up, I was obligated every week to compose music for each of the shows. What I did (and I recommend this to all young students) is when you record a long cue, try to record in isolation, as many instruments as possible, and then mix it using different combinations. Just take something as seemingly ridiculous as drums alone, or drums and bass, bass and vibes. I did this and in one piece of music I could have an hour of tracks. That whole idea of individual tracks was a key for *Twin Peaks*. There was a lot of repetition; people got used to hearing those themes, but the sounds were different.

Lori Eschler Frystak: David talked to me about wanting to take a new approach to the music. He likened it to "sort of painting around the bushes" with the music. I thought that sounded intriguing. I didn't really know what I'd be doing, but I knew I'd figure it out if he hired me. After a while he smiled and said, "Well, you better get started, Lori. Don't let any grass grow!"

Angelo Badalamenti: All the way back to *Eraserhead*, David has loved to play and experiment with music and sound. He creates a remarkable aural experience. I would give David multiple music tracks which we used to call "firewood." I would go into the studio and record these ten- to twelve-minute cues; sometimes just synth stuff, or later on other projects I would do them with orchestral strings. I would orchestrate in the lowest possible registers for the celli and basses. David would take what I had recorded, this "firewood," and do his magic.

He would slow these things down to half speed and then he would even do it again at quarter speed and create what he feels is a beautiful thing. It worked on *Twin Peaks* like gangbusters. He would also edit them back in reverse; David loves doing it and it's so much a part of Lynch's world. I simply give him the firewood, but it's what he does with it and it works. The sound design can be subliminal where you hardly hear it, or sometimes you can get hit over the head with it.

Lori Eschler Frystak: I was the music editor, although the sound and music got pretty well mixed up together and I worked really closely with the sound editors. I was a little overwhelmed by all the variations of the music themes. Once I got to know the material I would sort of stash things and not use them for a while to try to keep things fresh sounding. I had free reign with the music, based on the directors' notes. I had a blast working with the music to play up the little nuances.

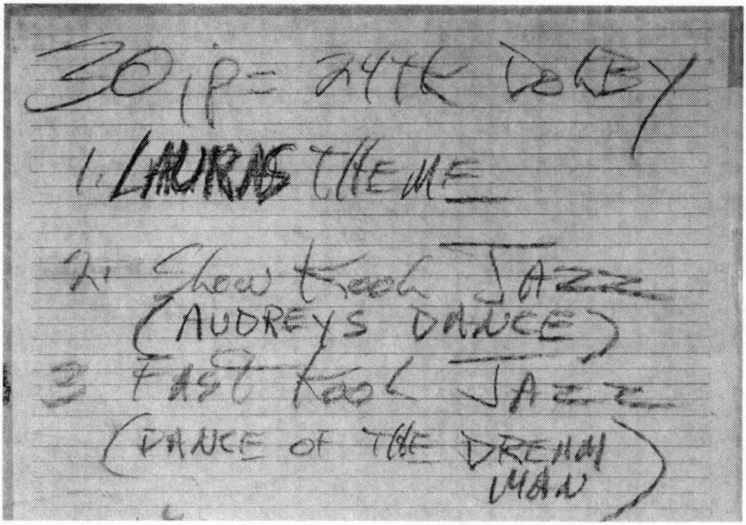

Assorted master tapes of the Twin Peaks soundtrack

Caleb Deschanel: You were able to take this library of music and combine cues because they would be in the same key, so you could come out of one into another and blend these things. Maybe they weren't intended to go together, but you could put them together in ways where you would have this lively tune and underneath in the same key you had this droning tone that was suggesting something else. The music had such a distinctive melancholy and darkness and sort of teenage angst pain to it and wonder and certain desire.

Lori Eschler Frystak: I loved the timing of the visual material. The scenes would savor each mood or a moment. The pacing was great fun for music placement. Everyone took the pacing very seriously. I also loved the dark themes: the night exterior scenes lit entirely by flashlight, the rich tones that prevailed from art direction to color timing to music production quality to final sound mix. For the first half of the first year, David was there almost all the time, sifting through, adjusting, and sometimes eliminating sounds and music. We didn't get a lot of sleep that first season.

Angelo Badalamenti: I've got to tell you that "Audrey's Prayer" which is played as an instrumental of "Questions in a World of Blue" has always been special to me. There were many different compositions and orchestrations that I did that contained melodic hints (or motifs) from that song that served perfectly for emotional scenes. It always affects me and it works great.

Van Dyke Parks *(Harold Racine)*: After I was on the show I listened to some of the music and I respect Badalamenti's work, sure I do. I like any work that feels or has an unusual individuality and his work is highly individual and it was just the ticket for that show. It created an atmosphere as music can do for picture and it was just anything but ordinary.

Vinnie Bell *(guitars)*: Angelo was terrific, a great arranger. I love the way he wrote; it was always in good taste, whatever instrument he wrote for - it all worked out. I invented a lot of things for the guitar and sometimes I used my sound that made the guitar sound like it was underwater. He used to like that so I would do that whenever I thought it would meet the scenes of the music he wrote.

Angelo Badalamenti: Vinnie created his own sounds way before we got involved with synth samples and things like that. He's also a fine musician and one of the best studio guitarists, ever. He's been on hundreds of hit records. Vinnie played on my first recording session - I did a song called "Apple Strudel," I'll never forget it. After that session I said I'm going to hire this guy on every session I ever do. [*laughs*] He created beautiful sounds and played so perfectly, whether it was the jazzy things or the mysterious, off-center things. All the haunting qualities – he played these chords with a certain kind of vibrato that was so perfect for *Twin Peaks*.

Art Polhemus: The music was out of the East, and it was important that it was done with East Coast musicians. I don't know if they could have got it with West musicians at that time. The real heavy-jazz cats are out here (or they were at that time) because you had Grady Tate on the drums, Ron Carter on bass - so it sounded East Coast and it worked.

Angelo Badalamenti: The most outrageous thing (and it was David's choice) was I recorded just a snare drum with brushes. I had this great studio drummer named Grady Tate, David loved him too. I would give Grady a tempo and record to a click track. He would just play a snare and improvise beautiful little fills with the snare and if you listen to *Twin Peaks* you'll hear little cues that are just snare drum for a minute or a minute and a half. That takes (what is a little Jewish word called) chutzpah [*laughs*] and yet, there was nothing better for the scene. You didn't have to go over the top with the New York Philharmonic, you know what I mean?

Miguel Ferrer: The music was unlike *any* music you'd ever heard on television. Angelo Badalamenti just brought such a point of view to that score and it was so special, it wasn't just the same old Tom or Ted Post interchangeable TV music. This was so radically different and so evocative. It almost became another character.

Itchy Palms

Sherilyn Fenn: Audrey was like every teenage girl, completely obsessed in her own life. She was a loner and did what she wanted to do. It was like, "Ugh, can I graduate yet?" With eyes to the future - in walks tall, dark, and handsome future. [*laughs*] Like everybody, at the core of what everyone wants is love and she decided the special agent was it.

One of the bona fide breakout stars of Twin Peaks *was Sherilyn Fenn, cast as the sexy and cunning Audrey Horne. The impetus of Audrey in the pilot script was small, but Fenn's dynamic screen presence sparked significant character expansion and subsequent stardom.*

Mark Frost: I thought Sherilyn was brilliant. I've always believed that so much of directing and producing is about casting, getting the right person in the right role. Audrey on the page was based a little bit on somebody I knew, and I think I saw Sherilyn in a movie called *Two Moon Junction* and brought her to David's attention and then we talked to Johanna and arranged to meet her. The minute we did, we knew Audrey couldn't be anybody else but her.

Sherilyn Fenn: It was a poignant time for me. I was young, in my early twenties and I had talked to a manager that had said to me, "I think you try to be who people want you to be and I just want you to be yourself. That means if you as a person are kind of a bitch, then be that. If you are like a nerdy person, be that. Whatever you are, you need to be that instead of trying to be who you think directors want you to be."

So I read the script and I go to meet David. I thought, "Okay, I'm shy when I meet people. I'm not going to jump through hoops; I'm just going to do what this lady told me to do." David led the meeting and I was just kind of quiet and he asked what I thought of the script. I was young and trying to be honest: "Well, everyone's sleeping together. Yeah, it's good!" [*laughs*] I got home and the casting director who knows my manager kind of said, "She should have been more positive!" Long story short, a week later they called and said David Lynch is writing you a role.

The pilot was written and they added me into a few little scenes which were an eighth of a page. It didn't seem like anything and then we were doing it, Audrey just drops in and causes a little bit of trouble, poking holes in coffee cups and messing up her dad's life. It was so much fun. I never knew that it would turn into that when I read the pilot.

Lesli Linka Glatter: Sherilyn was effervescent, and it wasn't just because she was incredible to look at. She had a wonderful spirit about her. I loved that she could be so tough and sexy but unbelievably vulnerable and fragile. So many of the characters were not what they appeared to be and Audrey fit that bill. I love the end of my first episode [5] where Audrey Horne comes to Dale Cooper's room and looks incredibly innocent and beautiful and dangerous. Audrey was such a troubled young girl who happened to be absolutely gorgeous, but ultimately, she just wanted the simplest things - to be loved.

Sherilyn Fenn: I got the pilot before I met my teacher that changed my life, Roy London. I shot the pilot without Roy and then I started working on the show with him and we streamlined it a lot. He really made it clear to me: the idea of being very, very aware of what I am working on or what's screwed up in my life and having the ability to put that on film, between the lines. After the pilot I had grown my hair out and I went whining to David and Mark: "Don't let them cut my hair!" They said, "Leave her alone, she was barely in the pilot, it is okay." [*laughs*]

Jonathan P. Shaw: There's a scene where Agent Cooper comes to town and he meets Audrey for the first time. He's having breakfast and she comes up to him and asks him a few things. It was so well played by both of them and it was so well written. There was a playful attraction between them and an underlying humor... and a very sexy Audrey! It was so simple, but beautiful. Those were the moments that really intrigued me as an audience. Beyond what we do as an editor, I think as a fan, "Is that cool?" That was a pivotal scene for me. Simple and so well done, and something about the grapefruits? Freshly squeezed! [*laughs*] What innuendo!

Sherilyn Fenn as Audrey Horne

Sherilyn Fenn: Audrey was negotiating how she could get what she wanted, like any young woman. Audrey was so in love with Agent Dale Cooper. She's certain this is the one; this is her prince: "We're going to take over the world together," in those kinds of grandiose, young girl things. She was a virgin. That was a big thing. I remember David said, "Audrey's still a virgin. People might think these things because she's strong and you look a certain way, but she's a virgin and this is her first love."

Kyle MacLachlan: I think Sherilyn and all the women on *Twin Peaks* were first of all incredible actresses. There was a real range of looks and sort of personality and character - all of course gorgeous and very, very watchable - but also very interesting. The women of *Twin Peaks* were celebrated on the cover of *Rolling Stone* which was pretty impressive back in the day.

Sherilyn Fenn: They actually planned to hook Kyle up with Joan Chen, but by the time we did the first season he's at the Great Northern and he runs into Audrey and it worked. People liked it and they turned the story in that direction. It was so fun, Audrey loved Cooper and when I think about it, it makes me smile; I feel warm inside. It was her first love: [*gasp*] "There he is!" It was just fun. We had fun playing together. There were not a lot of deep, intense moments. We were just playing.

Sara Markowitz *(costume designer)*: The evolution of Audrey Horne was interesting: beginning as a girl smoking in the bathroom of school in her tight sweater and pencil skirts to working at Horne's Department Store then to One Eyed Jack's undercover as one of the prostitutes. There was a maturity in her costumes, although a softness always evident as daddy's little girl through a soft fabric of a blouse or bow in a headband. The loss of the black and white saddle shoe was also a sign of maturing.

Don Amendolia *(Emory Battis)*: Sherilyn was just a sweetheart, so beautiful! Skin like porcelain, you couldn't believe anyone was that beautiful in person. She was a dear, sweet gal. Emory Battis was funneling women through the perfume counter to work at One Eyed Jack's and David Lynch was directing the episode. I'm there as a customer, all tied up. I'm blindfolded, in silk pajamas and painted toenails; it was just a weird thing. There was a cowgirl with blue hair and a vacuum cleaner. It was all a part of Emory's crazy sexual need.

She's on top of me, forcing me to tell her something, I can't remember what it was. She was supposed to be choking me and she just couldn't do it. I kept saying, "It's okay, Sherilyn. Choke me! My hand is right here off camera. I can tap you if you're doing it too hard." It's harder to act like I'm being choked than it would to be really choked. She's so sweet and tenderhearted, she just wouldn't do it. [*laughs*] She was a darling. I loved her!

Richard Beymer: Sherilyn and I didn't sit around and have coffee together. It was a strained relationship. [*laughs*] I was disappointed that David didn't have us do some more fun things together. There was a setup of her working at the house of ill repute where I'm knocking on the door to come in and obviously have sex with one of the gals and it's her on the inside. I knocked on the door and then it picked up to the next season. I thought they could have played with that a lot more, but maybe the network thought it would be going too far.

David Patrick Kelly: Sherilyn was just a wonderful, emotionally present actress. I enjoyed her so much in *Wild at Heart*. The one scene she had was very gripping, so just from my first sandwich scene she was really creative and just perfect for that role. She was also from the Detroit area, she went to school in Grosse Pointe where my niece went and so there was a real hometown feeling of working with Sherilyn.

Caleb Deschanel: Sherilyn had this wonderful sort of Marilyn Monroe-esque quality about her, being both innocent and very seductive at the same time which I thought was sort of amazing. With all the young actors, it was kind of like *American Graffiti* because they were all sort of undiscovered actors you had never seen before. They were all really talented and they had all pretty well established the personalities they were.

Intent on helping Agent Cooper in his search for Laura Palmer's killer, Audrey infiltrates One Eyed Jack's in episode 6. To enter the brothel, she ties a cherry stem in a knot with her tongue to impress the madam, Blackie (Victoria Catlin). The suggestive scene was met with raves from the audience and the media, heightening the national profiles of both Fenn and Twin Peaks.

Sherilyn Fenn: I thought it was stupid; I didn't understand at first. I didn't go to college and they said people do this in college. I said, "*Who* does this?!" [*laughs*] David was out and about doing something at that point and I remember having conversations with Mark about it. He said, "Sherilyn, I promise you, just do it. It's really going to be funny. Have a sense of humor and it will show what she can do." It just turned into something I never would have expected.

Caleb Deschanel: I actually remember it on *The Tonight Show* being part of a monologue. It was a big scene, or at least people were able to read between the lines. I remember during the fifties there was a time period when the US would censor all this obvious propaganda coming in from Russia and all the other subversive stuff would get through. I felt in a lot of ways that *Twin Peaks* was that kind of show that had this wonderful way of expressing itself on a much more subliminal level.

Harley Peyton: I'm at a restaurant with some friends and one of them shows me this trick with the cherry stem. I put it in the script two days later. We're shooting it in a few weeks after that, then it's on television, and then John Leonard is writing about it in *New York Magazine* a month later. The immediacy of that... and this is before the Internet, God save us. It was a lot of fun and that scene was one of those moments where you feel like you just nailed something.

Wendy Robie: When Harley Peyton and Bob Engels wrote an episode, I would sort of jump with glee to see what they were going to do. I remember when I read how Audrey takes the cherry stem and ties it into a knot; I read that and fell out of bed laughing so hard. It was like, "I got to read that for the first time, I got to be on set when that was being shot," I was that kind of fan.

Sherilyn Fenn: In between seasons in May or June, my manager and I had to go to New York for something and people shouted my name on the street and that was when I realized the show was a success. It scared me a little bit: "Audrey! There's Audrey!" I remember the moment, asking, "Are they talking to me?" My manager said, "Yes they are, babe."

We were in our hotel and got locked out of our rooms in our pajamas, so we went down to the bar and learned how to tie cherry stems. [*laughs*] I thought I better learn how to do this! It was all fake on the show, but within the year David Letterman had asked three times for me to be on the show and I had said, "No, no, no," because I knew he would ask me to tie a cherry stem and I had no idea how. [*laughs*] It was a trip. It was amazing.

The Legend of Margaret Lanterman

After a few outrageous cameo appearances as the Log Lady during the first season, Catherine E. Coulson became an unlikely celebrity. The Log Lady was received with widespread amusement and curiosity as the character and her dear log received parodies on Saturday Night Live *and* Sesame Street. *Part mystic and part messenger, the Log Lady was an idea that lingered in the minds of both David Lynch and Coulson for nearly fifteen years before the character came to life.*

Catherine E. Coulson: We were shooting late at night on *Eraserhead*; we always shot at night at the stables of the Doheny Mansion where the American Film Institute was housed in Beverly Hills. I would wear my glasses late at night when we were working and he [David Lynch] was always very fond of wood because his father was a research botanist (I think that was his title) for the US Forest Service.

So we're shooting that scene where they're making pencil erasers – I think that's when it happened – but somehow we started talking about a TV show. At the time David thought about doing a miniseries and among film students at the time that wasn't the really cool thing to do, but he was interested in that format.

David got this idea for a TV series that would be called "I'll Test My Log with Every Branch of Knowledge." He said I would be a girl who would carry a log with her; it would be Ponderosa Pine because that's what his dad did his thesis on. She would carry the log from expert to expert, and that expert would talk about the wood and we would then learn about the wood and learn about what those people did.

So the idea was, for example: I would go to a dentist, and he'd clip a little blue towel on the log and the dentist would probe the rings and talk about dentistry as well as the wood. There would be a different expert every week and that was the idea for the series. It was one of those ideas that he floated in the middle of the night. Once in a while we would revisit the idea.

So time passed and David and Mark Frost got the pilot. David called me up and said, "Are you ready to do the Log Girl for this pilot?" and I said, "Yeah, I'd really like to – it would be fun but I don't think she's a Log Girl anymore!" [*laughs*] In fact, I think it was fourteen or fifteen years later after Eraserhead when he called, so we decided we'd call her the Log Lady.

I got flown up there to Snoqualmie and got the clothes we talked about – the plaid skirt and the logging boots and he put me in the pilot flipping that light switch. I think that character was well received so they just kept writing in places for the Log Lady to appear. We made up a lot of the backstory for her, and figured out a lot about her husband and the fire, and put a picture on the mantle of her husband and the story grew and David and Mark kept writing and the rest is history!

To this very day, Coulson is the caretaker of the same log she carried throughout the series. Fittingly, the log's origins stretch all the way back to Washington State.

Catherine E. Coulson: It was from a stand of Ponderosa Pines. Where we were shooting in Carnation near Snoqualmie, Washington, there were not a lot of Ponderosa around, so the prop man who went to procure it had to drive quite a way to find the right log. When we were on the set where I flip the switch before shooting, they brought a number of different logs for David to check. The one he chose for me had these two little branches. I always say, "No trees' lives were lost," they just severed one branch. It was very, very heavy because it was newly cut and it was oozing sap which made me feel a little bad. But David said, "You should have the log." That was a nice gesture; I'm glad to have the log.

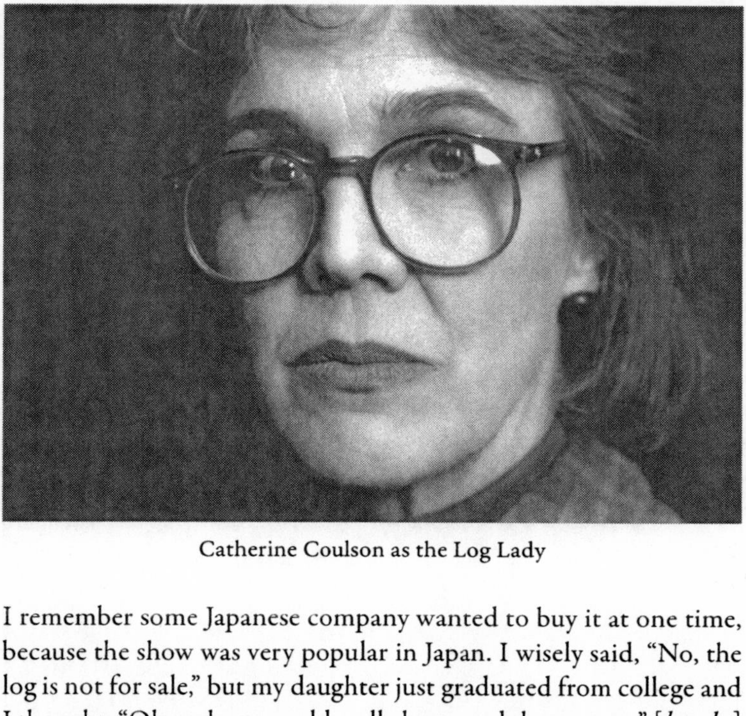

Catherine Coulson as the Log Lady

I remember some Japanese company wanted to buy it at one time, because the show was very popular in Japan. I wisely said, "No, the log is not for sale," but my daughter just graduated from college and I thought, "Oh gosh, we could really have used that money," [*laughs*] but I could never sell the log.

I brought it down to Los Angeles for an autograph show and actually had to FedEx it and it made me incredibly nervous because I just don't let it go off on its own. I went to the Federal Express office and they asked me what its value was, and I said probably about $275,000.

I have been told that number at one time. They said it would cost at least $800 to insure it so I just did the regular $50 insurance. They were really puzzled by what the heck is in this box, but I didn't tell them. I didn't want to take a chance it would disappear.

Before 9/11, I was able to put it in the overhead compartment and I remember the flight attendants saying, "Oh, we love your work, can we have your autograph?" and when I told them what was in the overhead compartment they would go crazy: "I can't believe we've got the log on the plane!" You can't take it on board anymore because I was told by TSA [Transportation Security Administration] that it could be used as a bludgeon. So I can't fly with it now anyway because I would never check it.

Magic Carpet Ride

May 21, 1990, brought thrilling news to the world of Twin Peaks. *After David Lynch's* Wild at Heart *won the elite Palme d'Or award at the Cannes Film Festival, Mark Frost appeared live before a national television audience on* The Phil Donahue Show *with Mädchen Amick, Dana Ashbrook, Eric DaRe, Piper Laurie, Sheryl Lee, and Peggy Lipton.*

After coyly fielding a few questions from the audience, Frost announced that Twin Peaks *had been renewed for a second season on ABC. Two days later, the first season finale aired to audiences. With viewers still clamoring to know "Who killed Laura Palmer?" throughout the summer, Lynch and Frost turned* Twin Peaks *into a multimedia sensation.*

Mark Frost: I had fond memories of some merchandise from shows I liked from the sixties. I got a briefcase from *The Man from U.N.C.L.E.* that was my proudest possession as a little kid and I just thought, "Wouldn't it be great if we could create some stuff that people really liked?" So the book [*The Secret Diary of Laura Palmer* by Jennifer Lynch] became the first idea we developed and it became a big success, the number one New York Times Best Seller for about six weeks.

Ken Scherer *(former chief operating officer, Lynch/Frost Productions)*: I dealt a lot with Tony Krantz over the years and we put in a lot of merchandising contracts, licensing, and published the three books [*The*

Secret Diary of Laura Palmer, The Autobiography of FBI Special Agent Dale Cooper: My Life, My Tapes by Scott Frost, and *The Visitor's Guide to Twin Peaks*]. The soundtrack had been started by the time I came on board with David and Warner Music. I worked with promotion people when we rolled that out and handled the media. As you can imagine there was a great deal of scrutiny from the press. We were pretty self-contained.

Michael Saltzman: We started licensing things like the books and not a lot of television series have licensed products from their TV shows. I think that was really unique and I tip my hat to Tony and Mark and David for getting into that. A business was really started. Yes, I'm sure there are shirts that say *The Dick Van Dyke Show* or *I Love Lucy* but we really were in the business of promoting it with *The Secret Diary of Laura Palmer* and things like that.

Philip Segal: One of the big linchpins [of conflict with the network] was this diary and the intent to produce the diary as a book that you could purchase that would reveal the inner secrets of Laura Palmer. It made the network crazy! The idea the book contained more information than the show just spiraled them off the planet even more. In return there was this sort of conspiracy on the part of the production company to keep the network from the inner sanctum of the creative and spiritual center of the show.

Ken Scherer: Jennifer [Lynch] was on *Good Morning America* and the book sold like gangbusters. It sold worldwide, maybe half a million copies. For its time and its nature it was a huge success for us. She labored over it and there were some wonderful moments of crisis where she thought she had it or she didn't have it. There were some wonderful editors in New York that just loved the show and worked her through it and it was a home run. Actually, there were three books and the one I liked the best was the one nobody saw – *The Visitor's Guide to Twin Peaks* - only because we had such a hoot creating this fictional town out of David and Mark's heads.

Mark Frost: The promise we made to ourselves was that we didn't want to do anything that was schlocky or cheesy, only things that captured the spirit of the show. We personally reviewed every product we were going to be associated with and I was certainly happy with what we came up with.

Ken Scherer: There were talking logs (which were not produced) and so many insane things. We had so much fun; you can't even begin to understand how fun that is when you can think of the most absurd thing and it's not absurd enough.

The worst fight I ever had with David Lynch was over the t-shirts. I think we had twelve or thirteen different t-shirts out there at one time; I still have a couple. The licensing group came to me and said they want to do a Twin Peaks High School gym shirt. I thought, "This is great; this is a no-brainer." I thought I had run it by David, but I think there was some time pressure so I just did it. When the prototype of the shirt came in to approve, I sent it over to him. He went fucking ballistic: "This is too commercial!" I thought I was going to lose my job, I really did.

ABC rebroadcast the first season for summer viewers as anticipation mounted for a second season. Sitting on the cutting edge of pop culture, Twin Peaks *attracted the attention of the highest-grossing feature film director of all time.*

Harley Peyton: After the first season a lot of crazy things happened, like me and Mark sitting at Steven Spielberg's house convincing him to do the opener for the second season. That was all ready to go. This is a long story, but my first wife [Tricia Brock] is and was Kate Capshaw's best friend so I knew Steven pretty well and he was a huge fan of the show – watched it every week, I mean a huge fan. Because we were friendly we talked about it a lot and he said to me in passing how fun it would be to direct an episode, so I went to Mark over the summer and said, "This probably is not a bad way to kick off the second season, right?"

Mark Frost: They invited me over to their house and we had dinner in the kitchen. Afterwards we sat down and showed Steven and Kate a rough cut of episode 7 (the one I had directed) and we talked quite a number of times over the next few months about him maybe coming on and doing the opening episode of the second season.

Harley Peyton: Steven just said, "I want it to be as weird as possible; it'll be so much fun." So whether or not he would have even done it, we'll never really know, but when Mark told David he didn't even hesitate, saying, "No, no, I think I'll direct the first one. Maybe he can direct later in the season," which he obviously didn't.

Mark Frost: When we actually sat down and wrote it David said, "I really want to do this," and I said, "Absolutely, that's your right and privilege." Steven went off to make a movie and we weren't able to find another time.

On September 16, 1990, the cast and crew took a break from the secretive second season production to attend the Prime Time Emmy Awards. Twin Peaks *was nominated in fourteen categories for achievements in a drama series, including Outstanding Series, Outstanding Directing (David Lynch), Outstanding Lead Actor (Kyle MacLachlan), Outstanding Lead Actress (Piper Laurie) and Outstanding Supporting Actress (Sherilyn Fenn). Shut out of all major categories,* Twin Peaks *received two technical awards: Outstanding Editing, Single Camera Production (Duwayne Dunham) and Outstanding Costume Design (Patricia Norris).*

Gregg Fienberg: I kid you not, I had never watched the Emmys in my life; I didn't care. I didn't know what they meant. They said we got nominated for a bunch of Emmys and I just thought, "Okay, is fourteen good?" I had no idea. [*laughs*] I know a lot more now which (looking back) was a part of the fun of it. It was just a lot of innocent people trying to make this really cool show.

Harley Peyton: I remember going to the Emmys and there was kind of a 'club' and they were on the other side of the lobby - shows like

Thirtysomething. I looked at Mark and said, "We are so not a part of this party." [*laughs*] We just didn't belong and we found out later when the awards were given we really didn't belong. It seemed to exist outside of the timeline of television. Even now in the fullness of time it feels like that.

Sheryl Lee attends the 1990 Prime Time Emmy Awards

Kimmy Robertson: Everybody was surprised it was nominated for anything at all. It was a huge honor which was really flattering. I was thinking we would either win it all or it would be: "We like you and want you here, but we're going to vote for something normal," which is what happened. There was a lot of pressure to figure out what to wear and all that. [*laughs*] I wasn't nominated and it was stressful for me! I don't know how people do it every single year. It's hugely stressful.

Sherilyn Fenn: For me it was such a huge personal validation to get a Golden Globe and an Emmy nomination. I didn't even know I was up for anything and my teacher woke me up at six in the morning to tell me. That stuff isn't supposed to matter, but I was proud and kind of amazed.

Wendy Robie: We all went to the Emmys and it was like a field trip. I went as James Marshall's date; he came over to the apartment and my boyfriend helped him hook up his tuxedo and sent us off. I was wearing a facsimile of a prom dress and off we went to the Emmys. [*laughs*] We sat up there, all of us together and Richard Beymer had snacks and granola bars to keep up our energy. Afterwards at the Governors Ball I danced with David and with Don Ameche. That was the peak experience for me of Hollywood glamour! It was a wild, splashy, wonderful thing that happened.

James Marshall attends the 1990 Prime Time Emmy Awards

The network television establishment turned a cold shoulder to Twin Peaks *at the Emmys, but the national media was still unofficially crowning* Twin Peaks *as the coolest series on television with Lynch on the cover of Time magazine and Sherilyn Fenn, Lara Flynn Boyle, and Mädchen Amick gracing the cover of* Rolling Stone *magazine. With all eyes on* Twin Peaks, *Kyle MacLachlan hosted the season premiere of* Saturday Night Live *and reprised his role of Agent Cooper in a witty send-up.*

Kyle MacLachlan: What I had was some really wonderful opportunities and hosting *Saturday Night Live* was one of them; it was a really memorable experience. I am still connected to Mike Myers and Lorne Michaels and some of the folks that I worked with. It gave me a chance to do some of the things I trained for in college, which was really fun too. I was trained to do regional and repertory theatre and this was like a little miniature repertory company and for an hour and a half you do these different roles on the run. It sort of sent me back to my theatre roots a little, which I enjoyed.

They really did a great job; I want to say the *Twin Peaks* skit was co-written by Rob Schneider and David Spade. Some of the cast members hadn't seen *Twin Peaks* so they were asking questions about this and that. It was also the first season for Chris Farley who played a memorable Leo. Mike Myers and I had three things we did together on that show: "All Things Scottish," "Sprockets," and of course he was Little Mike towards the end of the show.

Catherine E. Coulson: I was the only one who watched *Sesame Street* because I had a toddler at the time. One day I came in and said, "Guys we were all on *Sesame Street*," they did this episode called "Twin Beaks" which was really fun, they used this Angelo kind of music and all the Muppets had two beaks. There I was with my voice and my glasses, but it wasn't me, it was the Log Bird and she had two beaks and the log had two beaks. I wish I could find that, it really was incredible. The Cookie Monster was in it; it was just brilliant. So I brought it in and we all sat around and watched it. It was a really fun moment.

Tony Krantz: We thought we were on a magic carpet ride. We were changing the face of TV. We were changing the face of pop culture. It was the show everyone was talking about and it had the most Emmy nominations, I believe. It was so incredibly exciting and for me as a young agent who was thirty-whatever, it was a game changer for me because everyone knew my role in having put that show together. In my community among the agents, no one had ever done anything like that. I was functioning as a producer basically through my role as an agent and I will forever look at that as one of the great moments of my life and as far as my resume that I adore.

Timing is Everything

Richard Beymer: I don't remember it being so successful, actually. I mean, I don't remember like waking up the next day and getting phone calls saying, "We have a massive hit here." It may have looked like it in retrospect, but the network didn't like it.

After months of positive press and acclaim for Twin Peaks, *David Lynch and Mark Frost were under increasing pressure from ABC executives to wrap up the Palmer case and move the series forward. With dissipating ratings toward the end of the first season, the network demanded an imminent resolution to the mystery in the coming season.*

Angelo Badalamenti: "Who killed Laura Palmer?" As the first season was unfolding, only David, Mark, and God knew, and that was the tragedy of it. The great part was "Who killed Laura Palmer?" Nobody knew. Mystery was the key word for *Twin Peaks*. Other than the uniqueness of the piece, that was the question everybody wanted to know and people were getting fidgety. The bosses of ABC insisted – because the public was outraged - they wanted to know who killed Laura Palmer. But that was a mistake, once you announce who killed her - that was it, man. That's all gone and then you'll just be treading water. There's nowhere to go but downhill from there. They really had to keep that going.

David J. Latt: I think you get to the end of the first season and it's very difficult to both satisfy an audience whom you have kept on the edge of their seats and keep them engaged for the next year. There are very few shows that manage to pull that off. It was a tricky hand off and it didn't satisfy a lot of people, or that's at least the sense I got.

Chad Hoffman: I do remember discussions with Mark in particular saying that you need to resolve the murder sooner than later. I thought that if it played out too long the audience would get antsy and the thought that what you needed to do is that while you began to unwind the mystery of "Who killed Laura Palmer," you had to wind up another equally (if not more) powerful mystery that will keep people glued to the show and that was the nature of it all, these people in this place. You had to keep winding down and winding up various stories and my hope was that they would do that after I left.

Gary Levine: You can't tell mysteries without giving audiences some story satisfaction; you have to pay off some story lines. Otherwise the audience feels like you're making it up - you're treading water and there's no forward motion.

Philip Segal: There was a tremendous amount of pressure to reveal the killer. It was priority number one, but Mark and David didn't care. The network was caught up in the frenzy of the speculation and the mystery. It was a huge conflict and the pressure was tremendous and it fell on deaf ears. There were very high-powered meetings I was a part of where we definitely put the hammer on them to reveal the killer, and the truth is they never knew who killed Laura Palmer! That was the reality of that - it was sort of a nonconspiracy.

Robert Bauer: I think I spoke with David and Mark about Johnny Horne potentially being the killer. Maybe they didn't know at the time or it was just a good smoke screen, but it seemed like the conversations I had with them were about "Where are we going with the killing?" I'm gonna guess they didn't have a fucking clue at the time. They were just having fun doing what they wanted to do the way they wanted to do it on network TV. That didn't last too long, I'm afraid.

Sheryl Lee: I completely trusted David and Mark to have the right timing with revealing Laura's killer. To me, they are the visionaries. They are the ones who wrote it and were creating it. I've worked on a lot of network shows since then as a guest star or whatever and they are very controlling. They want women to look and act a certain way and they want the story lines to please their advertisers. It's a very limited way to work and it can be very frustrating.

Tony Krantz: David knew (and I assume Mark felt the same way) that the minute you reveal who the killer is people are going to move on to the next thing. The death of Laura Palmer was never supposed to overwhelm the show. It wasn't what the show was about, but when the show took off, the desire to solve that mystery was so big in the minds of the audience that it really overwhelmed the series itself and ABC absolutely insisted that we solve the problem.

Ken Scherer: I think David and Mark didn't care [who the killer was]. I truly mean that in a very positive way. I think they had a concept and they were tweaking the television model. One of the very first meetings I attended with David and Mark was with Bob Iger (who was then the head of the network) and his team and they pleaded with these guys to solve the mystery in the upcoming season.

They pleaded with them because they "knew the television model." Coming out of the meeting, nothing definitive was ever stated but it was clear to me these two guys were not about to do that. I think it was the mystery of not knowing that drove them.

Twin Peaks *was set to premiere its second season in a new Saturday night time slot. Throughout the eighties, Saturday night network ratings had declined with the advent of home video, but ABC justified this dubious decision in the press with research indicating that Saturday night audiences had long been ignored and ratings would improve with quality programming.*[1] *After asking former ABC Director of Research Alan Wurtzel if the Saturday experiment was a subtle effort to euthanize the show, he responded, "I simply don't remember. I would tell you if I did."*

Mark Frost: After we had all this success on Thursdays, when it had clearly become the show everyone talked about the next day at work, to move it to Saturday night felt like a kamikaze mission. The audience we were delivering to them wasn't home on Saturday night! We were giving them the exact numbers and demographics those outfits need, and they ended up discouraging them from watching. We never understood it and had no say on the matter, and I have my theories about why but 'it was what it was.' We were stuck with it.

Philip Segal: Thursday was considered a sort of loss leader in terms of ABC's programming strategy. We had young writers on Thursday and no matter what we did – if that show had a young cast it skewed very old. So the perception at the time of the scheduling department was that Thursday was full of fifty-plus viewers and they wanted to find a place to put the show where it could attract a younger audience. The strategy of Saturday was that it would attract a younger audience who were willing to watch the show before they went out on a Saturday night.

Michael Saltzman: From the very beginning I don't think ABC ever loved the show. I think they thought they could get a show like *The Waltons* or maybe a *Hill Street Blues*. Having a pedigree like Mark Frost, they may have thought they could create a show like that and when they finally saw it they didn't know what to do with it.

Mädchen Amick: The whole time it felt like the network wasn't behind it. They were unwilling partners in having a show going that far beyond the realm of what television was supposed to be at the time. I think they were thinking, "What did we get ourselves into?" For me, every episode we were on television was kind of a miracle.

Peter Michael Goetz: I've done over two hundred episodes of television and you always have the executives with their suits watching on the sidelines. They are conservative and want to be careful. When you step beyond certain boundaries to be funny, they are worried about the general audience - the common denominator - reacting to it in a proper way. *Twin Peaks* did not go for a common denominator.

Al Strobel: The suits also didn't like the idea that David and Mark had 'final cut' approval. When we were shooting the scene where the cops catch up with Gerard coming out of the shower wrapped only in a towel, the set was crawling with angry suits. "We can't show a half-naked amputee," they argued. "Families will be watching. Put him in a wet t-shirt." They finally got David on the phone where he was filming *Wild at Heart*. David told the suits that he had 'final cut' and the t-shirt stays off.

Gary Hershberger: I really, truly felt the network didn't know what to do with it. They thought, "We've unleashed the lion out of the cage... now what do we do with it?" They moved it to Saturday and to all of us actors it felt like it was where all the great shows went to die. They moved it there for a reason and I think they just didn't know what they had. There was no reason to move it from Thursday; at least I thought it was doing well.

Mark Frost: The main thing we were fighting was that the network had no idea what this thing was – they did an okay job marketing it after David set them straight on the direction to take – but they almost seemed determined to kill the show.

Ken Scherer: ABC really didn't want the show and I know that for a fact because even before I got the job with Lynch/Frost Productions I had a meeting with a leading ABC executive. In the course of doing my business for the American Film Institute, I mentioned David Lynch and *Twin Peaks* and the guy rolled his eyes.

Mark Frost: Bob [Iger] was the point man for ABC on the show when Chad Hoffman left; he was running the network at the time. So at big points of discussion or decision he was always the guy that we met with. Honestly, I always found him to be a very straight-ahead, straight-shooting guy even when we were (in their eyes) in trouble when we had a ratings decline. He was up-front about it and never tried to color the truth in any particular way and I appreciated that.

Ken Scherer: I will give a lot of credit to Bob Iger and Ted Harbert because they wanted the show. If you look at what Iger has done subsequently, he's somewhat of a risk-taker, even in what he's done with Disney. I think corporate New York hated it and didn't think America would respond and I think they got pissed off when they did. I just think corporate suits hate being wrong, so they tweaked time periods on us and they moved it around.

Again, from a corporate perspective they didn't own it and they had no stake in it. The show was a big family. Mark and David owned it, which is why I always felt ABC was kind of not committed to the show. It did nothing for their bottom line except draw ratings and advertisements.

4.

SIDE B

Fever Dream

Production on the second season of Twin Peaks *began in mid-July, 1990, as David Lynch and Mark Frost plotted the series' path into the future. Network politics and a media circus raged on as the impending demands of a twenty-two episode order required the generation of new and engaging content - all while sustaining the extolled caliber of the first season.*

Mark Frost: Season two - by virtue of having all those episodes in front of us - had to be launched more like a traditional show than season one. We had written all episodes of season one before we started shooting, or at least certainly had them laid out. With season two we had to go back to the starting line, start from scratch, write stories, and get going quickly. So we didn't have the same amount of thinking time and felt the pressure of knowing we had to make that many shows and having to generate that many stories. David wasn't around as much because of *Wild at Heart*, so he and I didn't have each other to rely on quite as much, so it was just a different vibe.

Harley Peyton: The second season wasn't something I was thinking about a lot [during the first season]. I hoped there would be a second season, but I had never worked on a television show so it was all new to me! Then the second season came along and they made me a producer which thrilled me and spoiled me forever. It was an interesting balancing act in the second season and it had some highs and lows, but I certainly remember it fondly.

David Lynch directs David Patrick Kelly

Directed by David Lynch, the second season premiere picks up directly where season one ends and reveals the respective fates of many characters. As Agent Cooper lies shot and bleeding in his hotel room, a visit from an elderly room service waiter (Hank Worden) coincides with Cooper's vision of the Giant (Carel Struycken), who offers three clues to the identity of Laura Palmer's killer.

Mark Frost: When the idea of the Giant came up we knew he was part of this dream realm that was becoming a big part of *Peaks*. We needed entities who could color in and infuse that space with otherworldliness. This is mythological/fairy-tale territory so a giant was a perfect figure for that purpose. When we cast Carel the way David shot him we were able to find linkages between the characters inhabiting that realm, and helped us deepen that part of the story.

Kyle MacLachlan: I just remember reading it and thinking, "What's the next moment after Cooper is shot?" and I thought that the idea of him being visited by the Giant was really genius and I thought we were starting off on a great foot. I don't remember much about the filming, I just remember Carel was obviously very tall and the fact that Cooper wakes up - I was glad to see he wasn't finished! Also, the old fellow Hank [Worden] came down the hallway and he was an old cowboy.

Carel Struycken *(the Giant)*: It was the first episode of the new season and there was a lot of discussion going on that the network where *Twin Peaks* was being shown, they were kind of nervous about not having control and they wanted to push it out of its timeslot. So when we were shooting and Hank the waiter shuffled in I thought, "Oh my God! This is taking way too long. It's the first new episode! People are going to change the channel and it's going to be another argument for the network!" [*laughs*]

So I was kind of concerned about the show, if it was starting out that slow and if it was going to be okay. Halfway through that shuffle David Lynch yells, "Cut!" and I think he's going to tell him to walk a little bit faster. [*laughs*] Then he said, "Hank, the way you're walking...

I want you to do it a lot slower!" So that was kind of my first great David Lynch experience. He didn't disappoint when we first met. Everything was really "peachy keen." [*laughs*]

Stephen Gyllenhaal *(director, episode 27)*: I had seen a lot of the episodes, not all of them, but it was the first introduction of the Giant and I remember thinking this is the finest - not just piece of TV - but piece of cinema I'd ever seen. And that was pretty cool, I've gotta say.

Duwayne Dunham *(editor, episode 8)*: David really set the tone for the ensuing episodes with the Giant, which was so interesting to me and only David could pull that off. To have this large guy appear the way he appeared is not an easy thing to do - to make something appear like a dream or a vision and have it be real at the same time. As long as the mythology held the prospect of whoever killed Laura Palmer was associated with this, it made sense to me.

Michael Horse: I'm the most un-new age guy in all of freaking Berkeley, but if you grow up in a traditional Native community you know there's spirits wherever you go and there's always a battle between good and evil. I knew where it was going. Both David and Mark know the psyche of the human spirit. A lot of the Native ceremonies we do have characters that are bigger than life and they are basically showing the community that these things exist and they are part of the human condition.

Mark Frost: I wanted to inject a level and layer of metaphysical material and David was all for it. That planted the show's roots a little deeper in the ground and that was part of what we were presenting: life is not just a series of events that happen to you, it's also on another level a mythological experience, during which you are constantly receiving messages from or making contact with your subconscious. No one really knows for sure, do they? That territory has never been charted and I think it gave it a deeper sense of mystery beyond the obvious.

Inspired by the same free-wheeling spirit and open collaboration of the prior season, the early hours of season two install a haunting tone and slink closer to the revelation of Laura Palmer's killer.

Phoebe Augustine *(Ronette Pulaski)*: One story that comes to mind is when we were filming the hospital scene when Ronette remembers [Laura's murder] and is thrashing. I think David felt bad for me because I was actually getting bruised up pretty badly during filming so he pulled out a stick of gum and placed it on top of the camera and told me that I could have it when we were done. I remember that now whenever I'm chewing gum! It was all pretty challenging. I really try to identify and get into my roles and Ronette's world was not a comfortable one to get into.

Miguel Ferrer: There are so many scenes I like. I think it was the first episode of the second season where that guy [Big Ed Hurley] is talking about how his wife's eye was shot out. He's doing this really serious speech and I'm doing my damnedest not to laugh because it was hysterical and he was doing it so straight. Lynch saw me turning red or something and he said, "Albert, if you think it is funny then laugh!" I said, "Really?" and he said, "Absolutely." So I didn't have any lines, but we're laying out this tragic event where his wife lost an eye and I'm just hysterically laughing. That was a lot of fun.

Ray Wise: I remember the scene when I come into Ben Horne's office and he's there with his brother. I say, "I'm back! I'm okay!" and then I start to sing [*laughs*] and they go into their little goofy dances. I think Ben jumps up on the table and his brother starts doing these weird somersault gyrations. It was so bizarre and I thought totally of the moment, it was just right. It was crazy.

David Patrick Kelly: We were very creative on the set, like with the whole dancing sequence when Laura's father came in. We came up with that on the spot. My great teacher Marcel Marceau used to put a stool for me backstage and I would see some of his performances. The worm dance came from my training right there: "L'ecole

International de Mime." Some of his proudest mimes had very dark hearts, so even that was in there too.

Richard Beymer: I was in the corner doing a little shuffle to loosen up the new shoes they had bought for me. David [Lynch] saw it and said, "What are you doing?" and I said, "Oh, I'm just loosening up these shoes. When I was a kid I used to tap dance and I was just remembering a few things." He said, "Great, we'll use that in the next scene!" I said, "David, this is the scene where I'm with Leland and my brother and I am negotiating a murder!" He said, "Oh, it'll be great!" Once I got the handle on what David liked and what he was wanting and that it didn't have to have a deep reasoning - all of that became a lot more fun to work with David.

Dana Ashbrook: I loved all the Briggs stuff - that was my favorite stuff to do. Charlotte Stewart and I are still friends and Don [Davis] and I were still friends up until when he died [2008]. With Charlotte, her energy is love. Getting to work with her was such a joy and Don made me better in most scenes I had with him, honestly. He's a great actor. He really helped me be better and I loved every scene I did with them.

Mädchen Amick: One of my favorites is when Bobby and I are feeding Eric [DaRe] in the coma (the baby food) and then Eric hiccups and spits the food all over me. [*laughs*] Getting the three of us together on set was always trouble.

Eric is so the complete opposite of the character. Eric was such a big lovable sweetheart and so sometimes it was hard to separate how great and sweet he was, but they [the directors] would set up the scenes well and the scenario and talk us through it. Just the way it was written, it was really frightening. So we just kind of had to follow what we were told to do and it always came out right.

Dana Ashbrook: Harley Peyton wrote that party scene [episode 13] which is so great. I read it and just hoped I did it justice. It was fun, we had a good time doing it, and I really thought that Eric did a great job. He had a hard job letting me fuck with him while he's catatonic. It's not easy to be pulled on and prodded and all that shit.

Lesli Linka Glatter: Well, eventually Eric got his comeuppance ...playing a character who's paralyzed, not able to move a muscle and having to not anticipate anything as he takes a total nosedive into the cake, to the glee of Dana and Mädchen. How often does a director get material like that?

Beast Incarnate

Frank Silva *(Killer Bob)*: [The] first thing I have to say is that Bob was an accident. He was never, ever there from day one. It was a whole, unbelievable accident. It basically happened during the original pilot. I was a crew member, the on-set dresser in the art department.[2]

The unbelievable birth of Killer Bob has been recounted many times over the years by David Lynch and various members of the cast and crew. Almost every recollection of this event includes a different twist, adding to an urban legend that has grown since 1989.The only certainty is that Frank Silva entered Twin Peaks *as a crew member and was immortalized as the series' most menacing villain.*

Grace Zabriskie: Most of my memories are of moments that had little if anything to do with me. Being there, watching, when something went "wrong" and seeing David turn the mistake into something better than it would have been had the mistake not occurred. My favorite mistake was Frank Silva's mistake. No one is supposed to move about on set, so long as sound is rolling. Frank needed to grab something (a prop, maybe, or a cup of coffee), knew he could be very quiet, and was off camera. Or so he thought.

The shot was on me, lying on a couch against the wall, grieving, drugged out. Frank was in the hall outside the room. He needed to cross the doorway to get what he needed, but the doorway, which was in the same wall that my couch was against, wasn't in the shot, so there should have been no problem. But there was a mirror above the couch. Looking at the shot, David could see the mirror above me, and see that it was mirroring another mirror across the room...and that *that* mirror was bouncing back the image of Frank trying to sneak across that doorway.

Frank Silva

So that's what David saw, in the mirror above me on the couch; Frank trying to sneak past the doorway. Someday we'll have to do a PowerPoint presentation, or an animation of the way this happened, so that everyone can take pleasure in this most fabulous 'mistake.' And, while they're at it, see a bit more profoundly into the miracle of David seeing what was there, as opposed to what shouldn't have been there.

Sheryl Lee: I loved Frank so much. None of us could forget the day that he was behind the bed and ducked out of the way and the camera panned back and got him and David and Mark went off and wrote a whole new character and pages of dialogue. That was one of the coolest things I had ever seen. David was open to looking deeper into that and not just immediately writing it off and saying, "Cut! Frank, get out of the shot. We've gotta go again." He has this amazing ability and it taught me so much. It is one of the greatest things I learned from David and Frank is the greatest example: being able to surrender to the creative energy that is bigger than all of us and to trust that magic is at work.

Kyle MacLachlan: Frank had this long hair and this very particular face; he was one of the sweetest guys you'll ever meet and just a lovely, lovely person. He was a very hard worker who created really beautiful scenic stuff and work on the set. David just thought, "Oh, this could be interesting." The fact that David was open to the idea of him as this specter was just a genius thing that just happened and David was willing to expand *Twin Peaks* into another area simply because of this vision.

Ray Wise: I didn't find it as terrifying because I knew Frank and he was such a gentle, sweet guy. It was totally against his nature to play that snarling Bob character. I knew Frank very well and I knew it would be very hard to respond to his performance and be frightened by it.

He had long, beautiful, salt-and-pepper hair and a face that looked like it could have been carved on the head of a nickel. He looked like he could be on Mount Rushmore with that face. He was just a very strikingly physical looking character and I think that he was absolutely everyone's idea of what that kind of a malevolent spirit would be. But no, I couldn't be frightened by him because he was Frank. [*laughs*]

Phoebe Augustine: I remember how cold I was and how I had to carefully walk across the railroad ties without looking down [in the pilot]. While we were shooting the bridge scene, one of the crew was frightening to me. He wasn't doing anything scary – he just had a very scary aura about him.

I called David over and asked him who that was and if he had to be on set because he was frightening me. David quietly said, "Well, don't tell anyone, but he's the bad guy." It turned out to be the late, great Frank Silva! I met him later on and he was such a sweet guy – nothing like what I imagined during the scene on the bridge or how he was as Killer Bob.

Frank Silva: I never knew what I was going to be in the series. It was one of those things where they'd call me at the last minute and say, "Could you be on set? We need you." And I'd go, "Well what am I going to do? And they'd go, "Well, I don't know. I'd say, "Does David know?" And they'd go, "I guess." So I'd walk in and I'd go, "David, what am I doing?" He goes, "Well I'm not sure yet." [3]

Miguel Ferrer: That's pretty incredible; the guy was a prop guy and all of a sudden he's an actor and he has a SAG [Screen Actors Guild] card and he's Killer Bob? As a person he was so unlike the persona of Killer Bob. He was a gentle, sweet, kind, soft-spoken guy and he became this thing and it was fucking scary, you know? It was amazing.

Frank Silva: All the times I had gone in, David was the director. And I had known David for a long time, our relationship and friendship is there, and I feel real comfortable with him. Of course I'd get nervous, but I understand him. So, when they called me to go in, they said "We need you here for one of the episodes." And I said, "Oh, okay, what am I doing?" "Well, umm, we don't know exactly, yet, but just come in." And I went in and it was Tim Hunter directing. I went, "Oh no! This is, like, really scary! A real job, with a real director!" [4]

Tim Hunter: Bob was an absolutely sweet guy and he wasn't terrifying at all on the stage. I think I made a mistake with Bob by trying to make him too terrifying. I've got him mugging a little bit and that could be my fault as much as his, and then I remember seeing what David did with him when he revealed him and it was so subtle and so scary. It just sent a chill through your spine, whereas I was trying to pump the guy up. I don't think it worked as well and I always thought that was one of the many measures of David's genius, how he could hit stuff like that without even trying.

Jonathan P. Shaw: We were in the editing room and not privy to everything. The word came back that the gentleman who played Bob was actually a set dresser. So he was very well cast, but I remember one particular evening I was working late at night by myself at a studio in Hollywood.

There was a knock at the door, so I got up and walked out to the end of the hallway. Its pitch-dark and I turn on the light and there's Bob! [*laughs*] He's there to drop something off! That startled the heck out of me. I'd never met him and there he is behind this glass door! Man, that was something. [*laughs*] It was another part of working with David. What a scary guy! And so well cast. Did he ever speak?

Killer Bob is a curious oddity throughout the first season of Twin Peaks, *only appearing in a "Have You Seen This Man?" flier and in brief visions of Sarah Palmer and Agent Cooper. Killer Bob's increased presence in the second season remains ambiguous, but the character sinks deeper into the series' fabric with every sporadic appearance. Frank Silva passed away on September 13, 1995, at the age of forty-four*[5] *and remains a touchstone of the* Twin Peaks *narrative.*

Al Strobel: The world will never know as gentle and beautiful a man as Frank. He knew he wasn't a highly trained actor but was delighted that he had so much to offer our project. After doing his 'scary' thing he would break out into a muted giggle. He is dearly missed.

Leslie Morales: Frank Silva was my on-set dresser and one of my dear friends until he passed. Frank was one of the sweetest guys in the world. To just look at him he looked kind of evil or scary, but as a person he was exactly the opposite from how he visually looked. He knew what he looked like and how strong of an impression he made and he was very grateful for that moment in time where he was a celebrity, or something.

Whenever he wasn't working as an actor he was working with me, so we worked together for a few years after *Twin Peaks*. He gave wonderful dinner parties; he had a wonderful home. He was working in an antique shop and I went into see him and saw something I really liked and for Christmas he gave it to me; I still have it in my house. That's just who he was. If there was something you loved, he found a way to get it for you. You're asking me questions and it kind of chokes me up. He was a deeply kind and sweet person. Frank was my buyer at times; he was great at finding things. When I'm working on a set I'll still say to him, "Frank, I can't find it," and within twenty-four hours whatever we're looking for will appear on set.

Together Forever

Twin Peaks *fuses improvisation, beautiful music, a surface of serenity, and a creeping threat of terror in its finest moments, including a scene in episode 9 with James, Maddy, and Donna singing the longing ballad "Just You and I" in the Hayward living room.*

James Marshall: David said, "I would like you to sing. Do you want to do it? I heard you play guitar. I've heard you're good!" So I said, "Sure what vibe do you think?" and David said, "Well think of a vibe, Angelo will be at this part of the stage on the set. I'll see you in half an hour." So there was a piano on the set, I think it was Donna's house. It was just funny because that's where the song was performed, and where it was written.

Angelo has that vibe - he's so bubbly and energetic and fun when he's working. He said, "Okay, James, what do you think?" and I said, "Well I'm thinking fifties, but... you know that longing, sort of like doo-wop but haunting slow love ballad, like "Only You." That type of thing, but really longing. It's kind of like John Lennon with his slap echo."

So Angelo starts doing fifties rock n' roll on the piano and everybody had their necks up, searching for the words. David starts singing, [*in the style of The Platters*] "Only You..." and Angelo's singing "You" and playing chords and David sings, "Just You..." and then "Just You-ou-

ou-ou-ou" and I-i-i-i-i-i." [*laughs*] So we were having fun and cracking up and searching for the words and David began finishing the words "together, forever."

So they said we'll meet at this studio. Be ready to play guitar. So I get there and its fricking recorded already! Angelo said, "We have a guitar player, we did this and that, we just need you to sing." I was all bummed out, thinking I was going to play guitar and do the whole thing, not just sing it. I wanted it high falsetto, but it was ultra-high falsetto. It's in the key of C, and I struggle with it. It took three extra takes. If only it had been my key! David said, "I thought you could do this!" [*laughs*]

"Just You and I" is ironically bound to one of the most frightening moments in all of Twin Peaks, *as Maddy experiences a horrific vision of Killer Bob stalking her upon the song's conclusion.*

Sheryl Lee: I remember getting to go into the recording studio with Angelo Badalamenti, who I just love so much. I was so shy about singing that, but to be able to work with Angelo and David in the recording studio was such a thrill; it was so fun! So my memory of that scene is different than the viewer's memory of that scene.

Because of playing Laura, that sort of sheer terror that you might witness as a viewer was in my subconscious all the time because that was part of her life. Those moments don't stick out to me as much because they were through lines - it was always there. To the viewer, there's times when it's there and it's not there, but to me, playing Laura, it was always there.

Frank Silva: Sometimes he [Lynch] wouldn't even say that much, it would be generalizing, like the scene with Maddy, Donna, and James. David would say, "Well… I think I want Frank to walk into the room, and maybe leap over the sofa!" That was it, and he'd tell the camera man, and so they'd light it.

Then they'd call the first team – that's first team on the set. I was standing there, and David walked up to me in the dining room of the Hayward house, and he'd say "Frank, just walk in, blah blah blah... you know what to do!" Then he said, "Action!"

Instead of leaping – I just didn't feel comfortable leaping – I just crawled over it. As I started crawling over it, and got over the sofa, David said, "Keep crawling." So I kept crawling, and he didn't say anything. He didn't say, "Stop." He didn't say, "Cut." I kept crawling, and I kept crawling, but I was always taught that you're not supposed to look at the camera, or look at the lens of the camera. So I crawled to the side of the camera, just alongside of the camera. And David said "Cut! That was great, Frank! Do it again, and crawl right into the camera!" And so we did it in two takes. I crawled right into the camera. [6]

Natural Selection

The dawn of the second season warranted new horizons to shed the skin of the first season and progress into the future. Appearances and attitudes were also shifting behind the scenes and on camera, informing a new chapter of the series.

Harley Peyton: What happened over the summer was a lot of the actors decided they wanted to make changes to their characters and Audrey decided she really didn't want to be a sort of fetishized sex object in bobby socks and saddle shoes. She wanted to be more like Katharine Hepburn and that's a quote, if I remember it.

Meanwhile, Lara Flynn Boyle didn't really want to be this perfect and absurd distillation of goodness and a sweet girl-next-door type. She wanted to wear sunglasses and smoke cigarettes, and you get that, you're sympathetic to that, but we had only done seven episodes! So it was a little soon for that to be happening.

Sherilyn Fenn: I felt like some of the other characters were trying to do what they thought Audrey was doing. It seemed like Donna's character was changing: Lara starts sucking on cigarettes and: [*dramatically*] "Oh, James!" [*laughs*] That's when I made different choices. I started to wear little jackets and tried to move her more (in her mind) towards being a business woman. No more of this little girl stuff. That's really the subtle hand I was working with to keep it fresh, for me.

Sherilyn Fenn and Carla Fabrizi

Episode 10 offers an unexpected left turn for Albert Rosenfield when he angrily rejects another physical confrontation with Sheriff Truman. In a jarring monologue, Albert refers to himself as a "hatchet man in the fight against violence" and compares his vigilant manner to Ghandi and Martin Luther King, Jr.

Miguel Ferrer: Well, first of all, it's the best speech anyone has ever asked me to do in my entire working life as an actor. It's the best speech I expect ever to do in my entire life. It was unbelievable, and Mark didn't call me first to say, "By the way, you've got this crazy turn." I just got the script like I got every other script. I'm looking at it and looking at it and all of a sudden [*pause*] I see this speech and I said, "Oh... my... God. It's genius." I really wanted to do a great job and it just completely shocked me and shocked everybody else. You know, it just came to me without any warning and I still think it's the best writing I'll ever have the privilege of executing in my life.

Robert Engels *(screenwriter, episode 10)*: I remember that speech, but I don't remember where it came from. That's distant to me. Miguel was so good at that, so terrific with that stuff. That's another good example; you certainly realize you have a guy that can do this kind of thing. A lot of it is getting a good actor and then you know they will crush that. There's a real unique quality to him.

Lesli Linka Glatter *(director, episode 10)*: It's so funny because I haven't seen these shows in a really long time, but now that you bring up some of these iconic individual scenes, I so remember Miguel's amazing performance, so dry and straightforward. I think that scene was done in one shot and I only did a couple of takes because Miguel was so impeccable. Fantastic scene and great, great writing.

The independence of each director continued in the second season with Todd Holland (The Wizard) *and Graeme Clifford* (Frances) *shepherding respective episodes. The directors' latitude to add personal touches and concepts to the shooting scripts supplied each episode with refreshed ambition.*

Todd Holland *(director, episode 11)*: Leland Palmer was being interrogated by Sheriff Truman and that's all it said. The script was very plainspoken. So the stages were available to me and I sat on that jail set and I looked around and thought, "How does this show begin?" I sat in Leland Palmer's chair and I just looked forward at this acoustic tile and I got this idea that the whole thing starts in Leland's head.

You're deep inside, it's black, there are voices, you're turning in a cave and as it pulled back it revealed you were in the acoustic tile. I came up with all of it on my own and I thought, "That's how this episode starts, in Leland's mind," and I would pull back to reveal him in this rattled state being interrogated. I pitched my take and they completely supported it. That was essential because it was a really complicated shot to pull off in that day and age.

Graeme Clifford *(director, episode 12)*: There was very little conversation such as "this is the way we do it." You were able to direct your episode the way you saw it and give it a little personal stamp. I got the feeling sometimes that David let the episodes dictate what was going to be coming in the future. It was very much a stream of minimovies rather than the customary experience of directing an episode of a well-established series. And no one was there "just doing their job," we were all there because we loved the series and wanted to be a part of it.

So once you get in behind the camera you try to emulate what has gone before and bring your own little touches to it where possible. My little touches are to do with performance because I love actors and I love working with actors. I'm very character driven, so my concentration is trying to get interesting and emotional performances.

Caleb Deschanel: I could go to David and suggest (for instance) the scene where Ben Horne and his brother are in jail and they talk about when they were kids and this girl (Louise Dombrowski) came in and was dancing on the rug. I got this image of these little boys watching this girl and not quite understanding the sexual attraction, but it still being part of their psyche. I just had this idea that it would be great to do a flashback and get a couple of little boys and this girl dancing.

Most of the time if you ever come up with an idea that's new to a show, they don't want to do it because it means throwing the production into some kind of turmoil and people have to figure stuff out. In this case, it was great because David could say, "Yeah, let's do it." What was funny is that David Fincher's sister (Emily) was working in the office and she ended up being the girl in that scene who is dancing on the rug. That's a little bit of behind the scenes information. [*laughs*] I really love that scene.

Todd Holland: I pointed out to them it hadn't rained in *Twin Peaks* since the pilot and that it should rain in this episode. It wasn't in the script at all. Not a lot happened in the episode; it had a great opening and there were a few comic things like Lucy and Andy's pregnancy scare, so it was my pitch that we do this 'weather opera' where the storm approaches, the storm builds, it hits in act three, and then the denouement, wherein the aftermath the storm breaks and it passes. It gave the episode a nice 'frame' emotionally.

I wanted the episode to end with a real sense of power and foreboding – so that's why I decided to smash the camera to black with the flashlight hitting the floor in the fight between Hank and Jonathan at the end of that episode. That was the denouement of the storm - the rain has stopped, the thunder is receding, and you think everything is struggling to return to normal. But it turns out - as with all things *Twin Peaks* - nothing is anywhere close to normal.

The power goes out in the Double R Diner and there's a mysterious assassin in the darkness with a warning for Hank. The Asian assassin dude was Mak Takano, an actor and martial arts instructor. I see him around town teaching MA [martial arts]; he's a good guy.

Mak Takano *(Jonathan Kumagai/Mr. Lee)*: Todd specifically wanted a toe-to-toe kind of thing and he asked me what I was thinking. I said, "This guy is a lethal killer. He's an assassin and he's very diverse in killing people with his bare hands. Hank is twice the size of him, but he's not going to be able to do anything to this guy. Let's keep it short." Todd really liked it and suggested that I throw him over the counter to make it more dramatic. It worked out really well, and then we did the "blood brother" thing. I was really trying to intensify things and I actually smashed the flashlight. [*laughs*]

Chris Mulkey: I do all my fights in all the movies, and when Mr. Lee comes to the café for the first time, we do our thing and he flips me over the counter and I land behind there. For some reason one of the stuntmen said, "No, I have to do this." He rolls off the counter and totally fucked his back up. [*laughs*] I had to help him out and said, "You should have let me!" It was hilarious. It was as simple as falling off a chair.

In the summer of 1990, Twin Peaks' *tight circle of screenwriters grew to include Barry Pullman and Jerry Stahl. Pullman had no screen credits up until his hiring, while Stahl had spent years writing for the prime time hits* Moonlighting *and* Alf. *Pullman wrote three additional episodes and the hiring of Stahl resulted in total catastrophe.*

Mark Frost: These experiences were night and day. Barry Pullman was the one guy I hired cold. I read some stuff of his and I really liked him and he became a solid contributor to the show for the time he was involved and I worked with him again later. We've stayed friends over the years. Jerry Stahl was the complete opposite.

Harley Peyton: I remember Jerry Stahl for all the obvious reasons that are probably in his memoir [*Permanent Midnight*] (which I haven't read, so I don't know his point of view). He was this weird, smart, sort of hipster guy who had worked on *Alf* which we all thought was sort of weird and we thought the perfect sort of person to write an episode of *Twin Peaks*.

Mark Frost: I only hired him because my agent (I think it was Tony Krantz) pleaded with me to give this guy a job. From beginning to end it was an absolute car wreck. He was a mess, in the throes of addiction at the time and I discovered later he was shooting up in our restroom in the middle of meetings. He would take a bathroom break and go get high. He turned in a completely incomprehensible, unusable, incomplete script a few days late and as I recall there were blood stains on it.

Harley Peyton: He would be late, we would get mysterious phone calls, and then we couldn't find him. It was the only time in the history of the show where Mark Frost said, "No, we're taking credit on this." What was handed in was essentially so worthless that we sort of had to start from scratch.

Mark Frost: Later, in his memoir he slammed me for mistreating him. I got as angry as I've ever been in my professional life when I read what this clown had to say about how he'd been mistreated while he was taking money for work he didn't honor and doing heroin in our bathroom.

Phoenix

The revolving door of talent in the second season saw a variety of interesting names from prior decades of cinema and television, including one Michael Parks, a notorious character actor of the sixties and seventies who resurfaced in Twin Peaks *to play the sinister Jean Renault.*

Mark Frost: Johanna Ray brought his name up. I had loved Michael Parks in the sixties, one of my favorite actors. He had a really cool short-lived television show that I loved called *Then Came Bronson*. I think it was on NBC, kind of a one-man 'Route 66.'

Randy Barbee: I was a kid growing up in the late-sixties and *Then Came Bronson* was one of those shows that changed my life. When I got out of college a few years later I literally bought a motorcycle and rode all around the country, lived off the land, the whole thing. Michael Parks was my hero. I got a casting sheet and I couldn't believe it! I couldn't sleep the night before he came in!

Michael Parks *(Jean Renault)*: I had not seen *Twin Peaks*. I was living down in New Orleans and Johanna called and asked if I could do a Canadian accent and if I wanted to do *Twin Peaks*. It didn't pay hardly anything, but she said it would be fun. I don't audition. I haven't auditioned for fifty years. So I came out twice from New Orleans I guess. I did two shows and then I did another three, I think.

Mark Frost: It turned out Richard Beymer knew Michael from that era. They were young stars in Hollywood around the same time and Richard thought there was never a better actor in that generation and said Michael was also the one guy in town everybody was terrified of. He was like [Marlon] Brando in a way, he didn't take any prisoners, and he didn't compromise. He was also a genuinely tough guy and I thought that was a quality I wanted to see in that character.

Michael Parks as Jean Renault

Michael Parks: French Canadians, they have a wonderful dialect. It's not as "flavorable" as the real Canuck, it's that French Canadian; it's fun: [*in Jean Renault's accent*] "Running a whorehouse, it's Montreal you know?" It's funny because when I arrived, that's what attracted me. So I get out there and I was staying at the Chateau Marmont and they picked me up and brought me to the valley.

I got there early and went to the food wagon to get a coffee and a rolled tortilla or something. Out comes this gal director I didn't know and she said, "It's so wonderful to have you! What attracted you to the show?" I said, "The French-Canadian dialect." She said, "What dialect? The other two brothers didn't have that dialect." So I said, "That's their fucking problem." She introduced herself as the director and said, "I'm sorry." So I said, "Well you better go check it out." She said okay and ran off. She comes back and says, "Mr. Lynch says do whatever you want to do." So I said thank you.

Lesli Linka Glatter: Michael Parks, man. You know, he was playing a bad guy and he was able to bring that without effort and it made him (I think) very terrifying. He didn't play it with a heavy hand; it was very light and underneath the surface. I do think it made him terrifying. He had strong ideas, but that's never a problem to me, I find that interesting.

Todd Holland: Michael Parks insisted on speaking so slowly with that French-Canadian accent. Nothing I could say to him changed anything in his performance. I just could not get him to speak more quickly. He actually ended up forcing our cutting pattern in post because we had to cut away simply to tighten up the dialogue – even in his death scene. He's a very intense man who chose to be very intense when he met me. He's the only person on the entire crew that really came at me with a chip on his shoulder.

Graeme Clifford: Michael was great fun to work with. He relished his role and was full of ideas. I loved his accent! [*laughs*] He loved it too and used it when he was not on camera. I would say, "Michael, can I talk to you about this?" and he would say in his best French accent, "Oui, mon cher, what would you like?" [*laughs*] He'd be sort of jokingly in character all the time, as far as the accent went anyway.

Miguel Ferrer: Michael Parks was just a great guy; I think I made a fool of myself being a "slabbering" fan because way before *Twin Peaks* my favorite TV series was *Then Came Bronson*. Which was, just to me, at that age was just the *epitome* of cool, so anytime I was around him I was kind of reduced to a babbling super fan. I don't think I made much sense any time I talked to him.

Michael Parks: Most of my stuff was in chunks with certain people, you know? I got to meet Russ Tamblyn too! He just knocked me on my butt when I saw *Seven Brides for Seven Brothers*. It just killed me, his dancing. And what a nice cat Richard Beymer is. The Ferrer kid, they were all real nice. It's good because I can give you years of idiots. It's always good if it's true. If it's not, I won't talk about it.

Don Amendolia: He was amazing to watch. I actually was worried; I thought, "Gosh, I can barely hear him from three feet away." I could *barely* hear him speak. And then you see how wonderfully he came off in the show. He was very private and quiet and I watched him very closely and I thought he was pretty chilling. He killed my character, actually. [*laughs*]

Mark Frost: I've never worked with a more professionally prepared actor in my life. He was picture-perfect on take one of every scene I ever did with him. He was interesting and quirky and riveting. I loved working with him and I was happy for him because that kind of led the way for him get back on his feet, with [Quentin] Tarantino then casting him and he's been working a lot ever since.

Michael Parks: I don't go back and watch my stuff. I thought I did a good speech in my last episode [20]. I remember that, hunched down on my knees. It was real and in character. It's funny - I had to watch a movie I did not too long ago because Tarantino begged me. Quentin loved the *Twin Peaks* show, and liked a lot of my stuff. He's got an incredible collection of everything I've ever done. He'll say a line out of one of the movies [*laughs*] and one time it was from *Twin Peaks*. I call him the video savant.

Michael Horse: Parks is a pretty tough-ass guy and of course, a big icon to me. There's a scene where they got him and he's dead. I forget who was directing, but they said, "Hawk, you kind of kick him to see if he's dead." I looked down and Parks looks up at me like, "Kick me and I'll rip your throat out." I said, "I'm not kicking Michael Parks. He's dead, trust me!"

Kyle MacLachlan: One of the fun things about *Twin Peaks* was the ability to bring people in, people that either David or Mark had a fondness for and have them be a part of the show. I always thought that was a great thing. To see these character actors come back who were obviously a big part of the creator's young lives was really fun.

Ray Wise: I really enjoyed the scene that took place at the sheriff's office in one of the conference rooms with Royal Dano, he sort of looks like Abraham Lincoln. I believe he actually played him at one point and he was a great character actor, especially as the lightning rod salesman in *Something Wicked This Way Comes*, a great Ray Bradbury story. I was just thrilled to be in the scene and actually have dialogue with him because I had admired his work in movies from the time I was a little kid. I was a bit starstruck with Royal in that scene.

Mark Frost: We always added little asides when the opportunity arose, whether it was references to old movies or people's past work, like casting Clarence Williams [Peggy Lipton's *Mod Squad* costar] in a story line, which became a complete no-brainer. So we added a small moment where he and Peggy encounter each other in the diner - that was part of the fun of the show.

Nobody was using this word then, I don't think I'd even heard it, but this is a meta-level of conception, that in the show became a 'show within a show.' It became organic to our process. We knew we were making fictional narrative entertainment and we were also paying homage to things that tread similar thematic ground in the past.

Tourists

A number of guest stars and surprising casting choices illuminated new characters during the early hours of the second season. While their appearances are brief, their impact is etched deep in the Twin Peaks *canon. In episode 10, Lenny Von Dohlen joined the show as Harold Smith, a homebound recluse and melancholic guardian of Laura Palmer's secret diary.*

Lenny Von Dohlen *(Harold Smith)*: Johanna Ray had brought me in and Lesli Glatter directed the first episode. I didn't know much about agoraphobia before they offered it to me. I had to look that up and thought, "Oh yeah, every time I contemplate getting on the freeway, I know exactly what that feels like!"

So I did the audition and I changed the last line of the scene where Lara Flynn Boyle says, "I'll be back." I was supposed to say, "Great, I'll look forward to it," or something like that, and instead I changed it to "I'll be here." And they seemed to like that.

Lesli Linka Glatter: Lenny seemed like absolutely the most appropriate choice. He came in and did a reading and we were all just like, "Oh my God, that's the guy." He found that sense of vulnerability. You really felt like he wasn't just playing that role of the shut-in, but that he was being it. There was a sweetness about him, but there was something else underneath where you didn't know what was going on. Having that layer made the character grounded and very human.

Lenny Von Dohlen: It was a completely insular world for me. I didn't know anything about what was going on beyond Harold Smith's world and I really didn't really want to know. I liked the hermetically sealed world because that was Harold's environment and so I didn't know much about what else was going on. I was really quite content to be confined to Harold's world, as much as I would have enjoyed watching other people work.

Harley Peyton: I invented that character Harold (who never left the house) and he was based on a series of books called *The Inman Diaries*. There was a man named Harold Inman; I think he was from Boston and this guy never left his house. He just kept these copious diaries about the world and the life he wasn't living. So I took that real thing and made up this character.

Lenny Von Dohlen: Tangentially I worked with both David and Mark on the series, but most of my conversations were with Harley Peyton who wrote a few of the episodes. We were in tune and he was so helpful in turning me into the 'homeward bound' society and getting me into that world, and I just took off.

I was excited to work with Graeme Clifford because I was such a fan of *Frances* which he had directed. He was very sensitive to the whole burgeoning world of my character and we worked very closely together and I felt very grateful to have him there.

Graeme Clifford: I loved Lara Flynn Boyle's monologue where she verbally seduces Lenny Von Dohlen. I thought she acted the scene magnificently! I remember at the time, I thought, "Oh my God, this is great." I love when I'm shooting something and what I'm watching just takes me out of the fact that I'm actually shooting [*laughs*] and I end up watching the monitor thinking, "I'm not filming, this is real," and I almost forget to call "cut." The scene was so well written too, and with Angelo's hypnotic music... great!

Lenny Von Dohlen: I remember Kyle came to our set one day while Lara and I were shooting one of the sexy and suggestive scenes with the orchids - and it was - we tried to make it pretty hot. Between takes she'd run over and jump into Kyle's arms as if to say "I'm just acting!" She was young, he was very sweet and supportive and probably got a kick out of all that.

Graeme Clifford: Lenny's performance was very emotionally twisted and demanding. He and I spent time refining that performance. I was very happy with the result. He was great! Quirky intensity was the key, mixed with pathos and compassion for his character.

Lenny Von Dohlen: I objected to that scene when Harold goes after Donna and Maddy because I thought there wasn't a violent bone in his body. I remember it was a last minute rewrite because I got the pages that day and they wanted something dramatic. So I thought, "What if I turn it on myself? He might do that, as a precursor to his end." But it made no sense to me that he would go after them. So you got that rather gruesome image! My daughter's in sixth grade and I need to put it in writing that she can't watch that series or the movie [*Twin Peaks: Fire Walk with Me*] until she's forty... or until I'm dead, [*laughs*] whatever happens first!

I have to be honest - I didn't keep up with it after Harold met his end. There was a mourning period, even though I knew going in that Harold would meet his demise. I didn't know how that would take place, but I knew as I was creating this person that there were these bookends. It would begin this way and end this way, so it gave me permission to create within those parameters.

The character of Catherine Martell was still presumed dead as the second season began with Piper Laurie's name stricken from the credits. Laurie and the creative team went to great lengths to conceal her true identity when she rejoined the cast in episode 11 as the fictitious Japanese actor Fumio Yamaguchi, portraying the mysterious Mr. Tojamura.

Piper Laurie: David called me at home and told me the plan of Catherine's disguise and that no one was to know – no cast or crew, not even my family - and gave me the choice of what kind of foreigner I would be. I thought at that point a Japanese businessman would be less predictable.

I love that kind of thing. My childhood was filled with pretend events I conjured up, getting into an elaborate disguise when I was about ten years old as an old lady, going across the street with my sister to the old folks home and joining them on the porch. That's the actor in me; I did day-long improvisations long before I got paid for it. So this was not hard.

Piper Laurie as Catherine Martell

The hardest part was when things were so funny and I couldn't laugh or I would give it away. Even if I went to a private place I could split the prosthetics that had been glued on me and which took four hours in the morning. If I laughed, the makeup would be ruined and there was no time to start from scratch. It was very harsh on my skin, all that glue, and the painful hour of peeling it off at night. They gave me a few days off to heal in between. I never actually asked for it. It just seemed to work out that way thankfully.

When you're trying to live the schedule of an episodic television show, there's no room for life, or to find out what's happening in the world. So my whole world was going to work, getting up before the sun, sixteen-hour workdays. Driving home in the dark from deep in the valley to Santa Monica and having only a little over an hour to shower, eat, study the script and try to fall asleep. I'd sleep perhaps three or four hours and then back to the valley and the converted warehouse that was our soundstage. I wasn't aware of the world!

Todd Holland: I was told that Piper would be in disguise and that no one else knew. At one point I was taken to a secret location [*laughs*] and I was introduced to 'Mr. Tojamura' and I knew it was Piper and she was in complete makeup, complete drag at that moment.

We came back and shot that scene where she goes to the Great Northern. We shot the scene with Richard Beymer and he had this big cigar in his mouth and he's looking at her. We rehearsed, we did the scene and he rolled the cigar in his mouth and he looked at me and asked, "What's up?"

Mak Takano: I'm Japanese, but I was playing a Chinese character. I looked at the cast list and there's this Japanese character with a Japanese actor's name next to it. They made a big fuss about it and I had never heard of them. [*laughs*] My uncle was a famous actor in Japan and my parents lived in Japan at the time. I'd go back quite often and I knew something weird was going on. We were shooting something and Piper Laurie comes in with all the makeup and stuff and it was like Mickey Rooney in *Breakfast at Tiffany's*! He plays that Japanese man on the upper floor and he's always complaining that there's too much noise. [*laughs*] I wasn't insulted, but it was definitely weird.

Richard Beymer: They fooled us all... for a few hours. She came on set with an interpreter. She was being directed and the interpreter would tell her what to do and they played the whole thing up. When she came on as a famous Japanese actor in Japan playing the part, she was introduced and we bowed. [*laughs*] We figured it out a day or two afterwards and the gag was up, but she stayed in character the whole time.

Piper Laurie: The first day I worked as Fumio Yamaguchi, great pains had been taken to disguise me and keep it a secret. Jack [Nance] seemed to have bought the made-up story about Fumio 100 percent, more than anybody else in the cast. There was something so naïve and innocent about him. After that first day he went to David and to Mark Frost and said, "Boy, is that new actor weird!" I tried not to engage in conversation with anyone because if people got close to me they could see the extremely heavy makeup.

One of the scenes Jack and I did was standing at the bar and having an outlandish conversation about Broadway musicals. [*laughs*] The dialogue was preposterous and I could hardly keep a straight face. We were dangerously close to each other, perhaps no more than ten inches apart and I think we played the scene well but I was sure he would know it was me, but he didn't! He just didn't get it. Thank goodness in the rest of the scene I could move away from him and sit down because I could hardly control myself.

I had a few scenes with Kyle when I was playing Fumio and I thought he didn't know it was me. It seemed he accepted me as the new Japanese actor, though he seemed to be avoiding eye contact with me, even in our actual scenes. He may have known about it. He's known David a long time and David might have trusted him with our secret and that's how he dealt with it. My instinct was he didn't know, I was just some weird guy! [*laughs*]

The front office kept urging David to wrap it up – tell us who killed Cock Robin and they quickly resolved everything in an episode. I was disappointed because it meant my story line of Catherine going into disguise was kind of thrown away at the end. I was disappointed, but it didn't take away from what we did.

David Lynch emerged from behind the camera in episode 13 as FBI Regional Director Gordon Cole, the nearly deaf supervisor of Agent Cooper. Lynch's portrayal of Cole left the cast and crew in pangs of laughter and affirmed the sheer unpredictability of Twin Peaks.

Lesli Linka Glatter: There isn't a favorite scene (of mine) because the whole experience of doing it was just incredible, but I have to say directing David Lynch as the hard of hearing FBI agent was one of the most memorable.

Mark Frost: Because David and I loved film noir so much we were constantly inserting references to the great nineteen forties film noirs like the insurance investigator Walter Neff, from *Double Indemnity*; even David's character Gordon Cole, who is a character that is mentioned but never seen in *Sunset Boulevard*.

Al Strobel: Being in the presence of David was very similar to the one time I met the Dalai Lama. His creativity and inner joy are infectious. Yet he makes everyone around him feel uniquely and equally valued. When David showed up on set [as Gordon Cole] I thought: "How *cool* the maestro came to play in our sandbox." As Cooper's boss he was hilarious. I especially liked the hearing aid gag. And what a great setup for the heavy stuff to come.

Robert Engels: My mom was deaf like Gordon is, so there's stuff from there that my mom says; that was kind of my favorite character I guess. "Give me the glad hand!" That's my mom's expression. My mom looked at it and said, "I don't know who that is supposed to be," and I said, "It's you!" [*laughs*] It always happens when you do that. Just because it's them they don't see it.

Duwayne Dunham: David and Kyle MacLachlan are very good friends, you know their history and there's no wonder to me that David was okay acting in this thing with Kyle. You know, David and Kyle did a really good job and I loved the scene in the diner [episode 25] and I loved the way Shelly played it with David. I just thought it was great. I will say I was intimidated by the thought of directing David Lynch, but I was much more relaxed at the idea of directing Gordon Cole!

Lesli Linka Glatter: There was a scene where Gordon Cole takes Kyle and Michael into the sheriff's office to have a private conversation, and of course he's screaming so loud that everyone in the police station hears it. Literally the crew was laughing so hard that we were crying; you were hearing all this noise off camera because we could barely contain ourselves!

Kyle MacLachlan: We laughed a lot of the time, and David had a very distinct and specific idea about who Gordon was and what he was doing. I pretty much let him lead the whole thing, you know. He was a lot of fun to work with, but it was very difficult for me to keep a straight face!

Back to Missoula

Duwayne Dunham: I remember one day early on sitting in the cutting room for *Wild at Heart*. David asked us all, "Who killed Laura Palmer?" and we all wrote our pick down on a little index card and sealed it in an envelope and stashed it away. We opened it whenever it was revealed.

After months of speculation and scrutiny, ABC announced that the killer of Laura Palmer would once and for all be revealed during episode 14, originally aired November 10, 1990. To continue an air of mystery on the set and protect the revelation from being spoiled to the public, David Lynch and Mark Frost commissioned three separate scenes with a different killer brutally murdering Maddy Ferguson in the Palmer living room.

Philip Carr Neel *(associate producer)*: When we mixed the different endings, David Lynch wanted curtains put up to block the view of passersby who might be working on another show within the facility. We were mixing the audio at Todd AO Studios in Hollywood and had to make sure outsiders couldn't see or hear what was going on or who the killer was. At that time everyone wanted to know. So David wanted the mixers to mix the show "blind" without picture (so as not to reveal the killer on-screen) which would have been very difficult for the mixers. I finally convinced him that we just couldn't do that. [*laughs*]

Lori Eschler Frystak *(series music editor)*: When we got to the dub stage, the mixers hadn't seen any of it yet because it was such a huge secret who killed Laura. When we got to that scene, the mixers just let the reel run so they could see the whole scene. I'll never forget at the end of the scene, the head mixer, Gary Alexander, stopped the reel and turned around to David and said, "I hate you!" He had grown to really love Leland.

Ray Wise: I was praying it wasn't going to be me because the whole idea that Leland would kill his own daughter was extremely distasteful to me. I had just had my own baby daughter in 1987, so that whole idea didn't sit well with me. I was hoping against hope it wasn't me. I didn't really want to leave town and I knew that if I was exposed as a murderer and taken into custody that I would go to jail for life (or whatever the punishment would be) and no longer be on the show.

The day that Leland dispatches Maddy was a long twelve-hour day and poor Sheryl Lee had to die three times because Ben Horne killed Maddy that day, Bob killed her, then Leland Palmer killed her so even the crew wouldn't know who the real killer was. I suppose you've heard that story.

Richard Beymer: Even though David knew I wasn't going to be the killer, he directed the scene just like it was going to be that way. He wasn't holding back or fluffing it off. He was actually directing, making it better, and changing things as we went. I'm vaguely remembering it now. [*laughs*] It's all a big blur. It's always fun to do those sorts of things.

Ray Wise: I saw a little bit of Richard Beymer doing it as Ben Horne. I don't think I saw too much of Bob's character doing it. I pretty much knew how he would do it. Frank was a wonderful guy, actually a prop man, and acting didn't come that easily to him. He did a marvelous job as Bob, but I thought it was kind of predictable what he would do. He sort of had one or two speeds. Neither one of them did it as well as me! [*laughs*] I say that tongue-in-cheek, of course! Stephen King said that was one of the most scariest and horrific moments ever on television.

Frank Silva: That scene was so horrific to do. I remember when we did the master of me doing it, I was so exhausted towards the end of the scene, because we had shot the master all in one sequence. At the end where I shove her head into the painting of Missoula, Montana – I f---d up the line too, I kept saying Missouri-we were both so exhausted, she falls to the floor, and I was so exhausted and so into it, I fell to the floor with her, over her body. It ended with me animalistic, over the body, kind of licking the body and hovering over the body. It was such an intense thing to do.[7]

Frank Silva

Sheryl Lee: To this day, that is probably my most difficult day of work I've ever had in my whole life. No matter how fantastic the actors and stunt coordinators, you can't go through a scene like that without hurting the next day. I had a doctor once who brilliantly taught me that when one is acting, the only part of you that knows that you're acting is your mind, and it's helped me tremendously ever since.

Every other part of you does not know that it's acting if you're going for the truth of the scene or the moment. So if you're crying, your mind knows you are acting but your body is still releasing real tears; it is still going through the chemical changes of the body. So if you are experiencing fear like I was that day and in that scene, the chemical changes my body goes through are the same that one goes through when one experiences real fear or whatever primal response it is we're having - we're really having it.

Grace Zabriskie: She [Sheryl Lee] gave everything she had, she gave more, she gave more than she could afford to give, and she spent years coming back. I can't separate "what her performance says to me" from what I know it both gave to her and took from her. The performance itself tells this story. No one walks away unscathed from work like that. But I could be wrong. I don't know that she thinks of it this way in the least.

Sheryl Lee: Playing Laura was a very painful place to live for a long time. It's hard, in acting school they teach you how to develop a character but they don't teach you how to let a character go. There were many, many nights of nightmares. At the same time, we would be doing some of the most torturous scenes, but because everyone had such a sense of humor and we felt safe doing it, we had a great time. [*laughs*] Nowadays, it's no different than everything that's on, but a couple of those scenes were really brutal.

Carla Fabrizi *(makeup artist)*: There were so many moments where they were doing horrific scenes and they would call "cut" and the actor would look over and wink and laugh. You had to find some humor in it or it would take you to the dark side. At the end of the night you were just exhausted.

I remember an awful scene with Sheryl where claw marks were left on the floor of the soundstage. She put her nails into the floorboard *that* severely to have an impression on the floor. There were some very intense, dark sides. I had about five minutes to figure out how they were going to pull the letter out of her finger!

Randy Barbee: I just remember it was really, really intense. I remember that Sheryl Lee went to a place that nobody should have to go to. She really reached an emotional peak and I was trying to look out for her a little bit to make sure she had her space. Ray Wise was a consummate pro that he could go and become this guy and in between takes he was fine, he was just Ray.

Sheryl Lee: I felt so safe with Ray and trusted him so much. God bless his heart. I'm a parent now and I can only imagine how difficult some of that was for him. Thank God that all those actors were so experienced and kind and supportive and really looked out for me that day. They were all just brilliant. They were scary! [*laughs*] They did their job phenomenally, but that was a tough day.

It wasn't hard [leaving the show] because we were talking about there being a third character. I knew that chapter was over, but I knew that working with David wasn't 100 percent over. Laura had died and I had come back and Maddy had died, so it was kind of like, "Let's see what happens." [*laughs*]

It's a strange, curious thing to play somebody who is known because they are dead. It's like people are seeing a ghost, so there's a lot of curiosity for me about that and what that means in my life. Right after it aired I went and did a play in New York because I knew I had to do some things different, or this is going to be it. I saw every script about tortured young women that could have been written during that time.

Lori Eschler Frystak: I spotted the scene with David and the assistant music editor for the second season, Rickio Woods. I wasn't shocked that it was Leland but I was mad. I didn't want it to be Laura's dad. We pulled some tracks that David wanted to try and added some extra layers. At one point we played the scene dry, without music. It was just too intense without it. Even adding the creepiest music we could find softened the violence and terror a little.

Scott Frost: It was an extraordinary hour of television. That one just left me speechless - that scene in the living room cutting back and forth between Cooper and the club. That was the kind of television *Twin Peaks* could be when it was really good. I knew the story and everything that was going to happen and I saw that and I was left kind of shaken. I can't remember ever having that experience with a television show, before or since, but [it's] one of those moments that happened on *Twin Peaks* that will never be repeated.

Philip Carr Neel: It was obviously very violent when Leland killed Maddy. With the ending of that episode where Julee Cruise is singing in that bar and everyone is sensing the violence, David wanted to make sure that that portion of the show played out. I think he mentioned he didn't want the network to unintentionally chop off the ending. It really said a lot about David, that he understood the balance of the good and the bad. It was really important to him that it aired properly and he told the network not to interfere with it.

Dana Ashbrook: One day I just came to the set to hang out and David said, "Oh, we'll put you in here!" I was just hanging out and suddenly I got sent to makeup and then I'm just sitting at the bar and he just told me to act really sad. I had no idea at that moment what was happening, that her father was raping and killing her. I had zero idea. The only people that knew were David, Mark, and Ray and Sheryl. It was a very select few that knew what the fuck was going on.

Angelo Badalamenti: If there was one favorite scene in the show that I think about and chuckle - is in the country bar [the Roadhouse] where there is screaming, yelling, and all hell is breaking loose and then there's a beautiful girl singer, Julee Cruise, with her delicate, plaintive voice singing that wistful ballad ("The World Spins") which is truly one of my very favorite songs that David and I wrote. In the real world, that combination of the bar where all hell breaks loose and Julee Cruise is singing would never happen! [*laughs*]

Miguel Ferrer: You know, I think it was one of the greatest moments in television history. I thought it was one of the most effective reveals and it was a real horror moment, and really hardcore for TV, especially back then. I thought the scene and the whole sequence worked brilliantly. It was scary, wasn't it? I mean, I remember saying, "Whoa! That is really scary!" and I was on the show [*laughs*] so I definitely can understand how people watching (especially at a young age) could get the crap scared out of them.

Philip Segal: It was sort of a mixed bag, really. I think it played at nine or ten at night, but obviously Standards and Practices were very concerned. It was watered down quite a bit, but when you're in a ratings war you do what you can to try and promote and provoke an audience into watching.

Robert Engels: That was never the plan [to reveal the killer]. The actual execution of it is pretty amazing. My seventeen-year-old nephew just watched the series for the first time and the murder scared the shit out of him. It worked in the sense of having to resolve that. You might think it's kind of unsatisfying we had to do it. No one wants to do what you have to do.

Other than saying you have to show who murdered Laura Palmer, they [ABC] were pretty benevolent that David and Mark were going to do what they were going to do. They were worried about network stuff like the broadcast code and censors, but nothing out of the ordinary.

Harley Peyton: I will say that that episode is one of the best on television I've ever seen. The way Mark wrote that script, the way David directed it, and Ray Wise's performance was just, oh my God, so unbelievable. Wherever that episode landed it would have been tremendous. I think it's foolish to think one could never answer that question. I mean, you're not really respecting your audience that way, but I think it could have waited till the end of the second season.

Sheryl Lee: It's really fun to talk about *Twin Peaks* and it was such a great show to be a part of, but ultimately it's about who killed this girl and wrapped her in plastic and was sexually abusing her. When you think of it like that, it's very sobering.

Vehicle

In a stunning performance by Ray Wise, the fragile Leland Palmer is transformed into a sadistic monster, unveiling the character's true nature under the influence of Killer Bob during episodes 15 and 16. Although Leland had been revealed as the killer to a select group of individuals, false scripts were still being distributed on the set to cloud the mystery's final destination.

Ray Wise: I've been working professionally now since '68, actually. I've done about eighty-five different stage productions, I've guest starred in probably over one hundred episodic television shows, I've been a regular on three or four series, a recurring character in seven or eight series, and I've made about eighty-five movies. I've played Caligula on stage, the mad emperor of Rome who was certainly one of the most evil people that ever lived, but Leland Palmer was quite a challenge back in 1989 when it all began.

Then, as each week progressed and I read the script for that week and saw some of the trials and things that Leland had to go through, it became increasingly more challenging and more fulfilling - and satisfying once I had done the work each week.

Kyle MacLachlan: Ray, I had loved from *Robocop* where he's one of the villains with Kurtwood Smith. I just loved that little group of guys because they were *so* bad. He's an actor of incredible dimension and he had this wonderful surface, a loving father kind of thing he got to play and meanwhile there were other things happening to him. I was just so impressed with his ability to do that - to carry both of those same things at the same time with this fearlessness. It was not a particularly nice character when the reveal came out. It was a role that could really ostracize him from people and he embraced it.

Caleb Deschanel *(director, episode 15)*: Ray was amazing. He could be both comic and scary at the same time and he could switch back and forth, like when he gets pulled over in the car and he is singing "Surrey with a Fringe on Top."

Ray Wise: That was a wonderful lighthearted moment on the show, and then immediately following that it looks as if I almost take Cooper's head off with my golf club, but I don't. [*laughs*] There were so many marvelous moments and as you mention them to me they explode in my mind. For that week, it was my favorite moment of all time and I had a bunch of them, and that's why *Twin Peaks* was such a special experience. I was able to open myself up completely and be in the game 360 degrees. I didn't allow any restrictions or any unnecessary prejudices color what I was doing.

Graeme Clifford: I saw every single episode and I thought Ray was inspired throughout. Ray is a very sensitive actor. He always wanted to explore further and dig deeper into his character. We would have in-depth conversations about the particular scene we were doing and how it fit into the story and how the many plot twists and turns might affect his character as a father, and indeed, as an actor! He engaged me in more conversation than most of the other actors did and was very serious about it. He was so motivated to do the best he could absolutely do.

Grace Zabriskie: Ray is what's meant by 'consummate professional.' Which I suppose wouldn't have to include a great sense of humor, but in Ray's case it does. I'll never forget seeing, one day in the makeup trailer that all the repeated bleachings of his hair (after Leland's hair turned white) made his hair start to fall out. And when your hair is supposed to have turned white all of a sudden, there can be no roots showing at all, and he wasn't through shooting those scenes yet, which meant he wasn't through having his hair bleached again, and I remember thinking, "This is terrible, what if he loses his hair because of this?" But everything grew back. He has great hair!

Ray Wise: They discussed me having a wig made, and then they felt that because of all the things Leland had to go through in the ensuing weeks that the wig just really wasn't going to work. So, I would have to go to a hairdresser and get my dark hair bleached out. That was a long, painstaking process because my hair being very dark, to turn it to white took five or six hours and a lot of chemicals. Finally, it turned out a beautiful white and I certainly looked different. But then after doing it week after week, I had to do my roots every eight or nine days probably.

Jonathan P. Shaw: The episodes I did with Leland where he cracks up were all practical shots; there was very little postproduction that we did after the fact. Most of it was practical which made it authentic. It also allowed the actors to play off that stuff. So many times they're acting up against a green screen and it loses authenticity. When Leland is going crazy in the living room, it's powerful stuff.

Caleb Deschanel: It's the perfect representation of insanity when you see Leland hitting golf balls in the house. At first, you think people do that - they have those little devices that send the golf ball back. The idea was to reveal it slowly. You see him hitting golf balls and you think, "Well wait a second, he's hitting them a little too far," and then you suddenly realize there are a hundred golf balls he's been smashing into the room. [*laughs*] We had the prop man get all these golf balls and then we had to go get more.

The kids [Lara Flynn Boyle and James Marshall] come in and see this and it doesn't register to them. It registers as odd, but it never registers to them that it is totally insane and that's a wonderful thing about the scene that is really appealing to me. If you think about it, that's the reality of the horror of violence [with] all these people who end up doing terrible things. Everybody says their next-door neighbor is a great guy: "He came and helped me with my lawn," or something. [*laughs*] The fact that we can be blind to the most obvious demonstrations of insanity is really sort of wonderful.

Ray Wise: My favorite moment comes in the Great Northern, in the lobby, and I believe Cooper has told me they've arrested Ben Horne for the murder of my daughter. Then I walk into the next room with a golf club in hand and Cooper and the sheriff follow me and they have some more words with me. I'm looking at the camera, not looking at them, and I make that transition from weepy Leland to maniacally giggling Bob, and that's my favorite moment in all of *Twin Peaks*.

Caleb Deschanel: They made a big effort not to reveal that it was Ray Wise. We had three different scripts with each one revealing a different person as the killer. This was before the days of the Internet, but even so there was enough interest in the show and enough subterfuge of people wanting to know what was going on that they were afraid it would get out, so we went out and shot these other scenes as well.

Mary Jo Deschanel: Because Caleb was directing he had the real script and knew what was happening. One night the AD [assistant director] called when we were out and left a message with our daughter Emily (who was twelve at the time). The message she got was about Killer Bob and she was completely mystified and frightened by it. She could watch the show but our other daughter Zooey who was nine wasn't allowed to watch it. But I think she did sneak in and see a bit of some episodes.

Grace Zabriskie: The inhabiting spirit of Bob, I see as part and parcel of a lot of what *Twin Peaks* might have been about. A metaphor for the half of life that is true, the half that is false, and the half that is truer than true.

Al Strobel: The woman I've lived with for the last twenty-five years is an internationally renowned exorcist. She has helped me understand that entities from outside of what we can normally perceive have the ability to affect our behavior. Physicists have proved that we can perceive only a very small percent of the mass and energy of the universe. These are themes explored through many of the characters in *Twin Peaks*, not just Bob and Mike (although they are perhaps the most overt).

Ray Wise: I played Leland (at least in my mind) as not responsible for any of it - as being completely possessed by Bob - and that's the way it goes in my mind. To me, Leland is totally an innocent and he was taken over by that malevolent spirit of Bob and did all those horrific things.

I think that he was basically an intelligent, caring, considerate, kind man. That's the way I played it: the grief stricken who loved his daughter dearly and could not bear her loss. He just obsessed over it and his grief took a variety of forms and he was just overcome and overwhelmed with the loss of his daughter and I could identify with that... and Bob was just something that came out of the woods.

Leland Palmer's homicidal spree comes to an end at the conclusion of episode 16. In a chilling confession, Killer Bob speaks through Leland Palmer, admitting guilt of the murders to Agent Cooper just prior to Leland's death. Upon Bob's departure, Leland tearfully pleads for forgiveness in the arms of Cooper in a flooded jail cell.

Ray Wise: I didn't want to leave the cast, [*sigh*] but then I was told that it was me and David said, "Ray, it's you. It was always you." I don't know if that was true in his mind the whole time, but then he went on to explain how my final moments would go and how Agent Cooper would help me with the transition from life to death, reading from *The Tibetan Book of the Dead* and I would see the white light at the end of the tunnel and my daughter Laura would forgive me. So it seemed (to me) to be very redemptive and he made it sound so good, so I guess I couldn't complain after that.

Tim Hunter was incredible and he directed that final episode of Leland's. I had a good time with Tim and I think he helped me do some of my best work in that episode.

Miguel Ferrer, Carla Fabrizi, Kyle MacLachlan, and Ray Wise

It was one of the most difficult scenes I did on that show, in Cooper's arms with the water sprinklers showering down on me. The water was beading down on my face, going up my nose and in my mouth and it wasn't easy physically doing that scene. But emotionally, my God, it really was sort of overwhelming at that moment. I felt every moment of that and it was a wonderful way for Leland to go out.

Tim Hunter *(director, episode 16)*: Obviously it was a terrific scene, a big cathartic scene. I just really tried to shoot it honestly and let Ray Wise play the hell out of it. And certainly the atmosphere gave him something to work with, [*laughs*] with the water coming down on him. I thought it was great for the show; I thought it was strong stuff and I just hoped I had delivered it. I know the performance was wonderful.

Kyle MacLachlan: I remember it was very uncomfortable because it was late and we had to shoot through the rain and all my hair that was slicked back was falling in my face. It was one of those very surprising endings that comes back to the character of Cooper and his compassion and understanding at that moment was very unusual in television. I think the expectation would be for something else and it went against that logic. He somehow realized there were greater forces of good and evil at play here and that the body of Leland was sort of at the mercy of these larger forces of evil. It was a very touching and surprising moment.

Michael Horse: That was really interesting to me because we were all in that room and I knew we were calling on evil. When Bob was going to come out of Ray Wise, the director said someone would go for help and I said, "I'll go!" I didn't want to be in that room when they were calling on that evil. It had become that real to me. I had a chance to get out of that room and I took it. It was uncomfortable.

Robert Engels: The series was built on Leland as much as it was on Cooper in a weird way. His performance was pretty amazing. Ray was a good sport. It's never cool when you're on a series and you realize you're dead, but *Twin Peaks* people come back all the time, [*laughs*] so I guess they told him not to worry about that. If there had been a third year, he probably would have come back.

Harley Peyton: That is one of my favorite episodes and I think it may be for a lot of people. It's extraordinary. The writing - I don't know if it was David's - but that was really Mark with *The Tibetan Book of the Dead*. It's classic Mark Frost stuff. That was Mark and David working very, very closely together and bringing the kind of magic they could bring, and maybe for the last time on the show. I'm not really sure after that how many times they actually worked together.

Miguel Ferrer: I don't know if the other guys have told you about the phony scripts they gave us. We got scripts marked:

"Top secret,"
"This is the conclusion of the show,"
"Here's the killer,"
"For your eyes only,"
"Don't share this with your friend,"
"Destroy after [reading],"
"Don't leave it anywhere."

Every page of every script was stamped with a number that corresponded to a certain member of the cast or crew so that if a story line or a page was leaked, it could be traced back to the source.

Anyway, we were handed the end of the story that day, the morning we got to work. They said, "Okay, give us those pages. Here are the real pages." [*laughs*] They gave us the bullshit pages and the morning we shot that scene we found out who the real killer was. It was just what I think you'd imagine. It was like, "This is it. Here's what it's all been building up to." But, you know, it was everything you'd expect it to be. It was... very emotionally charged and everybody felt it was the end of something special.

5.
SPLINTER

Wake

Brandon Stoddard: My biggest concern on *Twin Peaks* was where it was going to go. I kept pushing and pushing for a bible which would indicate where the series was going to go over twenty weeks. I never got it and I can understand why I didn't get it, but I knew it was key to the success of the show and that we were going to get in trouble, and we did. It killed me. It really hurt me because I loved the show so much and I knew right up front when we were making the pilot that unless we had a long-term series projection we were going to get in trouble. It was like watching a shipwreck.

The end of the "Who killed Laura Palmer?" era required the introduction of a fresh through line to reel in a wandering audience. Mark Frost and Harley Peyton both confirmed that the next primary story line was planned to romantically link Agent Cooper and Audrey Horne, but the arc was vetoed by Kyle MacLachlan.

Harley Peyton: The major determinate for the story lines in that second season was the big switch after Kyle refused to do a love story between Agent Cooper and Audrey Horne. That was something that we had been planning, we talked a lot about it, and it was something everybody wanted to see. Kyle had very specific objections: he thought his character would never do that, he thought she was too young. Whether or not the fact that he was dating Lara Flynn Boyle had any impact on that - we all had our questions.

Sherilyn Fenn: It's sad and everyone knows what happened. Lara was mad that I was getting nominations. She got on board as the central character and from whatever fate there was, it turned into people wanting to see more of Audrey, which I'm very grateful for. Kyle said no [to the story line] because she was giving him a hard time.

Harley Peyton: Mark said to me, "Look, we're going to have Kyle come up and we're going to draw the line and tell him he's got to do this. It's important to the show." So I remember my office was right next to Mark's and the walls were very thin, but you can't hear through them. There was no yelling or stomping their feet so I thought, "This is great, this is all going to be cool, we're going to get it and move on." [*laughs*]

They came out after it was over and said, "Ah, we're not doing it!" They drew a line for Kyle not to walk across and Kyle walked across it rather effortlessly, and that was that. So when that story went away, we had to scramble a little to find the spine for the second season. In some ways I think we were successful, in some ways less so.

Sherilyn Fenn: I remember David [Lynch] and I had dinner. He said, "Sherilyn Fenn, are you in love with Kyle?" and I said, "God, no, David!" [*laughs*] I said, "But Audrey loves him. The characters work! I don't like Kyle at all." And that was the truth. They made a big fucking mistake. Because of that the show got fucked up, really. They needed a more pivotal story and I would have been a part of it. It would have been so great! Then they brought in Heather Graham who was years younger than me which made it even funnier.

Duwayne Dunham: Cooper is an FBI man and Audrey's a high school girl. That just wouldn't work. What would that do to the character of Cooper? To me, even allowing him to start dressing like the locals significantly changed the Cooper character. I find it refreshing every time he gets back into that suit. [*laughs*] He's got his hair slicked back and it's like, "Wow, cool." But here's a guy who's totally by the book and into his job. That was the character from the beginning.

Kyle MacLachlan: Sherilyn was sort of the 'femme fatale' of the piece and her fascination with Cooper was sort of fun to experiment with, but it was also (I think) a direction and a diversion that was only going to play out for a certain amount of time - being that she was a high school kid. But, it was fun to watch that relationship and Cooper's reaction to it and what he was feeling certainly as a man and as an FBI agent and almost as a possible father figure... but not exactly.

Agent Cooper, post-Dead Dog Farm

Harley Peyton: Obviously, Kyle was so important to the success of the show – I mean, God, Agent Cooper? So it did not surprise me in the end when David said, "Okay, if you don't want to do it, then let's not do it." So his character ended up falling in love with a woman as equally as young from a *convent*. It was unfortunate, but it is what it is.

With production bound to a tight weekly schedule, the creative minds behind Twin Peaks *were admittedly in no position to initiate an omnipresent story to replace the Palmer case. Although the series was teasing the impending arrival of Cooper's archenemy Windom Earle, the cast and crew recall an ongoing struggle to find a new and satisfying trajectory.*

Miguel Ferrer: I don't really have clear memories after the killer was revealed, to tell you the truth. I think once the mystery was solved the show was kind of over for me.

Gregg Fienberg *(series producer)*: I do think when they were forced by the network to reveal the killer it was like, "Okay, well what story are we really telling now?" To me, when you start a show you have to have a deeper river (is what I call it) of understanding what the show is really about. I actually thought after the reveal that the show became a whole different show.

Philip Carr Neel: "Who killed Laura Palmer?" was practically a bumper sticker. It was a tough act to follow. I feel that what made it so successful until then is that they were on this trail that took them on all these fascinating directions and they really took the heart and soul out of the show. Everything that drew the viewers in to want to watch it was taken away. You solve that crime and you have to revamp and start another mystery. The network basically hijacked the show and said, "Come up with a new series." And that is unfair to do.

James Marshall: I thought James and Donna were just going to continue what they're doing and all of a sudden people are doing things all over the place. It just became sad in a way. It worked before because you had these Nancy Drew-type situations with an incredible innocence juxtaposed against this mysteriously dark part of life. It took away that dynamic and it was a mistake.

Robert Engels: I think once the murder was solved you couldn't write scenes that were about guilt; I always thought that's what drove the series. I don't know what David, Harley, and Mark thought, but I always thought that's what made the series work. You could always go pick a character from the town and they all felt guilty about what happened. That was such a wonderful thing, so that of course was gone. Looking back on it, that would be the most unsatisfying part of it - you lost kind of a weapon.

Mark Frost: I remember we were planning the Windom Earle arc, it was in the wind but we didn't get to it quickly enough. So we did a three-part interim story that wrapped up the Renault brothers and brought in the David Duchovny character. It was a little bit of a scramble after the single-minded hours leading up to the solving of the murder, so in some ways these were the weakest hours we produced.

There was a little bit of trouble because the year before we had written all seven episodes and knew what we were doing from beginning to end and began production with them already prepped, whereas once you're into the second half of a full season you're being chased by the production monster. I think we hiccupped during those particular hours. On reflection we might have done it differently. If I had to do it over again I would have moved Windom Earle right into the aftermath of that next episode or maybe jumped ahead in time.

Gregg Feinberg: I wasn't a writer, (so who cared what I said) but I remember at one point saying, "Maybe we should have somebody else die, another girl, another mystery." If Lara Flynn Boyle was dead in the next episode, they [viewers] would be like, "What the fuck!"

You're intrigued to know who killed Laura Palmer, but you're more intrigued by watching people react as more and more shit is coming up for all these people - which is what happens in most people's daily lives. Things come up and it all unravels. If they had given you more to watch and some other big secrets, you'd suddenly go, "Oh no, giving the answer of who killed Laura Palmer didn't make things better, it only made it worse." That's what should have happened.

Kyle MacLachlan: I think ultimately that the show suffered a bit from losing the sort of overwhelming through line, which initially was "Who killed Laura Palmer?" and that was a very strong objective.

Once that mystery had been solved, there wasn't another compelling mystery presented to capture the audience's imagination.

It's very difficult in television to write character. It's easier (I think) to write towards a completion of a goal. So once that goal had been reached and they discovered the murderer and everything, you were left with character. Even though there was a nemesis coming that Cooper had to deal with, I don't feel it was telling a story to hold the audience. The characters were still there and they were still interesting enough, but it's difficult to move something forward with quirky characters. There needs to be an overriding objective.

Paul Trejo: We always wondered what was going to happen after the killer is revealed. Nobody knew if it was Bob or what was going on. Leland was a shock, but it was kept quiet as to where the show would go. I thought it was interesting, particularly when those four or five characters walk in the woods prior to seeing the owl [after Leland dies]. I think Don Davis quotes a Shakespeare line: "Things are stranger in the world than in our philosophies." For me, it got a little off the rails when we brought in Windom Earle and I can't even really remember the story line, but I felt it was a little disappointing. It sort of became something that just didn't feel like *Twin Peaks* anymore. It felt like every other serial drama.

Tina Rathborne *(director, episode 17)*: My episode needed to have been an explosion - an unexpected rocket that was launched that would carry us through - and the FBI firing Cooper is definitely not that. It's more about him saying goodbye than it is recommencing from a story standpoint. It didn't feel powerful enough to regenerate the audience's feeling of "where's the puzzle?" The emotion had gone out of it for me. When I did my episode I was not very compelled to see the series to the end.

Laura's funeral scene was really a huge, emotional well, whereas Leland's wake I felt was pretty incidental, emotionally. So to me the two of them aren't in the same realm. The death of Leland carries the same weight as Laura Palmer, yet her funeral was not played up for any humor. The old brothers fighting in the wake sticks out to me as strange, which was a precursor to a lot of over-the-top humor. It feels like one of the moments where *Twin Peaks* changes.

Kyle MacLachlan: As much as Cooper loved Twin Peaks, I wish I had kept him more firmly on the FBI side as opposed to the Twin Peaks side. That is just me looking back and imagining what that would have been like: keeping him in the suit and really more as an observer of Twin Peaks as opposed to trying to integrate into the town. Whether or not that would have been a more interesting choice, I don't know.

Harley Peyton: I think there are some things we all wish we had done better. This is just my opinion: we probably fell in love too much with absurdist comedy along the way. As I've said in the past, what usually happens on a television show is the writers get bored writing the same thing every week and the actors get bored playing it. So over time things start to alter and change and not necessarily for the good. That usually doesn't happen till season five, [*laughs*] but everything on *Twin Peaks* happened more quickly.

Dana Ashbrook: That second season everything got a little different; it was just a little different than it had been. It got too spread out and a little too watered down because there was just so much going on, but you know, I had a good time, always. The only thing I wanted was more work, more to do. That was my only complaint. They struggled and got me working for Ben Horne, then they tried to put me with Audrey for a second, and I just - I don't know.

AVALANCHE

With no immediate primary story line to establish, Twin Peaks *began a rapid expansion as madcap comedy, science fiction, and new characters entered the fray. Episode 18 marks the debut of a cluster of guest stars, including Robyn Lively as Lana Budding Milford, Annette McCarthy as Evelyn Marsh, Joshua Harris as "Little" Nicky Needleman, and Dan O'Herlihy as Andrew Packard.*

Robyn Lively *(Lana Budding Milford)*: I remember when I came into the show it was a massive hit and I just loved it. I was a huge fan. So I get the audition and basically the character of Lana is this girl who all the guys are falling head over heels for. Because she's so beautiful, I thought to myself, "Okay, I'm going to be a little realistic here. I know this show has Lara, Mädchen, Sherilyn - the most beautiful women I have ever seen." I just thought, "I can't compete with that, but I can still be creative with this. I've got to stand out."

I kept reading the sides and I thought, "I know exactly what I'm going to do. I'm going to do it southern." Because I am from the South (I am from Georgia) I just thought that was perfect for the character. It all made sense because the southern accent on women is so charming and they were all crazy for her. I thought it would either go over amazing or it won't, but I've got to just give it a try - and they loved it! I was so happy! I could not believe I got it.

Annette McCarthy *(Evelyn Marsh)*: My former husband and I were very great friends with Steven Soderbergh and he came over with a video cassette and said, "You guys *gotta* watch this!" We watched it and I was not a fan immediately. I didn't like it right away, but it really grew on me. It's one of those shows you love or hate, and it grew on me. By the time my role came around and I auditioned, I was totally game.

I went in to audition wearing my best outfit. It was this skintight black dress and they didn't tell me anything. I got to meet with David [Lynch] and I remember he sort of asked me to be emotional. As an actress, it's very confrontational to just be crying in front of these people and I did! And he said, "You're on!"

Joshua Harris *("Little" Nicky Needleman)*: I was actually a random fan of *Twin Peaks* because my older sister was a fan. It would be on and I probably watched most of the episodes by the time I was on the show, so not many ten-year-olds were watching that show, involved in "who's the killer?" and all that. [*laughs*] By the time the audition came around (which I remember nothing of) I was actually pretty excited to go on it.

Robyn Lively: I loved the story line with the old man's brother hating me and then falling in love. He [John Boylan] was so delightful. What a charming, wonderful man he was. He was a bit exaggerated of a character, but he was kind and sweet and old and wonderful. I do remember being horrified - the script said they walk in on us as we are making out and I almost died. I just thought, "Oh my gosh, you've got to be kidding me. There's no way. I can't do that." So I was kissing his forehead and he had kiss marks all over his forehead. [*laughs*]

The show was always kind of teetering on the edge of being a little absurd anyway, so I was completely comfortable in doing a character the way I was doing. It just fit into that whole vibe of the absurdity of it all. It wasn't really a struggle at all to find that balance. I thought it was natural and fun; it was just a blast to be honest.

Annette McCarthy: It actually was a one-time kind of deal. I was supposed to do something naughty or tawdry on the show or something and they just kept writing and I was very pleased! Kissing James was like... actually I have to tell you, it was the real deal. He gave me that kiss and I went to Mars! I knew him for a little bit afterwards and he's a very good man. I remember watching our episodes together.

James Marshall: At the time I expected Donna and James to continue their romance because I felt there was a lot left to explore there. James and Donna didn't need to get married, but they should have been together and worked through the pain to figure out everything that happened - to hold up a level of innocence in their characters - but the writers felt different. So I was taken aback once the James and Evelyn story line began and Donna went off trying to be this hoochie girl.

As an actor, I focused on what was cool about the situation. It was a beautiful romance, and sexy in a way with a younger guy and this bold woman. It was totally fun working with Annette though, she was really cool. She was really fun and a really good actress, aside from being an incredible kisser! [*laughs*]

Annette McCarthy: I only worked for a few weeks, but I loved James. He was my favorite because we clicked and we worked very well together. It was really simple. As an actor or an actress, sometimes you don't really click with someone and it just doesn't work and it's a job. That was not the case with him. My scenes with James were a little overdramatic and some of the lines were pretty silly, but it was cute, what can I say? *Twin Peaks* was just so out there.

That one scene where James fixes my car and we drink champagne – we actually drank champagne and they took (I think) maybe twelve takes of it. I had to drink twelve glasses of champagne! At one point they had to take me to the dressing room and lay me down. [*laughs*] The production assistant screamed to get some sparkling water instead. After twelve shots I had to be put under. I mean, who was the production assistant on this? James and I were wasted. Wasted! We had to take half the afternoon off. If you look at my face when I say my lines, you can totally tell. [*laughs*]

Harley Peyton: I feel like James' trip into 'film noir land' didn't really land as well as we wanted it to, that's just my opinion. For whatever reason, that story felt more like a miss to me and I can't even tell you why because I haven't seen it in years. Listen, there were certain parts of it I liked a great deal and film noir is something I (as a viewer) love, so that was certainly fun to write, but it just didn't feel organic to the show quite so much and that it belonged to another universe. I guess there's nothing wrong with that I suppose.

Kimmy Robertson: I would run into actors who were desperate to be on the show - one of them being David Duchovny - who went so far as to ask me out and date me, basically. All the time we were dating and talking on the phone, I thought it was because he liked me and it wasn't until this year (2013) that I realized he was just doing that to get on the show. I didn't know anyone had that amount of fortitude to put up with me for that long. [*laughs*] How smart was he? It's amazing.

I took his resume into Johanna (Ray) and talked about him and said, "He's got something special, you can't really tell from the picture but you have to talk to this person. He's very charming." She said, "I would love to be charmed. I'll have him in for a general." [*laughs*] He has never asked me to be on his show.

Episode 18 also features David Duchovny's debut as the Drug Enforcement Agency's Dennis Bryson, a transgender agent now known as Denise. Over the course of three episodes, Agent Bryson proves to be a key ally of Agent Cooper during his suspension from the FBI. Two years after Twin Peaks, *Duchovny was cast as Special Agent Fox Mulder in the hit science-fiction series* The X-Files, *often referred to as a direct descendant of* Twin Peaks.

Mark Frost: I wanted to introduce a character that had transgender issues; I just thought it was an interesting subject that hadn't really been tackled much, certainly not on network television. I also thought it was an interesting dilemma for Cooper to have a relationship with a guy he had known as a guy but now preferred to be a girl.

David Duchovny as Agent Bryson

It created great comic tension for Kyle and David was fantastic. He was right out of Yale drama school; this was one of his first gigs. He was completely fearless and just embraced the whole thing and I thought he gave a very subtle and funny performance.

Kyle MacLachlan: I remember David was very comfortable dressed up and also very even-keeled; it didn't ruffle his feathers. He had a good sense of humor, he was a good sport about it, and it was a chance for Cooper to reveal his kind of acceptance of people. He was not a character that really judged, which I thought was very refreshing. David was memorable; he took it in stride.

Robert Engels: It was like, "We have to have another FBI agent, how can we make him different?" [*laughs*] Duchovny was so relaxed about that. He would get in his makeup and just go sit on the set. He wasn't going to send it up. He was a good looking gal, [*laughs*] which was an accident too. The key as I recall is you just take those guys and write them as straight as possible.

Harley Peyton: It was a very easy character to write because we just wrote it as naturally as possible, there was no attempt to make him weird or odd and the way Duchovny played it, it was like Gary Cooper in drag for God's sake. So it was sort of killer and I really liked it.

Duwayne Dunham: I often think about David Duchovny and how he approached that. I'm not sure I've ever worked with an actor who came so willing and so prepared, and just so open to playing that role. He didn't think twice about it. David played it straight - almost like he wasn't in drag, just going about his business. It worked and it was a delight working with him. I will always remember this sly little smile on his face.

Annette McCarthy: David Duchovny in drag - that is my favorite thing of all time. The fact we're in the same episode: "Thank you God!" By the way, he makes a pretty good looking girl, don't you think? He's adorable in that! There are many men that if you actually transformed them into women they look awful, but he really wasn't that bad! [*laughs*]

Caleb Deschanel: I hadn't really known him before that, but it was really gutsy of him to play that part. It was a great idea because it kind of foretold the future where society would be much more accepting of all sorts of different realities of human beings. With his performance, there's nothing about it that suggests anything but a normal FBI agent, you know?

Michael Horse: I love David! He's one of the smartest guys I've ever met. It was so funny, he came on as the transsexual and some of the crew guys were looking like they're a little uncomfortable. I was going, "Come on! He's playing a character!" I had my picture taken with him in drag and I did an [episode of] *X-Files* and I was in the makeup truck. I said, "Yeah, I used to date David's sister." I showed them the picture and they didn't really say anything. [*laughs*] David came in and they showed him the picture asking about his sister and he said, "That's me, you idiots!"

The Lucy, Andy, and Dick Show

Kimmy Robertson: When I was on [*Late Night with*] *David Letterman* he asked me something about the show and I said I had no idea because I'm not really on *Twin Peaks* anymore, I'm on "The Lucy, Andy, and Dick Show." We had nothing to do with anything. We had wine tastings, the fashion show, Lucy's pregnant: "Who's the father?" I don't know, it just felt isolated and I had no idea what was going on with anyone else; we didn't get full scripts. David was gone and Mark was gone and people who weren't on the wavelength were running the show. My frustrations took over and I said that on national television. [*laughs*] It's out there on YouTube."

Twin Peaks *is often propelled by a foreboding sense of mystery, but the second season love triangle between Lucy Moran (Kimmy Robertson), Deputy Andy Brennan (Harry Goaz), and Dick Tremayne (Ian Buchanan) provides many touching moments peppered with comic relief.*

Kimmy Robertson: Andy and Lucy were two people that were meant for each other from the dawn of time. They were sweethearts, each has a job to do and they meshed together. They were as close to regular people (I'm pretty sure) as you could get on that whole show. They were nerds, both of them. I think we were cast as nerds and geeks [*laughs*] doing their jobs and having a relationship.

Michael Horse: Harry was completely unique. Hawk would look at him, not with disgust, but to say, "Stick with me so you don't get killed!" [*laughs*] Harry was his own person, but he was a lot like Barney Fife on *The Andy Griffith Show* and I thought Kimmy represented all these wonderful eccentric character actresses that I grew up watching in the fifties. They were a hybrid of a lot of things David and Mark had seen, I think. David hires people to do what they do and pretty much lets them do it.

Kimmy Robertson: David and Mark were very careful with me and I know they must have been with Harry, because we talked about it. I can't speak for Harry but I can speak for me, and we were always serious characters and our characters were earnest and tried really hard and we never approached anything to be funny. I think the stuff that was written to be funny was funny because we were so serious.

Ian Buchanan *(Dick Tremayne)*: I'd never seen the show during the first season. I would whistle into the makeup trailer and there would be buckets of blood, fingernails, and yanks of hair all over the place. I would think, "What the hell?! What's going on?" "Oh, we can't talk about it!"[*laughs*] There was all this gory stuff and then there was our fairy-tale soap opera in the middle of it all.

I heard Bob Engels say they wanted to bring in this whole story that had nothing to do with the murder and the mayhem and the darkness. My character in particular was looking for trouble, whereas everyone else was surrounded by it. People have asked me before, "Where in the world did Dick come from?" I have no idea. For me, maybe he came from Canada because it was just across the border.

Lesli Linka Glatter: Ian was absolutely amazing for that role and I have to admit I had no idea that he was a huge soap opera star. I didn't know it until literally every woman in the office was like, "Oh my God." They were all a twitter. He totally inhabited that role. The first time he came in to the police station, I don't think anyone could help from smiling and laughing. It was perfect; there was nobody else you could imagine doing that role.

Ian Buchanan: The whole fashion show with the pine weasel was a lot of fun, I didn't think it would work and then I saw it and it was funny the way they worked it. I remember saying to myself, "I've really got to go for this, I can't even question if it's over-the-top. I've got to sell it and commit to this utter madness - to be bitten by the pine weasel and fly all over the place." I was working with the great David Lander who is a comedic genius and someone who I respect immensely. He gave me a few pointers on how to make it work. He basically said, "You've just gotta do it. You can't even think about it." [*laughs*] That was a long, but fun day.

Kimmy Robertson as Lucy Moran

Kimmy Robertson: At one point Lucy and Andy are talking and he decides to call Dick Tremayne to give him a piece of his mind. I say, "You won't hurt him, will you, Andy?" and he doesn't answer and I had a really hard time with that. I had such a hard time not laughing. I'm pretty sure we had to do several extra takes because I kept cracking up and Harry never breaks. He never would be out of character when he was working.

Ray Wise: The Deputy Andy character was just marvelous; he was really one of the more interesting characters in all of *Twin Peaks*. I loved all of his scenes; I just found them infinitely interesting and funny. He was always so sincere and you could tell he was feeling everything he was saying. All of his scenes with Kimmy Robertson were just wonderful.

Duwayne Dunham: You know, he was David's driver and that's how he got hired. He was great and he embraced that role and he was very good at it. He was very consistent. He was always in that character and he knew that character better than I did or anybody else, so you could trust him and rely on him.

Kimmy Robertson: Harry is the sweetest, kindest creature I think I've ever encountered on this earth. He's lovely, he's generous and sensitive, and he's misunderstood because he's so kind. I think he was driving David around and David liked him and said, "This is this person, I can write for this person." That's who David is, he gets people.

Joshua Harris: Harry's demeanor on the show was childlike, for lack of better references. I vividly remember blowing the whipped cream in his face. We literally did that one hundred times. He was great at pratfalls and being able to sell the Andy character. He was a really nice guy and I probably connected closely with him because all the gags I got to do were pretty much with him. He was a super nice guy.

Ian Buchanan: David Lynch brought this little snow globe of America and Andy represented a sort of Gomer Pyle, you know, those goofy cops from many television series like *The Andy Griffith Show*. I just loved that character. He was very earnest at his core and so endearing. I got such a kick out of it; I loved working with him. Harry was great fun. We became great friends.

Lesli Linka Glatter: There was something about Andy. He was such an amazing character: the cop who is moved by everything around him. He hasn't developed that harder surface to actually be able to deal with the job he's doing. Yes, it was comic, but it was always grounded in reality. There was a certain pathos in it and a reality of love not totally returned. I feel like it struck a chord in that way.

As Lucy, Andy, and Dick become further estranged from the central plot of Twin Peaks *in the second season, they provide their own brand of comedy in a variety of screwball situations which briefly include the mischievous orphan Little Nicky, whom they suspect to be a sadistic murderer.*

Kimmy Robertson: I loved Little Nicky. I thought he was really cool as a kid and I liked the story line because it brought Harry and Ian back into view and it sort of brought *Twin Peaks* back from all the places it was going. I liked the "curmudgeony" kid. Anytime a kid is making adults act goofy, I like it. I have to say at that time I wasn't sure what was going on and that seemed to me like the only thing that was kind of fun and weird in an okay way.

Ian Buchanan: Little Nicky was great; he was a great actor and I think he has a very good career as a producer now. I loved that whole idea of the mini-me: Dick in his ignorance, deciding it would be very appealing to have a little brother dressed just like him. I had a lot of fun with that. I think it was Harry's character who was more suspicious of him than I was. I remember him saying, "Little Nicky is the devil!" [*laughs*]

Joshua Harris: I was definitely engrained in it prior to being on the show - into this weird, dark dimension as all the fans were with the cult following. I have friends to this day that didn't know I was an actor and one in particular is a filmmaker and he was like, "My friends and I used to sit around and curse at Little Nicky when he was being mean." [*laughs*]

Uli and Annie

Episodes 21 and 22 respectively inducted two distinct names into the exclusive club of Twin Peaks *directors: Uli Edel and Diane Keaton. Edel was an acclaimed German export who had just directed the gritty feature* Last Exit to Brooklyn. *Edel's mercurial techniques garnered both high praise and blunt criticism from his collaborators on set.*

Uli Edel *(director, episode 21)*: *Twin Peaks* was actually my first American job after *Last Exit to Brooklyn* (which was a European production shot in Brooklyn). I moved to LA in 1990 when the movie opened. Two weeks later I met David Lynch at the Chateau Marmont hotel. We knew each other already from Munich, because I did the German trailer for *Dune*. I told him I had moved to LA and I was looking for a job and he said, "Wanna do a *Twin Peaks*?" And I: "Are you kidding? *Twin Peaks*, any time!" That's how I got my first job in Hollywood.

David wasn't very involved in the day-to-day shoot. You had complete freedom. He never interfered in saying, "I wish you would do it this way or that way," he just gave you his reactions to some of the rough cuts he saw and thumbs up: "It looks terrific." After that opening horror scene he came in and just said, "Uli, this is one of the best openings we've ever had on the show!" After that I felt completely free to do what I thought this particular show needed. Since that first horror scene with Mädchen Amick came out very well and everybody was really happy with it, the rest of the shoot was actually easy going. The only pressure was the tight schedule.

Jonathan P. Shaw *(editor, episode 21)*: I had seen *Last Exit to Brooklyn* and that's a very dark film. I was very curious as to what he would bring to this whole thing. He was so well suited - almost in the way I think the Europeans have a fondness in their heart for *Twin Peaks*. Uli embraced it.

Of all the directors I worked with, we stretched the material the furthest, always looking for an interesting way to play a scene and he was very encouraging of any ideas I had. I remember he said, "We're going to play this whole scene on his back. We're not going to see him turn around." We tried it and it worked. There was this macabre to *Twin Peaks*, an underlying thing and certainly Uli grabbed it.

Uli Edel: The other surprising thing was these commercial breaks. When you came from Germany you didn't have to deal with commercial breaks in those days. Here the cliffhangers were already in the script - and in one case I felt it was really hurting the scene when a few cops, guns drawn, [are] getting ready in front of a door to storm the room: "Cut, commercial break!"

I just changed that on the set. Now they all look at Kyle MacLachlan for his signal. Kyle would look at his watch and say, "Just wait another moment!" and the commercial starts. After the commercial Kyle [is] still looking at his watch: "Now let's go!" and they storm the room. It was completely improvised and it was funny integrating the commercial break into our scene. The crew loved it; David saw it a few days later and loved it too.

Russ Tamblyn: I didn't like working with him [Uli Edel]. I just thought he was too bossy and kind of sarcastic and he just wasn't very friendly. It wasn't a good experience for me. I think someone did almost come to blows with him; he was just that kind of director – in your face. He would say terrible things. I can't remember what he said, but I just didn't like working with him, bottom line. I was so glad when that scene was over.

Michael Horse: Uli Edel was a pretty tough guy. One time he said, [*strict*] "You go here, you go there." I asked the crew if this guy was really this good and they said, "Yeah, he is, Michael." I said okay, but if this isn't Emmy material I'm gonna kick his ass. [*laughs*] He was pretty pushy.

Ian Buchanan: Uli was great. He was very Germanic. I remember when Andy and Dick are at the police department and we are told the true story of Little Nicky's life. In the script it said we were upset, so we went for it, howling like babies. Uli was right in our faces: [*loud*] "Stop the noise!"

David Patrick Kelly: Uli was very inspiring. He runs a strict set. I remember specifically about Uli that there was a lot of comedy in these scenes. But like David, Uli liked to keep it serious on set so that the underlying reality of what we were doing came through. I really respected that a lot about Uli because sometimes it seemed as if comedy was overwhelming things, so to keep it serious and based in reality was really important.

Uli Edel: I had an office for the time I was preparing my episode and a day before shooting I had a very surprising visitor there: Diane Keaton. She said hello and seemed even more nervous than I. After *The Godfather* and *Annie Hall* and everything she was (for me) this big screen goddess at that time.

"Uli, I want to ask you a favor." "Any favor," I thought. "How can I help you?" "I'm directing the next episode and I'm asking if I could watch you direct your episode because I'm very nervous and I want to see how you do it." I said, "What an honor, Diane, but I'm not sure you can learn anything from me, you've worked with the best directors in the world!" [*laughs*] And she: "Just let me be there! Directing is something completely different from the job as an actress. Please allow me to sit behind you." So a few days into shooting she was visiting me on the set and sat quietly behind me on her chair, just watching me doing my job. It was quite a feeling!

As one of the most celebrated stars of Hollywood since the early seventies, Diane Keaton began a brief run of directorial roles in the late-eighties that included an episode of Twin Peaks *and its Saturday night ABC contemporary,* China Beach.

Wendy Robie: Diane Keaton was a favorite of mine. I think maybe it's just because she is such a wonderful actor, she understood Nadine so well. I remember she directed the episode that I come back from the wrestling tournament and get in bed with Big Ed and Norma. [*laughs*] I just climb in bed with them and tell them how the airplane slam was illegal, tough break, and so on. Then at the door, she's leaving and she has this little moment that requires me to say, "I know about you guys."

Well, Diane Keaton is talking to me about that moment and she just leaned against the door frame and she was sort of paraphrasing what to say and she was Nadine, she was! It was just something in her body. I mean, I had this urge to take off the eye patch and hand it over because she was brilliant. She completely understood.

Kyle MacLachlan: I was thrilled to work with Diane. I was and continue to be a fan of what she does. I think her work is exceptionally special because of her choices, and her inner world is so interesting to me as an actor. As a director, she brought that kind of playfulness that you need when you work on episodic television and you have a lot of long days. You're looking for any way to break out of the routine and she was all for that. I remember it being a very playful and creative environment that she brought with her.

Richard Beymer: Working with Diane, there were great expectations of it being incredibly exciting, but it appeared that she hadn't looked at any of the previous episodes. She was very involved (as I recall) in making the set look wonderful. There was the train and all that business with the war scene, but it looked like it was decorated by the studio.

I said, "Look, if I were to be doing all these things here, I wouldn't be having this look like you hired someone to come in and design this." And that didn't go down too well. It just felt like someone hadn't read the script. In fact, I remember asking her if she had seen any of the episodes and she didn't answer. I didn't have a bad time with her, but it was just like she was directing another series. It wasn't *Twin Peaks*.

Dana Ashbrook: She was great; I had a huge crush on her and she was not having it at all. It was fun to watch her and Beymer kind of butt heads over things. She had a real set idea of what she wanted to do and Beymer was very organic. I loved working with her; she was awesome. Diane Keaton, man! I don't know if she would remember me, [*laughs*] but I had a great experience working with her.

Harley Peyton: As a writer you're usually up in your office, but that was one of those days we all came down to watch because we just liked her and she was wonderful with the actors and took to this world as easily as anyone who worked on the show. With some directors you didn't get a sense they were doing anything different from the scripts, but in terms of visual imagination, she definitely did.

Piper Laurie: Diane Keaton was extremely nervous, with lots of nervous energy. I think this was her first time as a director. She wanted my character Catherine to speak at a pace that I felt was wrong. That made me nervous and that sort of makes me retreat and go in the other direction.

After comparing notes later on, the other actors especially loved working with her. It clearly was me. Months later she went out of her way to call and tip me off about something importantly negative with a house she heard I was thinking of buying. I thought it was very thoughtful of her.

Miguel Ferrer: She was prepared and happy to be there and she's an actress, so she knew how to talk to actors. I think it was early in her directing career and so she asked a lot of questions and wasn't insecure or anything like that at all. I've seen her a number of times since and she's just a lovely person. We didn't have any bad directors, we really didn't. We had some wonderful directors but no bad ones and that's the only series I've ever been involved with that I can say that about.

Paul Trejo *(editor, episode 22)*: Sometimes we would go to lunch at local restaurants and it was weird, I had never been in the presence of celebrity out in public before, so it was just the two of us. She drove really fast. [*laughs*] We would show up at a restaurant and quietly take a table. We would sit down and heads would turn and I had never experienced that before. She told me stories about growing up out here and starting out as a performer and working with Woody Allen. It was really fun.

David Patrick Kelly: Diane was just really great; there was a scene with Audrey I got to do - one of my favorite scenes where she puts me in my place. I'm working my evil wiles and trying to take over control of the Horne business and she says that ain't gonna happen. The way Diane worked that was wonderful, and the Civil War scene as well.

The thing about Diane Keaton is that in her work as an actress and director, she brings this idea of empowering women and I thought she brought that to the one scene between Jerry and Audrey. While being completely sexy, the characters she represents are totally empowered. Those two things are not incompatible and I think are very important to *Twin Peaks.*

Cracking Up

A surreal chain of mid-second season episodes focuses on Ben Horne and Nadine Hurley each suffering their own existential crisis. With both characters coping with inner torment and shame, they regress to other identities to face reality. Entering a downward spiral of emotional strife, Richard Beymer stretches the character of Ben far beyond a philandering tycoon.

Duwayne Dunham: One of my most favorite scenes (outside of the emotional reasons of shooting with David Lynch as an actor) is when Richard Beymer is watching home movies and his dad was founding the Great Northern Hotel. He played that beautifully and there are genuine tears. I loved how he played that. For me, good cinema is when you get lost in the moment and you're lost in the experience of what the character is doing. He was in that moment and I love that scene playing with the projector and he is doing the shadow puppets.

Richard Beymer: Of all the things in the series, that was my most fun scene, ever. I'm not quite sure what happened, but something clicked that day and that scene came out without me trying and I had never really felt that as an actor. There was a feeling of totally not being in the way of myself as an actor. I don't think I ever hit that note again. [*laughs*]

Duwayne Dunham: I shot the old movies because the car that's in that scene (the old Woody) is actually my car! We shot it on sixteen millimeter in Balboa Park right by the studio in Van Nuys. That was a fun scene. Richard was into it, everybody was into it, everything just came together and I loved that scene. It was great.

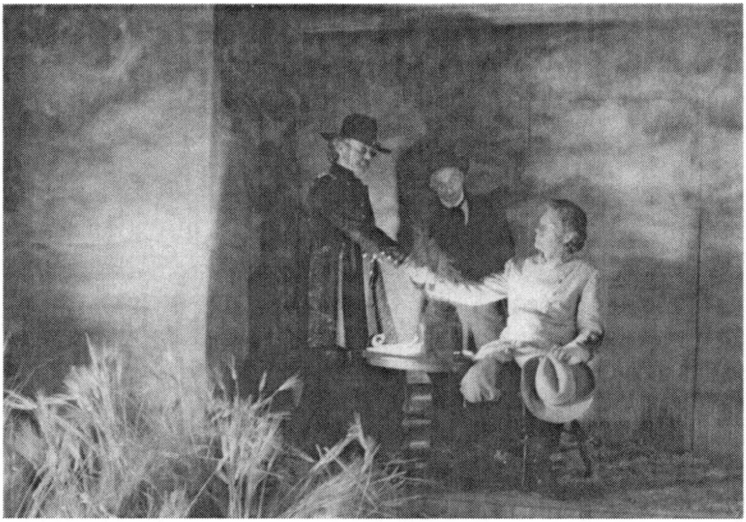

Surrender at Appomattox

Richard Beymer: The scene was supposed to end when Hank came in. He says, "Ben, you're out," and then he turns and leaves and that's it: "Cut." Duwayne let it go and I kept repeating, "You're out, Ben. You're out!" [*laughs*] and I figured he's about to cut the film and he didn't. So I kept repeating that and found myself walking to the desk, throwing things, sitting on the desk and making shadows on the screen, right? It was all just him letting it roll. Maybe he detected I was in a particular mood that day so he wanted to see what was going to happen. He could have left it on for longer; I would have just kept doing stuff. For me, Duwayne was one of the finest directors on the show.

Ben Horne's mental breakdown leads to an elaborate Civil War re-creation in his office, complete with costumes, train sets, and figurines. This story arc also offers memorable moments for the Horne brothers and an on-screen reunion of Beymer and his West Side Story *costar Russ Tamblyn.*

Mark Frost: I'm a big Civil War buff and I thought the idea of Ben seeing himself as Robert E. Lee – I mean, Lee is the poster figure for lost causes and a kind of doomed gallantry. That was an interesting aura for Ben to invest in. Ben has a very grandiose self-conception to begin with, so I thought it fit perfectly. It was also a way to do a kind of chamber piece about somebody cracking up in an interesting way and we had some fun with it.

David Patrick Kelly: The Civil War scenes were directed by Uli Edel and Diane Keaton. They were both really great. I danced at the end of one scene and am not so sure if it made it into the final cut of that, but it was great. There was a great men's store called New Republic where I got this green beaver skin fedora. I brought that in and Sara Markowitz approved it. It was a lot of fun and I thought the contrast between the Civil War and this bizarre business man was a wonderful thing.

Sara Markowitz: Richard Beymer and I had an ongoing wager. Richard was convinced in television that rarely was an actor's feet shown and in fact, he could wear bunny slippers and no one would know. So he wore off camera shoes unless his feet were going to be seen and the deal was neither he nor I could say anything to the director or camera man about putting his feet in a shot. Honestly, he was right mostly. [*laughs*] I don't think he ever paid me.

Dana Ashbrook: Oh my God, I love Richard. I loved him, and he's just a straight-out artist. Just getting to know him and work with him when he was going crazy with the Civil War stuff; it was fun to see him do his thing. I was a musical theater guy as a kid, so I just loved *West Side Story*. Working with him and Russ Tamblyn - it was a big thing - knowing they were still around and working and seeing that in person. I loved being around them.

James Marshall: Every few weeks I would sing a different song [from *West Side Story*] to Richard Beymer in the hall if I was walking behind him and he just hated it. [*laughs*] He didn't like it a lot, but once in a while I just had to because as I was growing up my parents played musicals nonstop on the stereo: [*singing*] "Maria, the most beautiful sound I ever heard." He would turn around really slowly and say, "I check if James is working in the morning and I brace myself for these moments." [*laughs*]

Russ Tamblyn: It was really nice to work with Richard again. We hadn't really gotten the opportunity to sit and talk about *West Side Story*, and it was during the filming of that Civil War scene that we got to sit down and talk about his experience, which I had never really talked to him about before.

Richard Beymer: It's always enjoyable to see Russ, and really we don't talk about the acting so much as the art that we're involved in. I don't know how much of it he's doing now, but he used to do these incredible collages, and it was really quite extraordinary work he was doing. He was very involved in all kinds of art with [Dennis] Hopper, Dean Stockwell and that whole crew. They were always into photography and painting and it was always fun to talk to him about what he was doing.

Uli Edel: At first I didn't even realize who these two gentlemen Richard Beymer and Russ Tamblyn were till Deepak [Nayar], the first AD, told me. "Oh my God!" was my reaction, "They are Tony and Riff in *West Side Story*?!" Only thirty years later, [*laughs*] that's why I didn't recognize them right away.

It was one of my favorite movies and having those two guys – I started to think, "What can I give them to make their scenes outstanding?" So Richard had his *Henry V* speech ("Band of

Brothers") from Shakespeare in front of all these tin soldiers [*laughs*] and he turns on the fan so this Confederate flag would flap in its breeze and he has this speech. Finally Russ Tamblyn as his therapist jumps up and joins him with the final "Look away, Dixie Land" song. It's surreal and in their dramatic, very theatrical performance, also touching. That's one of my favorite moments in the show.

Richard Beymer: Maybe you can find some places in television where this has happened before, but I've never seen it – where they allow a main character to go through major changes like that, right? I mean, they want to keep their lead characters being the lead characters. They might find out House [*House, MD*] is a drug addict after a while, but he's still House. This was allowing someone to just go through all sorts of changes which was really fun.

Wendy Robie charged through the first season of Twin Peaks *as a disturbed homemaker hell-bent on inventing silent drape runners, and her role of Nadine Hurley was set to become even more outlandish.*

After an unsuccessful suicide attempt, Nadine awakens from a coma in the second season convinced that she is a teenaged girl. Still married to Big Ed Hurley (Everett McGill), Nadine returns to Twin Peaks High School and tries out for cheerleading, joins the wrestling team, and romantically pursues her classmate, Mike Nelson (Gary Hershberger).

Wendy Robie: The first season was so different from the second, and all I did was befuddle Big Ed. I was like, "Okay, my job is to just stymie him, leave him aghast!" [*laughs*] I've always been a jock, so I can jump and leap around and be springy and everything, but I certainly don't have superhuman strength. [*laughs*] I can't mash a little metal bell flat or bend steel, but they did send me to this school, this sort of 'Bob's Circus' that trains people to do aerial tricks. There was this school in Van Nuys and I remember spending an afternoon there and it was really fun.

Wendy Robie as Nadine Hurley

Gary Hershberger: Well, I thought it was a little strange, [*laughs*] but I thought the whole season was strange, so let's go with it. It actually provided a lot of comedy for me and for the character because in the first season I am not funny; you're kind of scared of this guy. I was a little worried, like, "Gosh, are we taking this character too much to the left here? This is a total turn." But you know, you do what they give you and that's what they gave me, so I thought, "Okay! It's romantic comedy for me."

Wendy Robie: All of the wrestling scenes had to be me and it had to be Gary, but he was on a kind of harness. I couldn't of course pick him up and throw him around on my shoulders like that. He was being held up while I did that. That was really technical and it was challenging too! [*laughs*] I was really sore after that!

Gary Hershberger: I just remember Wendy and I got along really wonderfully. It was kind of a jump; Wendy must have been older than me at the time. It was great though. We got to do all these fun adventures together, the wrestling bit, and then we got in the accident and it looks like there's a Q-tip on my head... all this strange stuff at the hotel, but it was the second season and everything got more comedic all the way around. It was a fun, weird relationship to go through.

Wendy Robie: That whole second season it was like some insane eighteen-year-old stole my body in the morning, beat the crap out of it, and gave it back to me at night! [*laughs*] There was no other way for me to do it other than pretend like I could. There were many incidental wounds and sore knuckles.

Gary Hershberger: It was a pretty physical role, actually. We were doing real moves; they would throw me down and she would jump on me for half a dozen takes. I was in pretty good shape for the role, but I was always sore the next day. I had to bulk up a bit to play that role because I wasn't that size when I got it. I thought, "Oh gosh, I've got to be this big thug," so I was in pretty good shape for the pilot and the series, and my neck was always sore. They put me through a little training and I went right into it.

Wendy Robie: The lovely fantasy that Nadine got to play in the second season was like a little gift or reward for her, and that was fun. Then of course it all had to be taken away from her at the end when she comes back. She knows what she's lost in that last moment. That was doing her honor and that was all David because if you read that scene on the page it's funny, but he allowed her the tragedy that was due: the pain of that grief. She knows what she's lost and she can't live in her own fantasy anymore. That was David. I couldn't be anything but grateful.

Nadine looms large in my career. I was just a small part of the series, but if you put it all together over that amount of time it was a huge role that I was allowed to create. She loomed large, just to be playing a character for that long, but I do know that especially that first season it had to carry underneath it - that pain of Nadine. I had to carry that to do her justice. I've never played a character that hurt as much as she does. She lived in her own private firestorm of madness.

Death by Drawer Pull

Josie Packard remains cloaked in mystery throughout Twin Peaks *as she romances Sheriff Truman and fails in her attempts to murder Agent Cooper, Catherine Martell, and her own husband, Andrew. The character of Josie was initially conceived for another actress in the pilot script, but the blossoming international superstar Joan Chen (of 1988's Oscar-winning Best Picture,* The Last Emperor*) was destined for the role.*

Chad Hoffman: David [*Lynch*] was also going to cast Isabella Rossellini who he (I think) had a relationship with at that time and had also worked with in *Blue Velvet*. He brought her in for a meeting and we sat and we talked and I said, "Absolutely," but it turned out afterwards that there was a bit of a problem in that she could not commit to the whole series.

So Isabella very graciously bowed out and then Mark called me one day and said, "We've got the replacement for Isabella Rossellini." I said, "Who is it?" and he said "Joan Chen," and I said, "Well, she's a great actress." I had just seen *The Last Emperor* and I said, "But the woman you wrote was like an Italian countess! Joan Chen is not an Italian countess." [*laughs*]

Joan Chen: I suppose my agent called me and I went to meet with David Lynch. I think he saw me in *The Last Emperor* and he was looking for some of that exotic element: the character is the outsider in a small, very closely knit, almost incestuous town. So I was very, very happy.

Chad Hoffman: They laid out this tale of how someone had met her in Asia and she had come back with him and explained it away. She was all excited to do it so I said, "Okay, done. Let's do it." So that's how Joan Chen wound up on the show. I think that's probably the most surprising piece of the casting process in that we went from Isabella Rossellini to Joan Chen in the blink of an eye and it worked seamlessly.

Joan Chen: I didn't have much [input into Josie's character], honestly. I realized there was the same kind of element like *Blue Velvet* - that outsider in this little town. She was an unknown [and] she was mysterious, but I didn't reach out to Mark Frost as they were going along to have any input of my own. We didn't know where our characters were going until we got the script and went to shoot. I slowly began to realize that because I wasn't Italian, I wished they had just kept writing as if she was. That would have been more interesting.

Piper Laurie: The first time I saw Joan Chen was in the business office the first day I met with Mark with David. We sat next to each other in the waiting room and pretty much ignored each other. I didn't know who she was except that she was very beautiful and connected with the show in some way. Like myself, she too is not very social on the set, and I think shy. She's there to do business, the business of acting.

Joan Chen: I was a little bit scared of Piper. [*laughs*] She was this grande dame; she was very impressive and scary to me. She had that air - she was that old-timer from Hollywood, but she was very friendly. In the makeup trailer she was chatty, but there was this air that sort of kept me on my toes a little bit.

Piper Laurie: I thought Joan Chen was wonderful to play with. She gave me a lot to work with, especially later in those episodes when she becomes my housemaid! [*laughs*] To think about it makes me laugh. It was hard to shoot those scenes, they were so preposterous! I admired her choice to play her character in the housemaid scenes as very straight and humble.

Joan Chen: It just seemed natural; I didn't think it was a huge turn [for Josie to be Catherine's housemaid]. I think we all had that capacity in us – we would do what we would have to do. She was put in a position that she had to do that and obviously in her heart she knew she wasn't going to do it forever.

I think what's interesting is that throughout the show we didn't know what we were going to become or what else was there inside us. Looking back, I realized that we do all have the capacity in us as people - put in this situation where you would be doing this thing you would never expect to do.

Michael Ontkean: First time I saw Joan Chen she was leaning calmly and gently into an origami figure she was intently creating. I was instantly smitten. Obviously David was too. His introductory close-up of her in front of a private upstairs mirror perfectly captures the sultry, heart-stopping languor of her *Twin Peaks* character. It remains one of the signature images of the entire series.

As the sheriff, I intentionally fumbled lines in our scenes together just to create the need for extra takes. There are also certain spatial tricks one can employ that will, for technical reasons, require additional takes. I hereby confess to being shameless and unprofessional. At the time nobody busted me, but I may be delusional in thinking my lark went unnoticed on the set.

Chris Mulkey: Joan was just groovy, and talk about an actor who is willing to try stuff. The whole thing with the blood and cutting our fingers - I said, "We should really show the blood! We'll drink it!" and she said, "Yeah, let's do that!" That was a big mess. The papers went completely crazy when we did that, with AIDS and everything. It was a very big deal. Someone at the *LA Times* wrote something like, "Talk about irresponsible! Chris Mulkey and Joan Chen drinking each other's blood on *Twin Peaks*! What the fuck were they thinking?!"

Joan Chen: In the end the role got more stereotypical than not, but still, I loved the character and I loved every time I got to discover what she was like. It was a thrill to get the new scripts and say, "Who is she, really?" We didn't know who we were basically as the show progressed and as it went along: "Oh my God, that's who she really is."

I liked in the beginning how Josie would talk a certain way, but we lost it along the way. Because she married a very old man she would say things like "a cup of joe" or "top o' the morning" and I loved that. She came from Hong Kong and there was a certain old-American way of saying things that she picked up from her husband. I remember those sayings coming from this Chinese woman and I liked that.

Josie Packard makes her grand exit from Twin Peaks *in episode 23 during one of the more confounding sequences in the entire series. After Josie dies in Sheriff Truman's arms, the Man from Another Place and Killer Bob appear to Agent Cooper in a vision as Josie's face is emblazoned upon a wooden drawer pull in the Great Northern Hotel.*

Joan Chen: I remember I actually wanted out [of the show] because there was a film that I wanted to do. The film was a big failure, but I really was passionate about that story. Who in their right mind would want out of something like that? I asked to be written out and it was very naïve.

Wendy Robie: Remember Major Briggs was talking about extraterrestrials and the Blue Book Project? In most places they are examining the heavens and in the case of *Twin Peaks* it's beneath the surface and then they go spelunking in Owl Cave and all that stuff. I think there are areas there where the membrane is very thin and those are portals where you can see captive spirits down in there. Josie tried to break free, but she was captured in there. I thought that her spirit had been taken into the Black Lodge.

Joan Chen: I thought, "Oh my God, my punishment for leaving the show is to be trapped in a doorknob. It's like being sent to hell!" [*laughs*] But at the same time I thought it was very humorous. Who would think of that, that Josie now and forever is a doorknob? She still is.

Joan Chen and Jack Nance

Tricia Brock *(screenwriter, episodes 17, 23)*: That had to be Lynch and Frost. I don't remember writing that, but that's totally their sensibility. I can't take credit for it and that's completely them. I loved it; I thought it was so inventive. Whether it was effective or not, it was so far ahead of its time. I considered it a privilege to be part of it.

Lesli Linka Glatter: I first read that scene and it was like, "What?!" That was out there, even for *Twin Peaks*. [*laughs*] What I loved about the reality of *Twin Peaks* is that it examined human behavior in microscopic detail so you saw the humor of it, the absurdity and also the truth.

That definitely went to an extreme, and also the special effects were not that sophisticated at that time, so figuring out how to put her in the drawer pull was not self-evident at all. There were lots of tests; I remember seeing all these different versions of that until we came up with something that everyone liked. That was hotly debated, and rightfully so.

Harley Peyton: You know what, that's a David thing. That was one of those moments where I thought, "What the fuck is this?" I really felt in the moment that this is a jump-the-shark moment and it's just fucking stupid. It was totally David and nobody else. It was his thing, he wanted to do it and my memory is that Mark tried to talk him out of it. I could be wrong... but it's something I saw ten years later and went, "Oh, okay, that was sort of awesome."

Mark Frost: I think that was something David and I talked about and he had the notion that she [Josie] should be lost in another realm but imprisoned in a way and that it shouldn't be a physical as much as a metaphysical prison. We had decided at the end of her arc that we didn't want to do another melodramatic death; we wanted something that had some mythological feel, and the next thing you know she's in a drawer pull.

Todd Holland: I called Lesli [Glatter] up one night after an episode aired and said, "What's the deal with Josie turning into the knob on the nightstand?" And she just said, "I have no idea. That's what it said in the script, so that's what I shot." It made no sense to me at the time I watched it, but you would get those things in scripts and you just had to shoot them as is. It was the only time I've ever done that – no other show has ever required that kind of secrecy.

Usually a director knows every nuance of what a scene really means – so that you can imbue it with the proper subtext. But there you did what you were told without any sense of how it fits into the big picture. It was very different and, truth be told, actually a lot of fun.

Joan Chen: I thought it was a bit sad, but I was humored by it. I kept thinking I should not have talked to them or asked to be out, but at the same time I was very amused by it. What a way to go! [*laughs*]

Ghost Town

Warren Frost: It was a great experience and sometimes it didn't work as well as other times... but that's the business.

Sinking Nielsen ratings and rampant creative frustrations created distress on the set of Twin Peaks. *Select interview participants indicate that these issues stemmed from the physical absence of Mark Frost and David Lynch. As an overall apathy cemented within the cast and crew, fractures in the* Twin Peaks *family began to grow.*

Tony Krantz: I think the union with David and Mark was broken on a certain level by virtue of geographic separation, and as a result some of the more tried-and-true fundamental postulates of dramatic series storytelling were ignored. The big one was to keep the stories involving the main characters and there was a creation of additional characters and additional worlds and it started to spin out like a Russian novel.

Kyle MacLachlan: Both Mark and David had interests and projects and other things that were going forward. I really don't think that either Mark or David were made to babysit a show for any length of time and they created a writing staff and a crew and set them up to move forward. It's difficult in the world of television if you're not present every day. It's such an intense and focused environment and the expectations are so high that it's very difficult to step away, even for a short period of time to know where everything is. It's a tremendous juggling act with all these scripts and stories and characters. It's just not easy.

They were not around and there were always a number of questions that I and a lot of the actors had about the characters and their development and that was part of the process. We would discuss with the writers some of the directions and stuff like that and tried to make our way through as best we could. I think we probably could have used their input more. It was refreshing when David or Mark would return to direct an episode because we felt a little bit of the old magic again and that was fun. It was a little more difficult when they were not there holding it all together.

Mark Frost: I was always involved in putting stories together, but there was a period (I don't remember the exact sequence) around episode 14, 15, and 16 where I had to go prep *Storyville*. I was still rewriting scripts and giving input, but I wasn't as directly involved as I had been prior to that.

Harley Peyton: How do I put this diplomatically? David and I did not get along toward the end of *Twin Peaks*. Part of that was based on something very simple. David could call up Mark at eleven thirty at night and say change this and change that. So when Mark wasn't there (when he was making his movie) that became my job, but one thing David did not take well then was "no" because who says "no" to David Lynch for God's sake?

Todd Holland (who was a wonderful director on the show) called me at midnight and said, "Look, I had this whole opening shot planned for tomorrow morning." David had read the script and was giving notes as he should, but would not read them in what I would call a timely fashion. [*laughs*] So David called up and talked to Todd, so Todd called me saying, "Oh my God, he's completely changed my day tomorrow! Piper Laurie has to work tomorrow and now she's not available!"

It was a whole panic call at midnight (bear in mind we are shooting in six hours) so I said, "No, I'll make this decision. You shouldn't be put in this position. I don't like what it does to our schedule. Go ahead and shoot it." David called me and [*laughs*] screamed at me for sort of a long time. He was not a happy camper. Our relationship frayed a little bit after that.

Tony Krantz: The writers who were working with Mark and the dynamic and direction of the show was one that David really did not want to re-enter into because he felt alienated from his own show and he didn't feel that he was welcome. I think Mark felt to a great degree there was so much credit that was being given to David that he really wanted to take the ball and run with it in the second season.

Philip Segal: You have to understand the sort of architecture of the relationship between Mark and David. It was souring. Mark wasn't really part of the show and David really didn't pay attention to what was really happening. It was really a rebellious ship, so the writers did the best they could to keep the tone and spirit of the show up, but the heart and soul of the show was really not writing the show.

Caleb Deschanel: I sort of felt (from my own point of view) that the latter half of the second season got off track. There was something wonderful about the initial humor, but by that time Harley Peyton had pretty much taken over a lot of the writing on that. I honestly think that David - as much as he loved the project – I don't think he probably had any idea what it was like running a television show and how much work goes into it. I don't know how much of that was him stepping away from it a little bit or Mark stepping away, but I'm more thinking it probably came from the other writers who came in than it did from David. To me, it doesn't feel like David's sensibility.

Gary Levine: David Lynch is a moviemaker and I'm not sure he ever had honed the muscles of storytelling that goes on for years. That is a specific form and not all moviemakers can adapt to that form. He certainly presented a fascinating two-hour opening, but I'm not sure he saw all the years of storytelling the way he would see the shape of every minute of a movie he was crafting.

Mädchen Amick: I felt like the second season just ended up becoming writers trying to write like Mark and David. I could tell things were a lot campier and there was a different feel and a lot of guest stars coming in and out. I got a lesson pretty early in the business that once something becomes a hit, it can be the death of the artistic vision.

Kyle MacLachlan: They [Bob Engels and Harley Peyton] were both really committed to the show and to the vision that was David's and Mark's. I think they did the best they could to keep that unusual and offbeat kind of energy and dynamic going. Bob was very receptive to meetings with actors. I sat down a number of times with him to explain what I was thinking and they were very positive about everything.

Sherilyn Fenn: Bob and Harley were sweethearts. Everybody surrounding the show was. [*sigh*] I have nothing bad to say about those guys. It's just like Picasso starts a painting and then someone else comes in to finish it – it's not going to work. To do a show you need to have that original thing in place and have a commitment to sticking with it.

Todd Holland: My second episode [20] was different, I felt. *Storyville* was greenlit and Mark was very busy on that. I was told that David was dealing heavily with art exhibits in Japan. It was really Harley running the series at that point. Harley is amazing – but with the former core creative duo absent from the day-to-day, the series simply had a different feel.

Laura's murderer had been named and so the series was really facing its greatest challenges of maintaining velocity at that time. I always felt my second episode lacked urgency or the script lacked some centrifugal force. Even though my first episode was lighter, I thought it was better because it had the gravitas of that murder mystery binding it together.

Tony Krantz: The audience began attrition and once it starts, it's impossible in a relatively quick way (certainly within a season) to arrest that decline and then build it back up. In those days, the networks were not willing to take chances and let shows stick on the air for a long time if they were not working and the decline was just constant on *Twin Peaks*. There was no sense that there was a new kind of story engine that was building stories people wanted to see.

Robert Engels: There was always a kind of response to *Twin Peaks* on a minority level that we were saying "fuck you" to TV audiences, but that was never the case. You go big and sometimes it just doesn't work. It's kind of weird. You look back and say, "Well, that moment sucked," but you didn't think it sucked when you did it and saw the dailies.

Richard Beymer: It started turning into *Saturday Night Live*, for me. As you say, it went off the tracks - people flying and all sorts of stuff, right? David was very much involved in the first few shows and there is a place that he goes (for me) when he's right on and it's just a *little* off-center. There's a little strange thing in the scene, but it doesn't turn slapstick. It's just like, "*What*?" But, other people were directing and writing and so all that gets diffused after a while, I felt.

Tony Krantz: The show I was trying to get David to come back into had long since disappeared from his subconscious in the way it was during the beginning. It was pure David Lynch, it was of him with Mark. Mark was critical to the process and they were partners, but in the second season it was of a bunch of writers who were trying to do something quirky and funny and weird, but it was coming from the outside in as opposed from the inside out and the American public felt it.

Robert Engels: I don't have a recollection of Mark and David being *gone*, but by that point we all did the characters together. It's kind of like a writer's room - Mark and David had things they wanted to do and we would do adjustments to them. Mark always did the last pass through the scripts, always.

Michael Parks: I didn't really work with David. Mark was a sweetheart. Later after the series I worked with him on *Storyville* in New Orleans with Jason Robards and James Spader - nice kid. I didn't work with David at all. I saw him coming out of the bathroom once. He said, "I like your work," and I said, "Thank you very much." And that was it.

Robyn Lively: I did not work with David Lynch or Mark Frost at all, unfortunately. I think by the second season they were not present as much (I don't believe) on set that they were the first season, or at least when I was around I just didn't get a chance to ever see them much. Because I was a recurring, maybe it just so happened that they weren't around. I might not have a correct gauge on that. Obviously they were involved, but they were not on set when I was.

Annette McCarthy: Mark Frost was right there every day on the set - every day. David Lynch was definitely there less, but he was there in the casting and in production. Mark Frost was much more available. Nonetheless, you could feel David on the set; you could feel him right there in every corner. He was available, just not as much as Mark. He just wasn't admissible.

Harley Peyton: In Mark's absence, it was mostly me and Mark doing everything he could from a distance. I probably worked as much with Mark while he was gone as I did with David. I always thought of David as being his own orbiting planet that would check in with me from time to time, although his office was just across the lobby.

Tony Krantz: There was a restaurant in Los Angeles called Muse; it was one of my favorite restaurants as a young agent that I would go to. David and I would have lunch and dinner there. The second season was clearly spiraling out of control and David and Mark were not really talking to each other. David felt alienated from his own show. I brought the two of them together with me to Muse for dinner and I literally made them hold hands and I said, "Guys, you need to do this show together. This is magic with you guys together. Separately, it is not working." By that time it was too late.

6.

JAWS OF LIFE

Give Peaks a Chance

Ken Scherer *(former chief operating officer, Lynch/Frost Productions)*: We knew people were watching this show in mass numbers. We knew it from our fan mail and I wish the Internet had existed then because if social media was around we would still be on the air. But, we couldn't prove to this rigid network structure that kids were watching it in dorms and people were having house parties and the numbers lied beneath the Nielsen ratings. By the way, with the Nielsen ratings today we would be a home run, but then it was unacceptable.

The turbulent times of Twin Peaks *were not eased when the series won Best Drama Series at the Golden Globes ceremony on January 19, 1991. With no reprieve in ratings, an influx of new faces and meandering story lines continued to alienate viewers in the following weeks. While most of the fickle television audience had moved on from the* Twin Peaks *craze, the series had earned a devoted core of fans who were still celebrating every episode with coffee and cherry pie.*

Michael Saltzman *(former publicist, Lynch/Frost Productions)*: People were writing us letters. They were finding my firm and we didn't know how to respond or what to do with the letters. There were people sending pictures of themselves holding a log or asking for Catherine Coulson's autograph. We really weren't prepared for the fans. We got to this point where we would just save up all the letters in a big box and I would give it to a PA when I went to the set because we just didn't know what to do with it.

Mark Frost: One day I was sitting in my office after the first season and somebody came in and dumped a whole ream of paper on my desk. I said, "What's this?" and they said to take a look. It was printed pages from chat rooms on what the Internet was back in those days (whether it was AOL or CompuServe) of people obsessing about the show. It was quite an artifact to be presented with and tremendous to realize that something we put this much care and work into was affecting people at that level. I've always felt (and to this day feel) grateful for the support we always got from people who were really into the show. It was great to feel that kind of connection to our audience.

Sheryl Lee: Even though I was very shy doing the press and all that stuff, I really appreciated that the story line was causing people to ask deep questions. They weren't talking about what we were wearing - they were getting introspective and looking into symbology and hidden meanings.

There was a lot of thought going into the audience dialogue and I really appreciated that and it was always very interesting to me. Part of what I love about David's work is that something can be interpreted so many different ways and none of its wrong because we're looking at it through our own lens.

On February 16, 1991, ABC announced an indefinite hiatus upon the airing of episode 23, leaving the immediate future of the show uncertain. Former ABC executive Philip Segal disclosed just how close Twin Peaks *actually came to cancellation at this point: "Oh, very close. They [ABC] were just so frustrated at the whole thing. I think that because it had come out of the gate with such wonderful intensity and wonderful press associated with it, it was frustrating to them they could not get their hands around it."*

ABC's announcement was met with backlash from dedicated fans of the show. Two fans from Washington, DC, led a concerted effort to save Twin Peaks *from cancellation and formed Citizens Opposed to the Offing of Peaks (COOP). Members of COOP were tasked with barraging the executives at ABC to prove that there was impassioned demand for the show.*

Michael Saltzman: In pre-Internet days they were tracking us down and finding us, so it didn't surprise me that a core group of fans were angry that the show had been pulled off of the air. That being said, I didn't have anything to do with organizing that group, but it didn't surprise me because the core fans wrote to Lynch/Frost Productions constantly. It was a very passionate group of people who didn't mind putting twelve cents on an envelope and writing us.

Michael R. Caputo *(cofounder, COOP)*: I started watching it during the first show and by the second show we had started having friends over to watch it with us and it became kind of a social thing. I hung around a pretty bizarre crowd and they liked a bizarre sense of humor. One of the most compelling things about the show was you never knew what was going to happen next. We spent a great deal of time trying to figure out what would happen next and we were always wrong.

I think the vast majority of people that I got to know at that time were not TV watchers. I wasn't for sure; I was a busy young executive in Washington working twenty hours a day. It was crazy back then and the average people we met through the show were pretty bright young executives as well. I think most of them didn't watch much TV themselves.

This is pre-Internet as you remember and Keith Poston was my deputy. He was a young aide in my office. We were involved in public relations (actually politics) and we had the tools and we knew how to make things happen. In politics it's all about building coalitions, so we had the knowledge necessary to do that on behalf of the show.

When the show was cancelled, I called David Lynch and offered the service and he and Mark Frost and Ken Scherer enthusiastically accepted. We didn't ask for any money, but we asked if we could fund our operation by selling a shirt that was licensed (and if it was not licensed, they would look the other way) and David was like, "Why not? What the heck. Go for it."

Ken Scherer: I spent a lot of time on the road with it and it had this bizarreness about it because people were so fanatical. I guess they're still that way about shows, but you can do it electronically - you can text or e-mail or go on Facebook. This required you actually coming out to some place or writing letters or making phone calls. It was weird. It had the *New York Times* kind of sensibility. It was smart, sophisticated, and edgy and we knew the people watching were not your typical TV audience.

Michael R. Caputo: Back in those days, everything would cost money. Direct mail was forty-five cents to a dollar depending on what you were doing. Now with the Internet, if you have a list of emails you can do a lot of stuff with no money. Back then we had to start from nothing, so we spoke to reporters first. We organized COOP and we had people from different cities who were interested and some friends that were watching the show to help us out.

Keith was our spokesman because I was a spokesman for a major corporate lobbying organization in Washington and I couldn't have my name out there. We just knew that if Keith said something funny or obtuse (like the script of the show) we could get some traction. We were estranged from ABC immediately because of Keith's first quotation on the record.

A reporter asked him if he had one thing to say to Bob Iger. His response was something along the lines of: "Bob, today you remind me of a small Mexican Chihuahua." [*laughs*] It got printed in *USA Today*; it was actually a pull-out quote. Immediately we were labeled quacks. He had a job where he wouldn't get in trouble if he was out in the press calling people Chihuahuas.

We were immediately and literally buried in thousands of pieces of mail. It didn't start out like a trickle - it started off like a deluge two days after the story went out. It just kept coming and coming and coming. We had almost twenty thousand members in four weeks with individual postage stamps. That's a sizable and active force because every one of them sought us out and joined by mail.

I had friends at ABC because I ran the TV newsroom in the House of Representatives and there were a lot of ABC reporters that worked there. I got ahold of the inside telephone and fax lists of all the executives at ABC corporate. We would say to call this number between this time and this time and fax this number at this time. It was fairly well orchestrated because the guys who gave me the numbers told me we were getting exactly the effect we wanted. It was a lot of fun.

After weeks of letters, logs, and doughnuts showing up at the ABC corporate offices, ABC announced that Twin Peaks *would return to its original time slot on Thursday nights beginning April 6. With a small window of time to rebuild ratings, the future of* Twin Peaks *and its relationship with ABC remained fragile.*

Michael Saltzman: I think that networks bow to pressure whether it's over censorship or letters or anything else. To this day, I go into meetings and they'll say, "Twenty-seven people posted something on Facebook, what are we going to do about it?" and I just think, "Really? In a population of 320 million people, twenty-seven people complain and you want to respond to it?" I think they do pay attention to letter-writing campaigns, but to be honest I think the network had passed the *Twin Peaks* phase and just wanted to burn off the last six episodes and move on.

Ken Scherer: They kept moving us around the schedule and all that nonsense, so we took it on the road. I took the Log Lady with me to Washington, DC, and we held a viewing party at a bar and it was trying to draw press attention to the fact that this is how people watch the show. We were all having a good time and there was a guy there dressed as the Log Lady, so I went over to introduce myself. He said he was an MIT [Massachusetts Institute of Technology] graduate and he worked in the Defense Department and had this big job. He said, "I never watch television and I went to my friends' house the other night and they said, 'We've got to watch this show,' and I was really irritated they were going to watch a TV show. So I sat down and watched it and here I am." That's the kind of impact the show had for people. You either hated it or you loved it. There was no in between.

Michael R. Caputo: At the time it was a little bit quirky and embarrassing. I would be at a meeting in the United States Capitol and somebody would tell a senator in the room that I'm the guy doing the thing with *Twin Peaks*. [*laughs*] It was a fun thing; we just kind of went with it. At first I was a little bit shy about it, but after it came back on the air it felt like we had beaten Goliath.

Agent Earle

Twin Peaks *returned to the air on March 28, 1991, with a renewed focus on episodic storytelling as Agent Cooper and his nemesis Windom Earle (Kenneth Welsh) are embroiled in a deadly game of chess. Earle's intentions are explained in episode 21 when Cooper confesses to Sheriff Truman of a past affair with Earle's wife, Caroline (Brenda E. Reed, neé Mathers), that triggered Earle's crusade of revenge. As a demented master of disguise, Earle's path of destruction runs throughout the remainder of the season, destined to end in a showdown with Agent Cooper.*

Kenneth Welsh *(Windom Earle)*: I was doing something in LA, a miniseries or something in 1990 or so. Bob [Engels] said, "I'm doing this series called *Twin Peaks*. There's a part here that's perfect for you! Come on out to the studio and I'll introduce you to some people." That's where I met Mark [Frost] and a few other people and by the end of all these meetings they said, "You got the part!" David [Lynch] was not there; I hadn't met him yet. That's how I got it, through Bob.

Robert Engels: Ken was the main star at the Guthrie in the seventies. We became best friends eventually. He was in Shakespeare's *Love's Labour's Lost* that nobody ever does because these guys swear off love for a year. You read it and it is like, "Why the hell are we doing this?" The whole play was just sensational because of him. I'd never seen anything like that in my life and at the same time we had lots of fun together.

Windom Earle's cabin

Kenneth Welsh: I had no idea about it [*Twin Peaks*] when I was cast; I said, "Can I look at some of this stuff?" I'd taken a look at the first season and thought, "Wow, this is pretty far out!" When I got there (the first time I flew in to shoot) there was an announcement that they had invaded Iraq and another time there was the big earthquake in San Francisco. And so on these two occasions I was doing *Twin Peaks* when I arrived in Los Angeles. A lot of interesting twists and turns.

Uli Edel *(director, episode 21)*: In my episode I also had to introduce the new villain, Windom Earle. I remember there was this chess game and he played the flute. Kenneth and I were interested in introducing him with this aura of mystery so the audience would be in awe about this new villain. I think it was the scene in that cabin in the woods where we introduced him. You hear Windom Earle playing the flute and the Steadicam is moving towards his cabin like it's drawn or mesmerized by the sound of the flute. The idea was to give him as much mystery as possible in just the few shots you see him.

Harley Peyton: I came up with the name for Windom Earle, but I certainly didn't create the character [*laughs*] because the name Windom Earle is a mash-up of an old actor named William Windom and the character Mad Dog Roy Earle that Humphrey Bogart played in *High Sierra*. So that's where Windom Earle came from. Anything after Laura Palmer was going to be tough, but I thought that that was something that was a lot of fun. As a television villain, he had a lot of different interesting levels and there was something genuinely creepy about him.

Kenneth Welsh: Well, [I was told] a little bit [about Windom]. He had been an ex-FBI agent, his wife had been killed, and Cooper – a few things about him being on the run and that he was a master of disguise, which we decided. We kind of went from there in his pursuit of Dale Cooper. He would come on with these various disguises; Bob knew I was quite skillful at that so he kept throwing them at me! [*laughs*]

I would have access to the scripts unlike a lot of people because Bob knew I'd like to look at it and decide how Windom would appear, for example, at the library. I thought he should be English, and then when he was at the counter of the diner I said, "I'd like to appear as a fat biker." This marvelous woman who did the costumes (I forget her name) would come up with anything I wanted.

Windom Earle as the Fat Biker

Shakespeare often uses disguise in his plays as an element for villainy and for comedy. In that sense I felt like, "Yeah, he's [Windom] some sort of Shakespearean villain." I think there is a connection there. I've done so much Shakespeare; he's in everything I did. My favorite one I ever did was *Hamlet*, which I played at Stratford in Ontario when I was twenty-six in 1969. So imagine that, playing Hamlet in '69 in all that turmoil! I played it very much as a young man of the sixties. It was great fun.

Robert Engels: I think (but I'm not sure) he is Order of Canada; he's knighted there. It was cool to get him on the series. At that point he was in four or five Clint Eastwood movies, but no one had really seen him except for in Canada. It was great to have this terrific actor that came out of nowhere.

Kenneth Welsh: David [Lynch] was hardly involved at all, except from a distance. He would have approval of things. He disapproved of what I was wearing at the beginning when Diane [Keaton] directed. He said, "Windom should be all in black, all the time," and Mark [Frost] was in and out. Bob [Engels] mostly was very involved.

Windom Earle as the Log Lady

The one episode where Diane Keaton directed where I beat Eric DaRe with the Shakuhachi flute - that was a collaboration between Bob and I. In the original script it said I'd play the flute and Bob knew I could play. I said, "Bob, I know how to play it. It's very soothing. It's a beautiful Japanese instrument." They made an actual rubber replica and introduced the idea that Windom beat Leo with the flute. I had a constant collaboration with Bob. He is a wonderfully creative guy.

The sound man (whose name I forget) said, "Let's go and find a room and we'll practice, practice, practice." I had a conversation with Angelo Badalamenti and I discussed it over the phone with him. I was in Los Angeles and he was in New York. He said, "Okay, what notes can you give me?" and I gave him the notes and he composed this melody that I then recorded with the soundman. We went over it five, six, seven times... and it was perfect. But what happened in the mix is they went for something synthetic. It wasn't the sound of the flute at all. That was my one disappointment with the series. It would have sounded fantastic.

Jonathan Sanger *(director, episode 26)*: Kenneth was a terrific Canadian actor and David really liked him. He was totally into the character. He loved the idea of doing this and nobody really knew at the time where things were going. When you came on the show you basically knew a little bit about where the character was coming from, but you really didn't know that much about him.

It was intense, but he was very interested in the fact he had become this arch villain. Ken is a great character actor, but he really had the opportunity to do something different and outside of what he normally got to do. Believe me, he took it and really went with it. [*laughs*] I enjoyed working on the scene with Windom Earle in the house where he kills the kid with the arrow. I mean, all of that was a pretty unusual and fun thing to do. [*laughs*]

Kenneth Welsh: When I asked Jonathan where I should point the arrow, he said, "Right at him, that papier-mâché will stop it from reaching him." So I did, and he was right, of course. There was another protective layer underneath it. That's how I remember it, anyway. I do remember that the young man [Ted Raimi] playing my victim gave a very good performance.

I didn't really constantly work with anyone in particular; it was always with someone else. All the girls were fun. I enjoyed hanging out on the set with Russ Tamblyn because he was a big hero of mine when I was a kid. We didn't have any scenes together though, that I remember. I loved those early movies of his, like *Seven Brides for Seven Brothers*. He could dance like a motherfucker, and of course he was in *West Side Story*.

Eric [DaRe] was very compliant and easygoing and always along with whatever I came up with. He was also a very good foil for me because he would put up a lot of resistance if I had him in a situation where it was needed. He always seemed to enjoy it. He was a sweetheart, I thought. He wasn't an actor, he was a member of the crew at first, I believe. His father [Aldo Ray] was obviously a very well-known actor.

And I loved working with Kyle [MacLachlan]! Come on. Just being around him. We never had that much to do with each other, but a few years later I was driving home where I live and someone said, "Kyle MacLachlan is filming up the road here. I pulled up just as he was coming out of his trailer and he said, "Kenny! Come on and have a cup of coffee!" I said, "Sure, Kyle!" I worked with him again for a TV movie in Montreal. He was always great, a great actor. He did give me one bit of advice I wish I had followed. He said, "Kenny, there's something called Starbucks. Invest in it!" In 1991? Come on! I'd be a millionaire today!

Twilight

In the final hours of the second season, Billy Zane and Heather Graham joined the cast to heighten the drama as John Justice Wheeler and Annie Blackburn, the respective love interests of Audrey Horne and Agent Cooper.

Mark Frost: The character of Annie was central to the Windom Earle story and the idea was that this was an echo for Cooper, of the one thing he had done that he was most ashamed of: the affair with Earle's wife and this presented a chance for him to redeem himself. It was central to the Earle story line and I thought Heather was excellent, it was one of her first roles and I thought they had good chemistry together. As we conceived the Windom Earle story line and decided where he was going to take us, I was very involved.

Kyle MacLachlan: Heather was refreshing and bubbly and sweet. They brought her in kind of as a potential love interest for Cooper. Again, looking back I think it maybe wasn't the direction the character should have gone, although there was some very sweet stuff and you got to see other sides of Cooper and of her as they came together. It was a very sweet time for the characters. Heather of course has gone on to do great things and it was one of the first things she did. She was really talented.

Billy Zane *(John Justice Wheeler)*: At that time I was pretty well known as the go-to-guy for sociopathic behavior on film. [*laughs*] David and Mark Frost brilliantly cast against type; you had a show that was really filled with eccentric people for the most part (crazy to some degree) and they cast the guy who was known as crazy as the most wholesome in the show, which I thought was very clever and humorous and ironic. I welcomed it, I loved that there was this Gary Cooper-like sweetness to John Justice. He flies in on his jet to save an endangered species and for his goodness, he gets the great privilege of deflowering Audrey in a plane. [*laughs*] It was extraordinary.

Sherilyn Fenn: Billy's a really nice person. He's a cutie. I remember he showed up at the set at seven a.m. dressed up like Jim Morrison. [*laughs*] He's funny, he's a sweet person, but it wasn't right. That story line just didn't work. Those characters didn't work for me; I didn't like it at all. Heather Graham and Cooper didn't work. It was stupid. The whole thing was just a whitewash.

Anonymous: Billy Zane was a hot young actor and he was going to be the next young 'it' guy and Sherilyn Fenn basically was the 'it' girl and somehow they just clashed. I remember one day in rehearsal Sherilyn was going to cross the room to beseech him to do something and I think that Sherilyn felt he should come to her, and he disagreed. We cleared the set and I know we spent an hour or two waiting for one of them to agree. It was pretty much a contest to see who was the biggest swinging dick in the room. [*laughs*]

Billy Zane: There was a very kind of haunting moment which solidified the entire character arc, which was both an onstage and offstage experience. I think it's when the pine weasel (or whatever it was) got loose at a fashion show. I don't know what it was! [*laughs*] The situation was breaking down into a sort of screwball comedy and Audrey and I share our kiss in the middle of all that madness.

Right before we shot the kiss, the crew was glued to the television set because they were just announcing our entry into the Gulf War - the first formal warfare our nation had been involved with in decades. Right before we rolled, I remember a grip saying, "We're at war."

Immediately they said, "Action!" and the kiss had an urgency that was from another time. The kiss held a promise of peace, so we held fast to each other in that moment and it was informed with a beautiful desperation. We didn't know what the future would hold or what that meant. It was par for the course for the experience, which was cemented in some kind of mad, romantic, tragic blur.

Changes continued on the set as a slate of new directors including James Foley, Jonathan Sanger, and Stephen Gyllenhaal helmed select late-season episodes. Progressing with a mix of surrealism, mythology, and wacky humor, Twin Peaks *wore its own path until the bitter end of the season.*

James Foley *(director, episode 24)*: It was definitely an enjoyable adventure, but it as it came off without a hitch little is burned into my consciousness beyond tangling with a nasty looking ferret (who turned out quite tame). The only hiccup I can recall was when I was suddenly, inexplicably taken with the notion that one of the characters, I can't remember which, should be carrying a blue suitcase. When I hit the art department with the idea I was met with some worried glances and some whispering among them.

Finally someone let me know that David did not want the color blue to appear in the series. My immediate reaction was to speak to him, but they let me know it was impossible as David was in Tokyo at an exhibit of his art and was unreachable there in the middle of the night. As I had only done features previously I was not accustomed to being overruled in aspects of production design, but it was clearly David's show. [*laughs*] I never did personally meet him and never saw any blue pop up in the episodes.

Kimmy Robertson: James Foley was incredibly warm and kind and trustworthy. He was all about making the show with the integrity of the original idea and it didn't seem like he was trying to promote his career by using an upside down camera suspended in a bowl of water over the set. He was lovely.

At that time it was starting to get really scary on the set because David was away and we were all scared we would be cancelled, reading the writing on the walls. I think that was one of the last times I felt where everything was okay: "James Foley gets it." It's very emotional to remember.

Jonathan Sanger: I came in to do an episode and I was particularly lucky that David acted in my episode too. David was a good friend of mine, so it was a great opportunity to just hang out a little bit on the set and the character [Gordon Cole] he had created was a tremendous amount of fun; we all enjoyed doing it.

Jonathan P. Shaw *(editor, episode 27)*: Steve Gyllenhaal was another great guy that came in; there was a whole boot camp of directors. He had another vibe and he was very enthusiastic. We talked a lot about the show itself. At times we'd take a break and it was still about this particular voyage we were on. That's a unique situation when you stop to take a break and you keep discussing the work because that means you really love what you're doing; very often you're like, "Let's get the heck out of here!" [*laughs*]

Stephen Gyllenhaal *(director, episode 27)*: I just loved the idea that I get to work with David Lynch, and he was open to doing whatever I wanted to do. I think I could have changed the script if I wanted to, but I liked what was there. I remember now, there was a whole thing in the script about a character feeling weird and I got more and more into 'the arm' part of it, and I really liked it. I thought, "We could shoot a close-up of it, or what if it started to shake and you couldn't control it?"

So I called David and asked him what he would think if some of the characters' hands shook just slightly. I think we even finished the episode with it. He said, "Stephen, I'm glad you have your thinking cap on properly!" [*laughs*] I didn't get to spend much time with him, but I thought, "That's just who he is."

Tim Hunter returned to direct episode 28, which concentrates on the Miss Twin Peaks pageant and Windom Earle's plot to harness the dark powers that lurk within the woods of Twin Peaks.

The Miss Twin Peaks Pageant

Tim Hunter: I wanted to see the cast and everyone one last time since the first two had been so special. I was sad to find that the actors had become cynical about it - quite a contrast from their energy and excitement doing the great first season material. Kyle MacLachlan was such a lovely guy - one didn't want to see him looking disillusioned.

David and Mark were largely off on other projects and the network was clearly rumbling they didn't know if they would sustain it because of its lack of commerciality one way or another and the writers had it - Harley Peyton and [Bob] Engels mostly. Gregg

Fienberg certainly always kept the thing running from a production point of view quite efficiently. It went off into surrealism, so I remember that it was interesting and inscrutable, but that the actual plot had gone into a place where it didn't really matter how they wrapped it up.

Everything was predicated on Frank Byers' unwillingness to do more than sixteen setups per day. The show looked great, but you hope for at least twenty-four setups a day on a TV show, even more. I didn't believe it when they told me, so I actually went over the production reports to see how many setups he was averaging and in fact it was steadfast around sixteen. So I had to reduce the scope of the coverage considerably. I watched Ozu's *Tokyo Story* and some other minimalist films and told myself I was directing a Japanese-style *Falcon Crest*. That's why I blacked the bad guy's [Windom Earle] teeth out in the opening - an homage to the Ozu-Mizoguchi pictures I watched [while] prepping for the episode.

Kenneth Welsh: God, I'm trying to think now...what did they do to me? Oh yeah! All that black over my face! Whoever the makeup artist was just went to town. Windom's totally out of his mind, and then he becomes the Log Lady [at the Miss Twin Peaks Pageant]. I loved doing that. I thought, "Holy shit! I look just like mom!"

Sherilyn Fenn: The pinnacle [of frustration] for me was when they had a beauty show or something and all the girls were dressed up. The whole show was starting to feel like it had lost its way. It wasn't character motivated. It was, [*sarcastic*] "Let's get the girls in a fashion show!" I just remember reading it and going, "No." It was the only time I ever went to David and Mark and said, "There's no way." They said, "But we have to have you there. Can you make an announcement for your dad's business?" And I said fine. That's why I wasn't up there. It was dumb. I hated the whole second season.

Kimmy Robertson: So I'm in the sheriff's station on the set waiting to shoot and down the hall past the entrance area there was always something happening, like people looking at you then turning away to say something in hushed tones. I call it the 'magic hall.' So down that magic hall one day, I see David Lynch and Mark Frost talking. I could tell they were talking about me and trying to figure out how to say something to me. I immediately thought, "Oh my God, they're going to fire me."

So they are walking up to me with shit-eating grins on their face: "We want you to dance on the show in the Miss Twin Peaks pageant and we want you to choreograph it." "Can I pick the music?" "Yes, that will be changed in post." I asked if it was a *Twin Peaks* dance or a real dance. They had evil grins, nodding: "Definitely a *Twin Peaks* dance."

So I went home and found "Mack the Knife" and put it on, choreographed the dance in two seconds, got my splits back, and went back the next day and did it. I have danced all over the world as a professional doing everything from Disneyland and highbrow to lowbrow. To actually be able to do my goofy dancing in front of cameras on a television show is the wildest dream come true, ever.

Robyn Lively: The contest was so much fun. I was raised in the south, so I knew all about beauty pageants and all of those things. It was one of those days where you think, "I can't believe I'm actually being paid to have this much fun."

I remember reading the script and it said, "Lana does 'jazz-contortionistic-exotica' dance." I just thought, "Oh my goodness, are you serious? I'm not a contortionist, how am I going to pull this one off? What am I going to do?" [*laughs*] They had this wonderful choreographer come in and we just worked on the dance a lot and I did the best I could. It was extremely intimidating when I was rehearsing my dance. Literally, the whole crew stopped working to watch me do my dance. I thought, "Hey fellas, you may not be impressed, but I'm going to give it my best."

Tim Hunter: There was that initial feeling of doing something wonderful and exciting, but by necessity giving way to more of a bittersweet feeling that it was the end. I think (objectively speaking) there was some feeling the story line hadn't lived up to the first season.

David still came in and did the last one of the series, so as far as we were concerned it was always a big deal when David was going to show up and get ready to do an episode. We all knew where the thing had gone, but we never knew where David was going to take it when he directed one.

Curtains

Twin Peaks wrapped production on its second and final season in March, 1991. Written by Mark Frost, Harley Peyton, and Robert Engels, the series finale episode of Twin Peaks *offers a dense and abstract hour of Agent Cooper's pursuit of Windom Earle in the realm known as the Black Lodge.*

Under the direction of David Lynch, the shooting script was largely ignored and rewritten on the spot as the scenes were filmed. The Black Lodge was realized as the red-curtained room from Agent Cooper's dream in episode 2, while the rest of the episode offers startling discoveries and grim fates to most characters.

Mark Frost: I've never questioned David's vision at any point in the process because his instincts are extraordinary. We knew it was going to be the last one, possibly for all time and I think I remember saying, "Do whatever you want to do here; use this as a map, not a set of directions," and he did; and when you've got a talent as singular as David, you don't question that. That would make no sense whatsoever.

Harley Peyton: I haven't read it [the finale script] in a while, but we all got together and wrote a part of it. In a perfect world Mark and David would sit down and write the entire thing, but I think David just came in and went, "Okay, fuck it. I'm just going to do it my way," and God knows he did. The results are one of the more amazing pieces of television you'll ever see. I must say I didn't spend a lot of time in the red room.

Barry Gremillion *(location liaison)*: One thing I can tell you that was a pretty funny and frustrating aspect of working with David Lynch is that as creative and strange as he is, he could be very vague and hard to pin down, especially as the show started getting "curiouser and curiouser."

Sometimes he tried to accommodate us as best he could. The show was by this time a bit of a mystery to everyone, but one day he delivered a classic line when we asked him about a script: "I wouldn't pay too much attention to that script if I were you." He said in that characteristic way he has of speaking.

When we pressed him as to specifics of what would be needed he answered, "I would just have everything ready if I were you." So we did. The last few episodes were very hectic as last-minute ideas came flying from David and Peyton and Mark and the other writers.

Frank Byers: The finale is absolutely brilliant. I remember we came into work [and] we had built the set and put in the base lighting and I did a lot of strobes and flash in that, if I remember. David said, "Okay, I'm going to rehearse, but I want to do this alone with the actors," and four hours go by. On television that is unheard of!

Brenda E. Reed *(Caroline Earle)*: David of course by this time was writing things as they came to him and was almost completely off script. He was sort of improvising in his head and he decided to write in more Caroline scenes.

I'm sure he had the whole idea and story line in his head, but it was amazing to witness the David Lynch creative process and be a part of it. He was reacting as things were happening on-screen and was inspired to try new ideas. I think that is the charm of *Twin Peaks*, it was so dynamic and constantly morphing and evolving into David Lynch's vision.

Carel Struycken *(the Giant)*: It was really David Lynch at his most genius because I'm not sure – I'm just guessing – but there wasn't much of a script. It was all on the spot and no one knew what was going on from moment-to-moment. After each little shot people were rushing him and saying, "What's next?!" He may have had a broad outline in his head or he may have known exactly what he wanted, but he had us all on edge.

The Giant serves Agent Cooper a cup of warm joe

Kenneth Welsh: I was doing this scene with Heather Graham in the truck I stole and David just said, [*yelling in David Lynch's voice*] "Windom! Forget what you were going to say. Grab her and push her head into the window and scream, 'Eight rainbow trout!' You hold the flashlight. When you speak, you put it on yourself, and put it on her when she speaks. These actors are great! Okay, let's go!" [*laughs*] He was very whimsical and a lot of fun.

Randy Barbee: We were in an old, abandoned bank building in downtown Los Angeles and there was this bank manager who was going to get a safety deposit box. He was a very old man, and he could not move quickly at all. David thought it would be interesting to just follow him as he walked across this enormous, cavernous lobby. He literally said, "Okay, I want you to stay with this guy," and then he told the guy to slow down! [*laughs*] We literally reloaded the camera and panned with this guy all the way to the vault and back. We ran out of film on a thousand-foot mag.

Sherilyn Fenn: I just knew Audrey wasn't going to be dead, which is all I really cared about. That's what they told me. It was bittersweet. David was back, he pulled it all back together, and I was just sad that it ended. It was upsetting.

Frank Byers: David came up to me and said, "I want to shoot this in reverse." I didn't even know they made a reverse mag! I'm dead serious. Where did that come from? God only knows. David explained it all and it was just surreal. It was so odd to be shooting it. Everybody was amazed with that episode. I can't believe it was even aired.

Carel Struycken: There were all these weird things going on and I think we stayed there all night, especially because people had been working nonstop. The people working every day, they were exhausted. I'm sure people were semi-hallucinating just from being so tired! [*laughs*]

There was one guy walking around with a beautiful wooden case - it was like a work of art full of contact lenses of different colors. He would walk to all the different actors that were waiting around and give them out.

Brenda E. Reed: I also loved setting up the scenes for the Black Lodge with David Lynch. Heather [Graham] and I had to have the same blood stains on our chest. As he was applying the blood on my dress I kept saying, "David, give me some more lines!" and he joked with me: "But you're saying a lot for a dead person!"

Ray Wise: Well, I was very surprised I was being called back for the last episode. [*laughs*] I guess it was a surprise to a lot of people on the cast. I remember putting in those white contacts was very strange, but I knew that I was dead and that I was playing a kind of spirit of what I used to be as Leland Palmer. Then it somehow figured into that netherworld of the red room, but the red room became much clearer to me when we did the prequel movie [*Twin Peaks: Fire Walk with Me*] after the series was over. Then the red room became (in my mind, at least) a clearer entity to me. But that last episode was a little strange.

Philip Segal: I just laughed at it because it laughed at us [ABC]. It made a mockery of us. It made a mockery of the television viewing audience when you think about it. It was so ridiculous. There was a part of me that thought it was brilliant and refreshing because it broke the rules and was so avant-garde and there was a part of me and part of the network that felt betrayed and felt this wonderful opportunity to keep something brilliant alive had just been destroyed by its creators.

Jules Haimovitz *(former president and chief operating officer, Spelling Entertainment)*: I thought David went off and did the same thing in *Dallas* - someone died, but the whole series was a dream that was going to stretch for some sort of esoteric ending. [*laughs*] David wasn't happy about ending it. I need to go back and watch it one more time and see if it makes any sense twenty-three years later.

Kenneth Welsh: I thought it [the finale] was fantastic. I hadn't seen anything so interesting since Pat McGoohan in *The Prisoner*. I thought it was really extraordinary, like when Bob burns me and sends me to hell. It was astonishing what David came up with. It was art, fucking art!

A harrowing sequence depicts Agent Cooper's confrontation with Windom Earle in the Black Lodge, as his visions of Caroline and Annie culminate with the appearance of Killer Bob. After Bob presumably destroys Earle's soul, Cooper's doppelgänger chases him through a maze of red rooms.

In the final moments of the series, Cooper awakens in his room at the Great Northern Hotel. He stares into his bathroom mirror and smashes his face into the glass, revealing Killer Bob grinning in the reflection. The credits roll one final time as a bloodied Cooper laughs, endlessly asking, "How's Annie?"

Frank Silva and Kyle MacLachlan

Harley Peyton: My memory is that I came into work and I basically said to Mark, "Look, I know how this should end. It's gotta be Cooper gets out of the lodge..." and Mark completes the sentence and says, "Cooper looks in the mirror and sees Bob." And we said, "Yeah, that's gotta be it." So I still contributed that, and I loved that ending. That might be my sole contribution to that script. [*laughs*] It didn't really feel like the end for anyone yet.

It was only toward the end where we started thinking about a third season when it was clear that Mark and David were going to make a concerted effort to wring one more season out of ABC. I simply do not remember [what was planned]. Bob is looking back in that mirror and you're going to have to figure that out - the doppelgänger is loose and Cooper is trapped in the lodge. We had those scenes in place, but I never went beyond that. My memory is they had a whole plan of what they wanted to do. Of course, it wasn't to be which is unfortunate for all concerned.

Kyle MacLachlan: Everything kind of focused down on those last few scenes. I felt like we were attempting to regenerate something that would possibly motivate the network to give the show another chance, and they thought by having this series of cliffhangers they would be able to do it. The strongest one, of course, ending with Cooper in the Black Lodge and what happened after that.

As an actor I was incredibly excited about the possibility of playing this duality (sort of like Ray Wise) and what that was going to mean and how I was going to do it. Looking back on it, it was the kind of story arc that probably wasn't compelling as "Who killed Laura Palmer?" but I felt it would be very interesting to the fans of the show because it involved the most beloved character.

Had it been introduced earlier in the season, I thought this could have been a catalyst to keep the show on the air. You never know, but I felt that it was a pretty good shot. Of course, we'll never know what happened or where things ended, but it was a great finish and I think a real shocker to a lot of people.

Rigor Mortis

Kimmy Robertson: In the second season there was a huge party down in Century City. They closed this four-lane street down on two sides of the meridian. They built the town of Twin Peaks and it must have cost millions of dollars. It was the affiliate thing where they say thanks for buying these shows. There was mist everywhere with the theme playing and Bob Iger came up to me. He grabbed me by the shoulders and said, "Kimmy! Look how much we love you guys! You're going to run forever!" I kind of knew him in a weird way because his lawyer was a friend of mine's dad. A few weeks later it was cancelled.

Twin Peaks *was officially cancelled from the ABC schedule on April 11, 1991. ABC allowed* Twin Peaks *to finish its run of episodes in April with the final two episodes set to air as the ABC Movie of the Week in June. In hindsight, the cast and crew share a range of emotions and conjecture surrounding the collapse of the series.*

Kyle MacLachlan: I think we were all aware of the writing on the wall. That's the thing about television - you can sort of chart the slow descent of the numbers and the interest. I think we were all disappointed, but the last half of the last year had been frustrating and difficult and it just didn't seem like the shows were as compelling as the first season and the audience seemed to be less and less interested in the stories and the direction the show was going.

Joan Chen: I wish I had been more aware, more knowing. I wish I had been more thoughtful and I've always wondered whether or not that would have made a little difference, but it is an interesting part for someone like me and that was the one TV series people remember me for. People remember me here in the US as Josie, so that's what it is.

Piper Laurie: I think I was disappointed [with the finale], I think very selfishly that the character I had invested so much energy and time in didn't get a proper send-off, but I understood why. I'm delighted I was in it, now that the hard work is over. I'm thinking about how ignorant I am about my own work. I've only recently begun to like my work in *The Hustler*. It's taken years to sit back and have some objectivity about it.

Warren Frost: It's always sad when something ends that everybody's had a good time doing, and it's the same thing like a long run in a play. You're thankful it's over and at the same time: "What am I going to do tomorrow?" but that's the actor's life. It was strange and wonderful at the same time. It was a wonderful get-together with a lot of good actors and a couple of guys that were writing scripts – I guess I would say they hadn't been written that way before. The story line was unique.

Harley Peyton: We never got a "no" from ABC. They were unbelievable. You can be sad the show was cancelled, but you certainly can't be angry. It's not like they were saying, "Please, do something else!" If I had a chance to go through and do it again, I think we all could have paid more attention and due diligence to our main characters and not brought in as many guest characters because I think it started to dilute the show. It was such a crazy time and the success of it was so insane. I wish we had been smart enough in the moment, but it's very hard to have that perspective then.

Jonathan P. Shaw: It was melancholy for me. By that point, we were wrapping up and it's like a trip to summer camp. You've been on this great trip, had a great time, and now it's coming to an end. It was hard to say goodbye. I don't know what else to say. I am not the network, but I felt for my particular taste it could have gone on forever. There was more stuff to do.

Dana Ashbrook: It lost its steam and the secondary characters and story lines they brought along just weren't as interesting. I don't want to fuss; there are parts that seemed overly silly to me or didn't work, but that's just what it is. You're out there writing, trying to create something, and it happens to come out that way. It's hard to say why it faltered. It's impossible for me to know.

Mark Frost: In retrospect I really wish we had [delayed revealing the killer], because the show might have gone on longer. But on the other hand it is what it is; I think it played out the right way. In a way we did keep the idea of the murder going because Leland died but Bob was still around and we found a way to continue, as we were hinting. In retrospect it was a mistake.

Tina Rathborne: You know that incredible scene in which the alien bursts out of Sigourney Weaver's guts [in Ridley Scott's *Alien*]? Well, that's my ideogram for Bob's role in the series and that could have been what made the second season very powerful. The reconfiguration that he could have created in Kyle would have been fascinating to me. That would have really been something I could dig my teeth into. The power of Bob is completely fascinating and sufficient to have carried the second season.

Scott Frost: I would have been surprised if it had continued. For me, the strength of the show was the core sense of ominous violence that can exist within a community and I think it got a little too crazy to work as a television show ultimately, for a large audience. It spun out of that. That core got lost and at times kind of goofy...and fun.

Robyn Lively: I remember everyone was so upset and to this day it was such a huge massive hit that I don't know what happened. Maybe it got way too strange. It may have lost the audience a bit, and then they changed the night. I think that was a huge problem. I'm not 100 percent sure, but I know there are many theories. I wish I knew because I loved it. I just thought, "Oh my gosh. This is great. I'll have this job for years." It was really an honor to be a part of an iconic show.

Chris Mulkey: I was frustrated about two things. That was episode 23 when I went away, so I was frustrated because the network kept moving the show around after we got so much notoriety. There were people who loved it and people were constantly calling me going, "What's going on?" as if I was responsible for moving the show around! Yeah, I wish I had that power! But I don't. I'm not sure if they were trying to reposition it or tag it on as a lead-in to another show or whatever.

Our final scene in the jail when I'm being sent back to prison was off the hook. It was really great writing, but you know, part of the motivation when I was playing that last scene was that I was really pissed I was being sent back to jail because it meant I wouldn't get to work on the show anymore! When you see that desperation and anger, it was pretty much that.

James Marshall: I thought it was sad in a way. I couldn't figure out why it was ending so fast. The way it went, the story lines should not have gotten the way they did and that's all I could think of at the time: "Wow, all of a sudden it's off the air?" That could have been a series that had stuck around for years and years. I was bummed out, but I did think the production of the finale was really intriguing.

Frank Byers: The network never wanted it. They didn't know what they had and they didn't know what to do with it. To be honest with you, I think we were dealing with people of low IQ. Seriously, they want to make the same thing over and over again. How it ever got on TV is beyond me. They could not control David and they were afraid of him. They couldn't get near him. With any television network, that's the kiss of death.

Carel Struycken: Usually when a TV show is made the 'suits' have a handle on stuff and they are able to steer things in a certain direction if they want to. They have control to a large extent, and it's also the reason why most TV is so utterly boring. They just had no clue about the show or the fans. It was like, "Solve the mystery!" and it made them very uncomfortable from day one. They were completely out of the loop and had no idea what was going on. They wanted to kill it, so they put it on Saturday night when nobody watched TV.

Todd Holland: For me it was scheduling. Look back to the airdates - I'm looking through them right now. The first hiatus goes from February 16 to March 28 and it airs for four weeks and doesn't come back until June! The airdate gaps in that show were so gigantic in season two and the show was so byzantine, that an audience didn't have a chance. Even I got confused and kind of lost interest and I knew that world really well. ABC did not know what they had. Why would they air it in June? Nobody watches TV in June.

Wendy Robie: When I got the sense that this magical time was ending, I just tried to stay in a place of gratitude and enjoy it for what it was, really essentially sucking the marrow out of the bone of that experience because I knew it couldn't last. I think that David Lynch and Mark Frost were meant to make *Twin Peaks* whatever it was and it would either go or stop.

Billy Zane: Perhaps it was a cultural phenomenon because it left the audience wanting more. You can only cram so much quality into something. You can overstay a welcome and I think part of that contributed to its limited run. You can run out of angles and stories if something is a little too gimmicky or too tiresome and in this case I think it wisely bowed and exited.

In terms of the pantheon of television drama, it was a great privilege to be invited into the club. It has certainly balanced the offerings in my résumé. It's just cool points forever. [*laughs*] You can't unring a bell fortunately, so it will resonate for a while.

David Patrick Kelly: Sometimes things just have a life and that's what you have to be content with. You can't expect things to go on further than they do. I think it's a combination of the will of the creators, because it's a very difficult thing to run a television show. These were all highly creative people who were moving on in their own lives, I think. It's a tricky thing.

I think maybe Mark Frost was more knowledgeable about television, but I think David wasn't that knowledgeable about it - about what requires a story to go on and on and on. It has to be novelistic and fascinating and this was novelistic, but it was a short novel and that's just fine with me. So while I was sad it didn't go on, it felt like a complete thing.

Gary Levine: I think it's very hard to sustain the level of novelty that *Twin Peaks* had. Part of what made it so interesting was that it was so refreshing, so different. Well, as you live with it week after week it becomes less novel and there are some inherent problems in a show whose allure is refreshing distinctiveness because you get used to it.

Michael Saltzman: There's a whole host of reasons I could tell you why the show didn't last, but I think (like a lot of things in life) it ran its course. There was a time and a place. It just all kind of fell together in a very unique way. In some respects it's never been duplicated in my life, but I also think lightning can only strike once and it seldom strikes a second time. I may never have another *Twin Peaks* again and I think it carried through all the experiences we had with the show.

As the Twin Peaks *family scattered, Mark Frost and David Lynch created the short-lived ABC sitcom* On the Air, *focused on a 1950s variety show struggling within the confines of network television. Around this time, David Lynch and Robert Engels also began scripting the feature film* Twin Peaks: Fire Walk with Me. *Directed by Lynch and released to theaters in the fall of 1992, the prequel film explores the last seven days of Laura Palmer and offers little insight into what a hypothetical third season may have entailed.*

Kyle MacLachlan: I think the general feeling was it is not getting better and there's really nothing we can do, so maybe it's for the best. Then we did the film which was a fun way to revisit the characters, although it felt like they lived on the small screen on television and not on the large screen in my mind. It seemed a little awkward somehow, to me. I was in kind of a small portion of the movie, but I didn't feel like I contributed much to the feature.

Sherilyn Fenn: I was being a brat about that [*Twin Peaks: Fire Walk with Me*]. First of all, I was already cast to do something else - *Of Mice and Men* with John Malkovich and Gary Sinise. David was really mad at me. It was the only time he's been really mad at me, but what could I do? I was really happy that they couldn't replace me. I love Sheryl Lee, but I always felt like "Who killed Laura Palmer?" was the doorway into *Twin Peaks*, to meet all these amazing people – young and old – that were really interesting characters. I was sad; God only knows what they would have wanted Audrey to do in that movie.

Richard Beymer: I was excited about it when I thought it was going to be the television show that was now expanded into a movie. I expected all the characters would be there and it became a whole other group of people. I was in it [the script] and they didn't shoot my scenes. I was very glad I didn't; I didn't like the scene at all. It was all about dealing coke and I thought, "Ben is crazy, but that's not Ben Horne." It didn't make any sense to me and I didn't like the script, to be frank with you.

Harley Peyton: I think a lot of relationships fractured temporarily over the second season and my relationship with David Lynch did not end particularly well. For example, with the half-hour comedy [*On the Air*] that was coming. I was hopeful to work on that show and I remember my agent calling and saying, "Yeah, that's not going to happen." I don't know if it was over that one moment, but it was unfortunate.

Oddly enough, that's when I think David and Bob Engels became close and would sort of chuckle the afternoon away in Bob's office. I think that's when their relationship became much stronger which I'm assuming is what led to *Fire Walk with Me*. There was no Mark Frost on *Fire Walk with Me* which was nonsensical to me. Although, I must say Mark and David have a tremendous relationship today.

Ken Scherer: I think the experience for all involved was so disastrous that it just died a death. I mean, the film – let's face it – it was not as strong as the series. I'm being diplomatic. I think that by then the division between the two guys [Lynch and Frost] was so wide that it was going to be hard and only time would bring them back together. I see Mark from time to time, but when I talk to him I do think there is a temptation to revisit it.

The only way – and I mean this – the only way it works is if the two of them can get back in Bob's Big Boy or Du-Par's or wherever the hell it was where they first started meeting over coffee. With all due respect to Bob Engels, Harley Peyton, and the other writers we brought in, there are only two guys that can tell that story and that's the truth of the movie. I always say the movie proves my point and that is it just was a collection of stuff – it didn't have Mark's brilliance to pull it together as a writer. They were on a wavelength and they were equal and that's what made it work.

Michael Horse: The magic of *Twin Peaks* is that it died before its time. It has that James Dean kind of thing going. People ask if it will be brought back and I say, "I don't know. I don't think so." I always had this concept that if they brought it back, Hawk would be the first to know that something is up. Hawk, as the wise elder, comes out of the sweat lodge and he looks up towards Twin Peaks and goes, "Oh... shit!" [*laughs*]

Everlasting

Nearly twenty-five years removed from its broadcast debut, Twin Peaks *lives on in the hearts and lives of its cast and crew, continuing to capture new audiences and prompt provocative questions. Those closest to the production of the series are united in their conviction of the enduring influence of* Twin Peaks *in the television medium and beyond.*

Mark Frost: I haven't made it a point to watch a lot of the show over the years, but I've seen enough of it to see that it still holds up. There is always something interesting going on and the look of the show was first-rate. I've always said we kind of kicked the doors in on what people thought was possible in a weekly series, but it would really take the flourishing of pay cable and eventually basic cable stations for that to fully flower.

What we were doing wasn't what the networks were (or to this day) interested in doing, but some of them are occasionally. But yeah, I think it is kind of cool to be thought of as the show that helped to get that ball rolling. Plenty of creative people over time have told me, "It inspired us to do what we did." That's always great to hear, that there's a legacy there that we all have a reason to be proud of.

Harley Peyton: There was something very seismic about it. It started a lot of changes that came later. When it vanished it was like it had never happened. I remember meeting someone from *Northern Exposure* and he said, "We always show writers *Twin Peaks* episodes to show them what to do and what not to do." [*laughs*] I think it was enormously influential and I'm perfectly comfortable saying that because the credit goes to Mark and David. They created something that was absolutely magical.

Miguel Ferrer: I think David Lynch approached television without realizing it was television, or without giving a moment's consideration to the fact that it was television. He unintentionally or unconsciously broke every rule of television and opened people's minds to what came afterwards, and I think the influences are very much still seen today. I remember that long shot in the pilot of that [*speaking slowly*] long shot of the telephone cord, just going down. You never saw anything like that on TV. It was so cinematic and it broke so many rules and did things that just weren't *ever* seen on television.

Mary Jo Deschanel: I think it was groundbreaking; it turned everything upside down where characters could be irrational and nonsensical. There was a sense of the dream being part of the reality and the reality part of the dream. There was a whole Eastern influence brought into small-town American life. They stayed ahead of the censors, always doing something that was subversive.

There was nothing like it until *Twin Peaks* and *Twin Peaks* just changed everything. It opened up all these possibilities and the influence is still there. I meet a lot of young people who say, "I know you from *Twin Peaks*," and they were three or four years old when it came out. It's a phenomenon.

Alan Wurtzel: I think it's very presumptuous of anyone to say any one show changed television, but this is clearly a program that was very different than the usual fare. It probably was the first program (and I don't want to use the term because it's probably wrong) that was sort of avant-garde. Today when you look at the landscape of cable programs and stuff, it's not odd to find programs that don't have that kind of mainstream sensibility, but in those days it was out of the mainstream.

So to that extent, it was probably the first program that really had that kind of non-traditional sensibility in a mainstream medium. Obviously there are movies and things that have always had that, but television is obviously designed to be very mainstream and appeal to a broad number of people. The fact it was on one of the broadcast networks was pretty extraordinary.

Jonathan P. Shaw: For a while *Twin Peaks* went its own way and wore itself out, but then it became something else where the sophisticated audience was getting what they came for. I think it was really a vanguard for that kind of material. I felt that was a strong indication of what the possibilities were and I think it's playing out still today.

Stephen Gyllenhaal: It was a magical piece of television. There was nothing like it and there's been nothing like it since. Even then the characters had an iconic feel to them, even though we knew the show was going off the air. I've been lucky to do a lot of stuff I'm really proud of and *Twin Peaks* is at the very top.

Sherilyn Fenn: It stands the test of time. For me, it's just a warm, proud, amazing thing. As an actor you touch people and there's nothing better. I didn't know what I was doing. I knew it was good when my brothers were like, "Audrey's just like you!" It tapped into something even my brothers recognize. [*laughs*] It was more than just a job. We all had a real connection on the show and as people and that connection doesn't die - and it's so cool. When really young people see it, it blows my mind. I'm glad they like it. [*laughs*]

Mädchen Amick: My kids grew up always hearing about *Twin Peaks* but have never really seen it, so when they were in high school in film studies class I was like, "Well, if you want to watch something classic that changed the business, watch *Twin Peaks*." They sat down and watched it one summer and they were hooked! They weren't sleeping because they had to get to the next episode. It's so creepy and so good and to know it had that effect (nothing impresses them) and for them to be like, "Wow, you were on the best TV series of all time," is pretty great.

Sheryl Lee: It's always interesting to me to hear (from a new generation's perspective) different questions and ideas, different thoughts. They're watching it in a very different time. It was groundbreaking then, but now they see everything on TV and they still respond to it. I love talking to them about that and hearing their questions.

Graeme Clifford: It still stands up in today's marketplace. My son watched my episode with me prior to this interview and he subsequently asked to watch every episode. I was surprised that it captured his attention so many years after it was first shown. It seems ageless. It has certainly influenced the current limited series trend, such as *Homeland* and *Americans*. However, to my mind there has never been another series as special and unique. It was a genuine "one-off," and I'm proud to have been a part of it.

Randy Barbee: I think it was obvious to all of us. We knew we were standing in the middle of history. Granted, it's not a world war, it's not the fall of the Berlin Wall, but it is entertainment history. It was a real benchmark that took us someplace else (literally) in our cultural development. There was a sense that we were doing something that hadn't been done before - that this is new and unique and people would write books about it. There was always that awareness.

Tricia Brock: It's amazing what a seminal TV show it is. When I met Andy Lincoln (who is the lead in *The Walking Dead*) he said, "What I hope our show even comes close to is *Twin Peaks*," and I sort of said, "Oh yes, I was a part of that," and he asked what I did. When I told him I wrote two episodes he almost fell out of his chair: "Oh my God!"

David Patrick Kelly: It was one of the great things I did; it was really good fortune. I was on the set of *Wild at Heart* and David offered it to me and I was skeptical. I really didn't know about going on a TV show. I was a stage and film actor and I remember Laura [Dern] being very supportive and saying, "You've gotta go on," and Nic Cage was talking about all the great things he had seen on television. He mentioned specifically Jack Palance doing *Requiem for a Heavyweight* (the television drama) and that inspired me. I thought, "Yeah, he's right." There are possibilities to do things in so many different venues and television was one of them.

I really enjoyed the impact that it had and David was really confident about it. He said, "This is really going to be something," and he was right. I'm really grateful to them for including me and for all the impact that it had around the world. Many of the HBO series learned so much from *Twin Peaks* about how to keep things going and what's required. With *The Sopranos*, David Chase has claimed he wanted it to be "Twin Peaks in New Jersey."

Ian Buchanan: If it wasn't for *Twin Peaks*, there wouldn't be *Picket Fences* or *Northern Exposure*, and I also remember David said, "If there hadn't been *Wagon Train* there wouldn't have been *Twin Peaks*." I look back at it with very fond memories. I really wanted to do something different and I'm really glad that's where I made a bend to the left. I'm very grateful for that opportunity and the way it turned out. Working with Lynch, there's no training in the world quite like that where someone gives you the capacity to see things differently and I'm very grateful for that.

Billy Zane: *Heart Shaped World* was number one on the radio and I remember listening to Chris Isaak as I was driving over Mulholland on the way to the studio. I remember pulling in and seeing Joan Chen having a cigarette in front of her trailer on her stairs. I mean, what an extraordinary time capsule and a great job. I just remember this incredible sexiness at the time; it was just something in the air. It was that particular song that was the world's soundtrack and what was afoot – it simply promised and delivered. It was a great privilege to work with all those talented and beautiful people at that time.

Like David, who has an interest in the visual arts and furniture design, I am a painter and I had my first exhibition in 2010 at Bergamot Station and soon after there was an exhibition of memorabilia from the show that attracted a huge and very interesting, eclectic fan base. I remember going to that opening and that was neat! There were some amazing pieces of art there inspired by the show. I think it was somehow curated by David to some degree. There were lines of people who were diehard fans of the show; it was like Comic-Con of the Pacific Northwest.

Dana Ashbrook: Personally, it's pretty much given me the one thing in my career that I really look back on and am super proud of and actually believe had an impact and broke through this sort of white noise of everything that's out there. I'm lucky for that to be a part of me. I think it kind of put a pressure on people to make more quality television, [to] make television that looks more like movies every week and has an ongoing story line that isn't always answered. Shows that followed it like *LOST*, or whatever - I don't think those shows would have existed.

Ray Wise: Leland is one of my signature roles and I'm very proud of all the work I did on that show. I still break it out at least once a year and watch all of it and I still enjoy it. There are definitely jobs I've gotten because I played Leland Palmer. The list goes on too long, probably. I remember for a short time after that show was over I would get auditions from people who just wanted to meet me. [*laughs*] I know it sounds funny, but I'm pretty sure it's true.

Sheryl Lee: I have a deep place of gratitude to the character of Laura and also to David for giving me the opportunity to play her. When I think of her, my experience is the whole thing - it's both seasons and the film - that whole life of that girl. I learned so much playing her in so many different areas of my life, mostly as an actress working with David and all those directors. I have curiosity, like, "What was our karma?" [*laughs*] That sounds like a corny question, but I cannot think of how else to articulate it. What was in my life path that that would happen? I give it to David and everybody that I worked with because they made me better and I am so grateful to have taken that journey with all of them.

Kyle MacLachlan: In the characters I've played, Cooper is probably the one that would be the most remembered. I say that now, but you never know. He's certainly one of the most memorable that I've ever done. You don't often get such rich and diverse characters to play (or at least I don't anyway) and in the format that is television you have a chance to go back and be in his skin for ten months at a time or as long as we had the series going.

It was my first television experience and it felt very good, but I didn't necessarily appreciate at the time how rare that opportunity really is. Having been around now for a while and having done a number of different shows on television, you realize how special that experience was. I wouldn't say I necessarily took it for granted because I enjoyed it, but I didn't necessarily appreciate it to the degree I would now.

Michael Ontkean: M.O. is an existential man. The concept of legacy is not part of my metabolism. I grew up below the poverty line in Canada without parents and without assistance from any government or any relative after the age of eight. Went to twenty-six different schools without graduating from any of them. As every day was a constant scramble, I never expected anything to last longer than a few minutes or a couple of hours. Still don't. So the notion of legacy is completely foreign. That's maybe the real pull of our make-believe world of acting. One gets to be a different person with different sets of people for the length of a working lifetime. You put on a mask to get behind all the other masks. All of them, including your own.

Richard Beymer: It was the best fun I ever had acting - being able to work with a lot of wonderful directors and David and Mark, of course. I was just getting the hang of it, really. It was a great job. I've never been handed such wonderful things to do and allowed to be so crazy. My career was usually roles of a leading man type guy - you don't get too crazy; you've got to hold it together. This allowed me to have some really fun experiences acting. It was nice to go through these different possibilities and have a character with such extremes.

Wendy Robie: I'm really glad that people enjoy it and that people keep rediscovering it. You wouldn't believe it. I get letters from teenagers in Liverpool, England. [*laughs*] Nadine touches hearts. I remember it vividly because it fascinated me and it was so intensely my life for those two years and I was very grateful and I had the best time. I will always be grateful to David and Mark.

Catherine E. Coulson: To this day people will send me pieces of pie at restaurants. I still do get recognized and I have eaten an awful lot of pie, especially cherry pie. In fact I would say it's not my favorite food anymore, [*laughs*] but I'm grateful for every piece that was sent to me!

Uli Edel: Like here in the States, in Germany it has a cult following too. Still today people say to me, "Oh, I saw you worked on *Twin Peaks*. That must have been exciting?" Well, I've done a lot of other stuff but people still ask me about *Twin Peaks*. [*laughs*] You can definitely see what an impact it had.

Annette McCarthy: I went to Italy fifteen years ago and this boy came up to me in a plaza and he recognized my character from the show. I guess it came on over there five years later. I thought that was incredible. It's very awkward, but the truth is that I am very proud of it. It is something I take great pride with. Actually, my cat is named Bob. [*laughs*] He is always creeping around corners.

Kenneth Welsh: It remains a gem. My son is twenty-three and students would come up to him at university and say, "You're dad is Windom Earle! Oh my God!" He got tired of it though! [*laughs*] He had enough of Windom Earle around the house. But I'm telling you, I loved it. People still come up to me and say "Windom Earle!" I'm not William Shatner, but Windom has some life. I guess I invested it with something rather interesting that people seem attracted to.

Ray Wise and Kenneth Welsh

Michael Horse: I live in the [San Francisco] Bay Area and I'll be in Berkley with my wife going to the movies. Young kids will follow us and they'll ask if I'm Deputy Hawk. When I say, "Yeah, I am," they go, "Cool!" [*laughs*] which I find really funny because I've done everything from *Walker, Texas Ranger* to *Malcolm in the Middle*. You don't get experiences (especially in television) to do something as great as that. If I never worked again, at least I did *Twin Peaks*!

Scott Frost: It's kind of frankly amazing to me that people still love it. It will invariably come up in conversation when people hear my history – whether it be someone that adores it or someone who goes, "What the hell were you thinking in the second season?!" It's always kind of fun to be involved with something that caught the eye of the country. It was like the network handed the keys of the asylum over to the writers, and the result was *Twin Peaks*!

Warren Frost: I still get fan mail if you believe that, from overseas. I'm not talking about fifty letters a day, but every once in a while I'll get a letter to sign something and I'm sure some of the guys that had bigger parts get a lot more.

It's strange - it's still going. We had friends of ours that were on the West Coast and they went up to Snoqualmie Falls, just because they were old friends and they knew about *Twin Peaks*. They went in the restaurant and there were pictures on the wall from *Twin Peaks*! When did it end? 1991? I understand there are *Twin Peaks* clubs. I don't know if they still exist, but I know they did for quite a while.

Duwayne Dunham: I can tell you, nobody thought it would ever see the light of day. David Lynch didn't think it would ever be aired. That's what he told me. He called me and said, "I want you to edit this thing. ABC is going to give us four or five million dollars and they're never going to air it. Let's go have some fun." Along the way, certain things happened... magic happened. You can say it derailed a little bit and it just got weird and goofy, but in the end you have to look back and say, "Wow, what a show." Nobody had seen anything like this on network television, ever.

Grace Zabriskie: The aftermath of *Twin Peaks* is where and when we are living now. All the writers who first quickened, creatively, watching *Twin Peaks*, all the failed attempts to imitate, the eventual successful results of the 'influence' of David's work, the new spaces there was suddenly permission or even a mandate to explore... we are still living in the aftermath, whether or not we know it, whether or not we ever actually saw any of *Twin Peaks*.

James Marshall: I think it blasted so many genres open. It was almost like *Twin Peaks* was the tree where all the branches of these shows came off of - like *CSI* and *The X-Files*. Can you even tell me one show where they were pulling letters out of fingernails before? *Twin Peaks* didn't change television with a sledgehammer because it wasn't intending to, but it shifted everything, eventually. I feel like I could turn on most shows at night now and see different aspects of *Twin Peaks*. I could question things all day and say, "What if it happened this way or that way?" It is what it is, and the fact that it "still is" is pretty darn neat. It was a blessing to be involved with. It's a work of art.

Angelo Badalamenti: *Twin Peaks* is just unbelievable. Whoever thought this outrageous program would take a hold on the world the way it did? When I say the world, I mean the world. I travel fairly extensively to many countries for various events and that's the first thing they talk about. Everybody wants to know more about *Twin Peaks*. It's one of those shows that will never die. What can you say? You've got to be grateful for beautiful things that happen in life.

Ken Scherer: It was by far the greatest experience I could have ever hoped for. Not because it had great fame, but because it was really good stuff. If you want to give eighteen hours a day of your life, you want to be involved with something that people are passionate about and that you can be proud of. There wasn't anyone attached to the project that didn't feel that and it started with David and Mark, two of the nicest people you're ever going to meet. It was a ride of a lifetime. The sadness is that it lasted way too short.

Kyle MacLachlan: I think that the show stands up as one of the great shows of the past thirty years. I don't think anything has been seen like it on television since. I know that it has influenced a number of people who are involved in television.

It was a combination of very creative people: David Lynch and Mark Frost and everyone involved (including the cast) combined with a sort of moment at ABC when they were looking for something unusual. How it made its way through that minefield that are the powers that make decisions in television is remarkable. It was sort of a perfect storm.

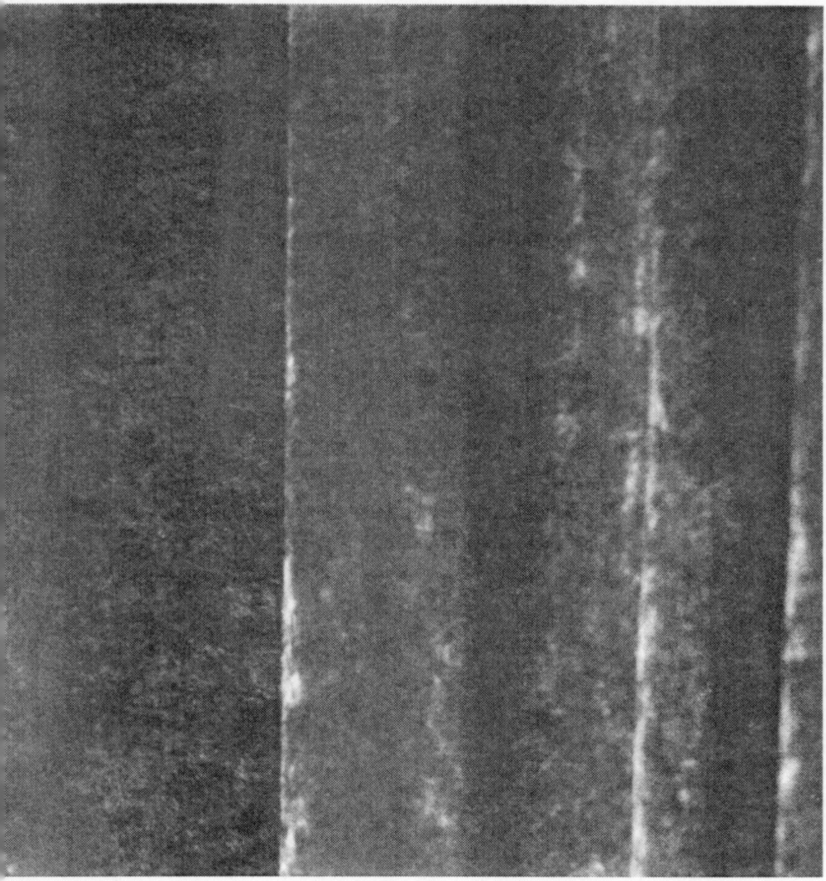

Acknowledgments

I offer my grace and gratitude to the individuals who helped me realize this book. Their gift of time and trust will never be forgotten.

My wife and best friend, Jessica Dukes, supported me in every way and kept me sane throughout this journey. I could not have managed all the highs and lows without her love and devotion.

When I first ran this project by Mark Frost, he replied that he was "happy to help in any way" he could. His cooperation was paramount to the creative process. I thank Mark for taking a chance on me and my dream.

Eben Moore aided me along the way in countless areas. We spent endless hours on the phone discussing concepts and cracking each other up. He also procured many photographs and provided vital feedback for innumerable versions of this manuscript. His dedication and insight were irreplaceable.

To Charles Ramsey, for his talents and friendship. His contribution to this book and its vision is a blessing.

Robert Engels and Harley Peyton were generous and patient in my extended interviews with them. Chad Hoffman, Tony Krantz, and Ken Scherer also offered invaluable insight behind the scenes.

It was a divine thrill to converse on the record with so many talented actors and actresses. Thanks to Kyle MacLachlan, Michael Ontkean, Don Amendolia, Mädchen Amick, Dana Ashbrook, Phoebe Augustine, Robert Bauer, Richard Beymer, Ian Buchanan, Joan Chen, Catherine E. Coulson, Lance Davis, Mary Jo Deschanel, Sherilyn Fenn, Miguel Ferrer, Warren Frost, Rick Giolito, Peter Michael Goetz, Joshua Harris, Gary Hershberger, Michael Horse, David Patrick Kelly, Piper Laurie, Sheryl Lee, Robyn Lively, James Marshall, Annette McCarthy, Chris Mulkey, Michael Parks, Van Dyke Parks, Brenda E. Reed, Kimmy Robertson, Wendy Robie, Charlotte Stewart, Al Strobel, Carel Struycken, Mak Takano, Russ Tamblyn, Lenny Von Dohlen, Kenneth Welsh, Ray Wise, Grace Zabriskie, and Billy Zane.

I want to thank all the directors who took a trip back in time with me. Here's to Graeme Clifford, Caleb Deschanel, Duwayne Dunham, Uli Edel, James Foley, Lesli Linka Glatter, Stephen Gyllenhaal,

Todd Holland, Tim Hunter, Tina Rathborne, and Jonathan Sanger.

The music of *Twin Peaks* is an enduring treasure. It was staggering to speak with the artists who brought it to life. Cheers to Angelo Badalamenti, Vinnie Bell, Julee Cruise, Lori Eschler Frystak, Kinny Landrum, Art Polhemus, and Al Regni.

To a tireless crew behind the scenes of the show, I enjoyed the stories of your art and craft. Thanks to Randy Barbee, Frank Byers, Carla Fabrizi, Gregg Fienberg, Ron Garcia, Barry Gremillion, Richard Hoover, David J. Latt, Sara Markowitz, Leslie Morales, Philip Carr Neel, Jonathan P. Shaw, Paul Trejo, and John Wentworth.

Other interview participants I wish to recognize: Gavin de Becker, Tricia Brock, Michael R. Caputo, Scott Frost, Gary Levine, Michael Saltzman, Philip Segal, Brandon Stoddard, and Alan Wurtzel.

Howard Miller and John Thorne permitted the inclusion of select interview excerpts originally published in *Wrapped in Plastic* magazine. I sincerely thank John and the late Craig Miller for all they have contributed to the *Twin Peaks* fan community over the years.

Alessandro Ago, Jim Bruening, Harmony Carrigan, Mischa Cronin, Brian Kursar, and Rob Wilson assisted me in varying areas of research and facilitation. Thanks y'all.

For their conversations, encouragement, and support: my parents Dr. Robert and Kimberly Dukes, my brother Peyton Dukes, Peggy Dukes, Gary Bullock, James Ciccarello, Pieter Dom, Harry Goaz, Richard Gold, Charles de Lauzirika, Tom Mayer, Rob and D'ann Lindley, Blake Roberson, and Connie Woods.

An extra special thanks to Danielle Badalamenti, Richard Beymer, Joan Chen, Annette Fabrizi-Coccarelli, Carla Fabrizi, Richard Hoover, James Marshall, Alan Light, *Rolling Stone*, and Ken Scherer for allowing the inclusion of their photographs.

Lastly, to Mark Frost, David Lynch, Tony Krantz, Chad Hoffman, Bob Iger, Brandon Stoddard, and the entire cast and crew – thank you for *Twin Peaks*!

Sources and Method

Reflections, An Oral History of Twin Peaks is comprised of interviews that took place between June, 2011, and February, 2014. All interviews were conducted, transcribed, and edited by the author. Assorted filming documents were supplied for reference courtesy of Mischa Cronin and Eben Moore. Exceptions include the following cited sources, previously noted in this manuscript:

1. Page 161, Carman, John. "On Saturday Nights, ABC Seeks Standing Date With Young Adults" *San Francisco Chronicle.* August 11, 1990.
2. Page 174, Miller, Craig and Thorne, John. "1993 Twin Peaks Fan Festival" *Wrapped in Plastic.* October, 1993: 9
3. Page 177, Ibid
4. Page 177, Miller, Craig and Thorne, John. "Killer Bob Speaks" *Wrapped in Plastic.* December, 1993: 6
5. Page 178, Miller, Craig and Thorne, John. "Frank Silva: A Remembrance" *Wrapped in Plastic.* December, 1995: 24
6. Page 182, Miller, Craig and Thorne, John. "Killer Bob Speaks." *Wrapped in Plastic.* December, 1993: 5-6
7. Page 204, Ibid

Census

The following is a list of individuals interviewed for this book, including a description of their role within the production of *Twin Peaks*, or otherwise.

Don Amendolia – *Emory Battis*
Mädchen Amick – *Shelly Johnson*
Dana Ashbrook – *Bobby Briggs*
Phoebe Augustine – *Ronette Pulaski*
Angelo Badalamenti – *conductor and orchestrations*
Randy Barbee – *series assistant director*
Robert Bauer – *Johnny Horne*
Gavin de Becker – *founder, Gavin de Becker and Associates*
Vinnie Bell - *guitars*
Richard Beymer – *Benjamin Horne*
Tricia Brock – *screenwriter, episodes 17, 23*
Ian Buchanan – *Dick Tremayne*
Frank Byers – *series director of photography*
Michael R. Caputo – *cofounder, Citizens Opposed to the Offing of Peaks*
Joan Chen – *Jocelyn "Josie" Packard*
Graeme Clifford – *director, episode 12*
Catherine E. Coulson – *Margaret Lanterman a.k.a. the Log Lady*
Julee Cruise – *Roadhouse singer; vocalist*
Lance Davis – *Martin Padley as Chet Weems*
Caleb Deschanel – *director, episodes 6,15,19*
Mary Jo Deschanel – *Eileen Hayward*
Duwayne Dunham – *editor, pilot episode, episode 8; director, episodes 1, 18, 25*
Uli Edel – *director, episode 21*
Robert "Bob" Engels – *series screenwriter and season two co-producer*
Carla Fabrizi – *makeup artist*
Gregg Feinberg – *series producer*
Sherilyn Fenn – *Audrey Horne*
Miguel Ferrer – *FBI Agent Albert Rosenfield*
James Foley – *director, episode 24*
Mark Frost - *series cocreator, executive producer, screenwriter, and director*
Scott Frost – *Mark Frost's brother; screenwriter, episodes 15, 21; author,* The Autobiography of FBI Special Agent Dale Cooper: My Life, My Tapes
Warren Frost – *Mark Frost's father; Dr. Will Hayward*

Lori Eschler Frystak – *series music editor*
Ron Garcia – *director of photography, pilot episode and episode 2 dream sequence*
Rick Giolito – *Mark Frost's brother-in-law; Jason Dimbo as Montana*
Lesli Linka Glatter – *director, episodes 5, 10, 13, 23*
Peter Michael Goetz – *Jared Lancaster as Evan St. Vincent*
Barry Gremillion – *location liaison, season two*
Stephen Gyllenhaal – *director, episode 27*
Jules Haimovitz – *former president and chief operating officer, Spelling Entertainment*
Joshua Harris – *"Little" Nicky Needleman*
Gary Hershberger – *Mike Nelson*
Chad Hoffman – *former vice president of drama development, ABC*
Todd Holland – *director, episodes 11, 20*
Richard Hoover – *series production designer*
Michael Horse – *Deputy Tommy "Hawk" Hill*
Tim Hunter – *director, episodes 4, 16, 28*
David Patrick Kelly – *Jerry Horne*
Tony Krantz – *former television agent, Creative Artists Agency*
Kinny Landrum - *synthesizer*
David J. Latt – *producer, pilot episode*
Piper Laurie – *Catherine Martell/Mr. Tojamura*
Sheryl Lee – *Laura Palmer/Maddy Ferguson*
Gary Levine - *former director and vice president of drama development, ABC*
Robyn Lively – *Lana Budding Milford*
Kyle MacLachlan – *Special Agent Dale Cooper*
Sara Markowitz – *series costume designer*
James Marshall – *James Hurley*
Annette McCarthy – *Evelyn Marsh*
Leslie Morales – *set decorator, pilot episode*
Philip Carr Neel – *series associate producer*
Michael Ontkean – *Sheriff Harry S. Truman*
Michael Parks – *Jean Renault*
Van Dyke Parks – *Harold Racine*
Harley Peyton – *series screenwriter and season two producer*
Art Polhemus - *engineer*
Tina Rathborne – *director, episodes 3, 17*
Brenda E. Reed, neé Mathers – *Caroline Earle*
Al Regni – *tenor saxophone*
Kimmy Robertson – *Lucy Moran*

Wendy Robie – *Nadine Hurley*
Michael Saltzman – *former publicist, Lynch/Frost Productions "and for anyone else who didn't have a publicist"*
Jonathan Sanger – director, episode 26
Ken Scherer – *former chief operating officer, Lynch/Frost Productions*
Philip Segal – *former programming director, ABC*
Jonathan P. Shaw – *series editor*
Charlotte Stewart – *Betty Briggs*
Brandon Stoddard – *former president of ABC entertainment*
Carel Struycken – *the Giant*
Mak Takano – *Jonathan Kumagai/Mr. Lee*
Russ Tamblyn – *Dr. Lawrence Jacoby*
Paul Trejo – *series editor*
Lenny Von Dohlen – *Harold Smith*
Kenneth Welsh – *Windom Earle*
John Wentworth – *series postproduction coordinator and associate producer*
Ray Wise – *Leland Palmer*
Alan Wurtzel – *former vice president of research, ABC*
Grace Zabriskie – *Sarah Palmer*
Billy Zane – *John Justice Wheeler*

Photo Credits

Cover and back photo by Charles Ramsey
Author photo by Jessica Dukes

1. Page 4, courtesy of Ken Scherer
2. Page 19, courtesy of Richard Beymer
3. Page 34, courtesy of Joan Chen
4. Page 38, courtesy of James Marshall
5. Page 44, courtesy of Danielle Badalamenti
6. Page 59, courtesy of Richard Hoover
7. Page 66, courtesy of Carla Fabrizi
8. Page 70, courtesy of Richard Hoover
9. Page 73, courtesy of Carla Fabrizi
10. Page 83, courtesy of Annette Fabrizi-Coccarelli
11. Page 90, courtesy of Carla Fabrizi
12. Page 91, courtesy of Carla Fabrizi
13. Page 92, courtesy of Carla Fabrizi
14. Page 96, courtesy of Richard Beymer
15. Page 107, courtesy of Richard Hoover
16. Page 108, courtesy of Carla Fabrizi
17. Page 120, courtesy of *Rolling Stone*
18. Page 134, courtesy of Danielle Badalamenti
19. Page 137, courtesy of Danielle Badalamenti
20. Page 142, courtesy of Richard Hoover
21. Page 149, courtesy of Richard Beymer
22. Page 155, courtesy of Alan Light
23. Page 156, courtesy of Alan Light
24. Page 168, courtesy of Richard Hoover
25. Page 175, courtesy of Carla Fabrizi
26. Page 184, courtesy of Carla Fabrizi
27. Page 190, courtesy of Carla Fabrizi
28. Page 197, courtesy of Carla Fabrizi
29. Page 204, courtesy of Richard Beymer
30. Page 214, courtesy of Carla Fabrizi
31. Page 220, courtesy of Carla Fabrizi
32. Page 229, courtesy of Annette Fabrizi-Coccarelli
33. Page 234, courtesy of Carla Fabrizi

34. Page 244, courtesy of Richard Hoover
35. Page 248, courtesy of Carla Fabrizi
36. Page 255, courtesy of Carla Fabrizi
37. Page 272, courtesy of Richard Hoover
38. Page 274, courtesy of Carla Fabrizi
39. Page 275, courtesy of Carla Fabrizi
40. Page 282, courtesy of Carla Fabrizi
41. Page 288, courtesy of Carla Fabrizi
42. Page 291, courtesy of Carla Fabrizi
43. Page 309, courtesy of Carla Fabrizi
44. Page 312-313, courtesy of Richard Beymer

CPSIA information can be obtained at www.ICGtesting.com
Printed in the USA
LVOW12s1504011114

411587LV00003B/16/P

9 780615 968834